Strategies of Survival

LEXINGTON STUDIES ON KOREA'S PLACE IN INTERNATIONAL RELATIONS

Series Editor: Jongwoo Han, President of the Korean War Legacy Foundation

This series publishes trailblazing research by pioneering scholars on contemporary Korean issues. Transformative events in the early twenty-first century have marked a watershed for South and North Korea in many areas, including political economy, democracy, international power politics and security, ongoing disputes over the past with China and Japan, and North Korea's nuclear and missile programs, to name a few. Furthermore, postmodern cultural influences and the global advent of digital technology have led to the diversification of Korea's culture, religion, sports, diasporic community, and inter-Korean linguistic differences, as well as the Korean Wave. This series aims to explore and dissect these issues to further understanding of contemporary Korean life and politics.

Titles Published

Strategies of Survival: North Korean Foreign Policy under Kim Jong-un, edited by Weiqi Zhang and Jun Take Kwon

Understanding Kim Jong-un's North Korea: Regime Dynamics, Negotiation, and Engagement, edited by Robert Carlin and Chung-in Moon

The Metamorphosis of U.S.–Korea Relations: The Korean Question Revisited, by Jongwoo Han

Diplomacy, Trade, and South Korea's Rise to International Influence, edited by Dennis Patterson and Jangsup Choi

The Construction of Korean Culture in Korean Language Textbooks: Ideologies and Textbooks, by Dong Bae Lee

Korea and the World: New Frontier in Korean Studies, edited by Gregg Brazinsky

Strategies of Survival

North Korean Foreign Policy under Kim Jong-un

Edited by Jun Taek Kwon and Weiqi Zhang

LEXINGTON BOOKS
Lanham • Boulder • New York • London

Rowman & Littlefield
Bloomsbury Publishing Inc, 1359 Broadway, New York, NY 10018, USA
Bloomsbury Publishing Plc, 50 Bedford Square, London, WC1B 3DP, UK
Bloomsbury Publishing Ireland, 29 Earlsfort Terrace, Dublin 2, D02 AY28, Ireland
www.bloomsbury.com

Published by Lexington Books
An imprint of The Rowman & Littlefield Publishing Group, Inc.
4501 Forbes Boulevard, Suite 200, Lanham, Maryland 20706
www.rowman.com
86-90 Paul Street, London EC2A 4NE

British Library Cataloguing in Publication Information available

Library of Congress Cataloging-in-Publication Data

Names: Kwon, Jun Taek, 1968- editor. | Zhang, Weiqi, 1983- editor.
  Title: Strategies of survival : North Korean foreign policy under Kim
    Jong-Un / edited by Jun Taek Kwon and Weiqi Zhang.
  Description: Lanham, Maryland : Lexington Books, 2023. | Series: Lexington
    studies on Korea's place in international relations | Includes
    bibliographical references and index.
  Identifiers: LCCN 2023004431 (print) | LCCN 2023004432 (ebook) | ISBN
    9781666922318 (cloth) | ISBN 9781666922325 (ebook)
  Subjects: LCSH: Korea (North)–Foreign relations–2011- | Kim, Chŏng-ŭn, 1984-
  Classification: LCC DS935.7778 .S77 2023 (print) | LCC DS935.7778 (ebook) |
    DDC 327.5193–dc23/eng/20230210
  LC record available at https://lccn.loc.gov/2023004431
  LC ebook record available at https://lccn.loc.gov/2023004432

Contents

Acknowledgments

I am grateful to my parents, who accompanied me on my trip to North Korea. Without them, I would have not started research on North Korea and this book would have not existed. I also thank my wife, Juan Ling, for her support during the difficult year of 2020 and her sacrifice over the years. Her support is integral to my career. I also want to express my appreciation to my son, George, who has been so kind and patient with me and let me complete work before playing with him. Lastly, I thank the Rosenberg Institute for East Asian Studies at Suffolk University for sponsoring this study.

Weiqi Zhang

I would like to express my appreciation to my parents, my wife, Misook, and my son, Samuel, for their unending patience and support.

Jun T. Kwon

Introduction

Framework of Understanding North Korean Foreign Policies

Weiqi Zhang and Jun T. Kwon

Questions about regime security in North Korea become more interesting as the Kim regime persists despite predictions that it could and should not. After decades of domestic economic mismanagement, and international isolation and sanctions, the North Korean regime, including today's Kim Jong-un and his ruling elites, are secure from the fear of forced removal from their power and govern without major challenges to their authority. Besides totalitarian and ruthless domestic controls, foreign policy also plays an integral part in the survival strategy of the hermit kingdom.

Despite being akin to a dynasty, the North Korean regime like other states pursues national security, legitimacy to rule, and economic prosperity to survive. For example, *Juche*, North Korea's official political ideology is composed of three fundamental principles: *chaju* (independence), *charip* (self-sustenance), and *chawi* (self-defense). The three principles cover the political, economic, and security aspects of the regime's interest. The three generations of the Kim regime tirelessly pursue these goals with different priorities.

Foreign policy is not only an instrument to achieve national goals but also an extension of domestic politics. It should be noted that, according to North Korea's Constitution, North Korean foreign policy follows the ideals of "independence, peace, and friendship." Nonetheless, like many other parts of the Constitution, these ideals are not always faithfully implemented by the regime.

This collection of studies examines how Pyongyang has managed its foreign policies toward key actors to pursue survival goals with a focus on the Kim Jong-un era and sheds light on the logic behind North Korean foreign policy behavior.

LEGITIMACY AND NATIONAL IDENTITY

Every political system attempts to generate and maintain its legitimacy. Through the support of the people, leaders can have their orders obeyed willingly rather than through the use of force. The key components of the legitimacy to rule are the belief of people in the ruler's moral right to issue commands and their corresponding consent to obey such commands. When regime legitimacy is created and maximized on the basis of inculcating a belief system, leaders need not be concerned with economic performance to satisfy people's material needs.

Identity may be defined as a concept of the self, a selection of physical, psychological, emotional, or social attributes of particular individuals. Identity provides a framework within which people construct reality and determine their positions on a wide range of issues. When state identity is formed as a basis for legitimacy, this identity unifies people, and at times, may serve as a strong basis for mass mobilization. Often, identity builds on common characteristics such as ideology, language, race, religion, beliefs, and a shared understanding of history. In an international context, this same identity can create allies or enemies of states that share or do not share these common characteristics. Identity, however, continues to change based on how both the domestic and international context change and how the population related to common memories of the past.

North Korea is one of the most striking examples of a system where national identity has been the basis of regime legitimacy, which is consolidated by the use of the foreign policy. Thus, identity is a key factor to be considered when one analyzes how preferences shape North Korea's foreign policy. When Juche ideology was proposed in 1955, Kim Il-sung meant to unify the nation under "Koreanistic socialism." To Kim Il-sung, political independence and consequential national identity is the most important goal because it is impossible to achieve self-reliance in economic affairs and national defense while under foreign influence.

One major challenge to the legitimacy and identity of the North Korean regime during modern times comes from South Korea. As a divided country, North Korea's legitimacy is rooted in the inter-Korean competition. Since the inception of the regime, North Korea has vigorously waged a legitimacy war against South Korea. For instance, while South Koreans view the Korean War as a political war protecting democratic values and institutions, North Koreans regard the war as the pursuit of political independence and a continuation of the nationalist struggle against foreign domination, first against Japan and now against the United States and its "surrogate" powers. This sentiment leads North Koreans to express pride that they served as their own representatives at the signing of the armistice agreement, whereas the South Koreans were represented by officials from the United Nations.

Such identity- and legitimacy-building in North Korea, on the one hand, contributes to regime stability and political unification. On the other hand, the dedication to the legitimacy contest has limited the political space for the North Korean government to explore policy changes because any change in the system to North Koreans implies system failure. During the post–Cold War era, with South Korean economic success being internationally recognized, Pyongyang's struggle for legitimacy and identity worsened due to economic collapse and had no choice but to open (in a cautious and limited way) for economic cooperation with South Korea economically under the latter's "Sunshine policy."

To enhance external legitimacy as a way to boost domestic legitimacy, North Korea focuses its legitimacy diplomacy on developing countries. In chapter 7, Dominguez reviews and analyzes North Korea's efforts in the past thirty years to improve relations with developing countries and international organizations. Analyzing the trend of relations between North Korea and smaller powers, Dominguez prescribes solutions to facilitate engagement with North Korea.

National Security

Security-related topics are often expressed in North Korean official documents and media as defending sovereignty, territorial integrity, and fundamental interests of the state. We use "national security" to refer to North Korea's security interests as this term is the most familiar to readers.

National security (territorial integrity and political independence), as the most important consideration of foreign policy for any country, is a significant domestic factor in shaping North Korea's foreign policy decision making. When a small country faces external threats, national security must be pursued at all costs.

In the case of North Korea, the struggle between the United States and the Soviet Union after World War II divided the Korean Peninsula into two separate governments, with each supporting one of the then superpowers. The breakout of the Korean War worsened the North Korea-U.S. relationship throughout the Cold War. Consequently, North Korea has considered the United States as an enemy of the state and perceived the United States as the source of an overwhelming threat. In North Korean national security policy, defending against U.S. aggression is the cornerstone, and security has been the theme of North Korean foreign policy toward the United States.

North Korea's pursuit of self-reliance in national security is complicated by the fact that it cannot defend against the United States single-handedly.

During the Cold War, Kim Il-sung carefully managed his relations with the Soviet Union and China to counter-balance the United States pressure and ensure economic stability on the one hand and maintain as much independence from the neighboring communist powers as possible on the other hand.

The unexpected collapse of the Soviet Union overnight made national security the most urgent problem for the North Korean regime. Losing Soviet support made North Korea vulnerable, especially when North Korea and the United States never signed a peace treaty to officially end the Korean War. As the United States remained the sole superpower in the post–Cold War era, North Korea has been increasingly suspicious of U.S. intentions and fearful of U.S. aggression. Consequently, *songun* (military first), one of the crucial components of the Juche ideology was elevated to represent the "new higher stage" of *Juche* and has been the official ruling ideology of North Korea. The difference between *songun* then and now is that *songun* then focused on conventional military capability whereas *songun* now stresses nuclear capability.

One direct result of the shift of priority from political independence to national security was that the North Korean military since then has become the dominant political force in the regime and society. Another result is the resumption of North Korea's nuclear program. In chapter 1, Kwon examines North Korean foreign policy on the United States and suggests that not only the adversarial relationship with the United States motivates Pyongyang to focus on national security at all cost but also the same adversarial relationship is used to serve the goal of the regime legitimacy and political independence in the domestic political context.

It should be noted that, under the *Juche* ideology, North Koreans are motivated to resist external pressure, not only from enemies but also from allies, such as China. China and North Korea have played important roles in each other's survival strategy. To North Korea, not only is China the only major power in the region that shares similar political ideology and has the capability to protect North Korea, but also China needs North Korea to serve as a buffer zone to keep the United States at arm's length. During the post–Cold War, however, North Korea's need for China becomes more urgent due to its domestic economic failure and immature nuclear deterrence capability. As a result, such unbalanced reliance makes North Korean leaders subjected to undesirable Chinese influence.

In chapter 2, Zhang examines the logic behind North Korean foreign policy toward China. Unlike what conventional wisdom would assume, he suggests that heavy reliance on China has made North Korean leaders wary of China's influence in North Korea. After all, the assumption under national security priority is that the Kims must remain the superior leader in the country. So, while North Korea needs China's support, the Kims have not hesitated to contain Chinese influence by either directly suppressing domestic political challengers or playing off between China and its competitors. In the meantime, North Korea proactively extends security allies. For example, in chapter 6, Levkowitz detailed years of cooperation between North Korea and Iran (and other states in the Middle East) on nuclear and conventional weapon technologies to develop nuclear deterrence capability and alleviate reliance on China. He also analyzes how the link between North Korea and Iran would affect their respective future denuclearization negotiation with the United States.

Economic Prosperity

Economic performance is referred to by the North Korean regime as the "people-first principle." Like the national security goal, we use "economic prosperity," a term most readers are familiar with, to describe the regime's economic goal.

Leaders' domestic concern about economic performance motivates them to be proactive in pursuing this goal with foreign policy. Hence, an examination of economic conditions and relations could reveal patterns of how the pursuit of economic goals of the North Korean government influences its foreign policies. One key component of North Korean identity is *Kansong Daekuk* (strong and prosperous great power). Under the doctrine, after accomplishing concrete military capabilities, North Korea needs to make an effort to pursue economic prosperity.

The pursuit of economic prosperity and economic independence can be hindered by the pursuit of the other two survival goals. For instance, the pursuit of political independence constrains North Korea from participating in international trade and trade diversification.

North Korean economy, which heavily relied on the Soviet Union during the Cold War, was disrupted by the collapse of the communist superpower. Due to the long-time tension between North Korea and the United States and its allies, international sanctions followed by the discovery of Pyongyang's nuclear program, and the great famine in the mid-1990s, economic cooperation with China became arguably the priority of the economic component of North Korean foreign policy. In the eyes of Pyongyang, even though relying on China is not ideal, the Chinese communist government, which also has a military agreement with North Korea, poses the least security and ideological threat in the region. From the Chinese perspective, a stable, communist, pro-China North Korea serves the Chinese interest, and China needs natural resources such as coal from North Korea to feed domestic industrialization.

To maintain Chinese economic support, North Korea has kept a positive political relationship with China. Nonetheless, as the North Korean economy becomes increasingly reliant on China, North Korean leaders seek to diversify economic partners. Some alternatives include Russia and Iran. In chapter 5, Gamerman reviews North Korea-Russia (Soviet Union) relations and shows that North Korea has actively improved relations with Russia to relieve its economic and diplomatic dependence on China. With Iran, in addition to cooperation on security, Levkowitz (chapter 6) points out that the arms trade also constitutes a key component of North Korean exports.

Additionally, to relieve domestic and international pressure, North Korea, despite brinksmanship diplomacy, can also be pragmatic and willing to engage with South Korea and Japan, two countries often depicted as enemies of the state in North Korean propaganda. Better relations with South Korea are pursued when the risk of domestic instability looms in North Korea. In chapter 3, Hong analyzes the inter-Korean economic relations and how the transition from a "military first" to an "economy first" policy under Kim Jong-un would affect the inter-Korean relationship. In comparison, the DPRK-Japan relationship is relatively marginalized in North Korean foreign policy because Japan does not pose as much direct security or identity threat to North Korea as the United States or South Korea. In chapter 4, Rao analyzed how the nuclear issue and the Japanese abductee issue have been complicating the bilateral relationship. Nonetheless, as a backup plan, improving relations with Japan becomes an option when the United States or South Korea is unwilling to engage with Pyongyang.

North Korea is isolated and to some extent has chosen to be closed to the outside world. It also has a unique political culture. But the logic behind its survival strategy is not too fundamentally different from other states, that is, North Korean leaders also pursue national security, legitimacy, and economic prosperity. The chapters included in this book examine how the North Korean regime pursues these survival goals with tailored foreign policies for different types of actors in world politics. We hope they could contribute to a better, more comprehensive understanding of North Korea.

Chapter 1

The Adversarial Interdependence between the Democratic People's Republic of Korea and the United States

Jun T. Kwon

REGIME SURVIVAL

Like individuals, states in the international relations are goal-oriented actors. Behaviors and policies of states (whether they are domestic or foreign) are dictated by the goals that they pursue to achieve. Unless you understand goals of states, you are unable to ascertain the behaviors of states, which may result in calling them unpredictable, provocative, irrational, immoral, and insane.

There are three premises that this chapter bases its analysis regarding different patterns of foreign policy conducts: (a) foreign policy is an extension of domestic politics; (b) foreign policy consists of strategic and tactical maneuvers aimed at achieving a set of goals of the political system; (c) in conducting foreign policy, also commonly pursued is the attainment and management of relative superiority in relation with other significant competitors. These goals of any political system, in order of priority, are security, identity, and prosperity.

Being not drastically different from any other country, the Democratic People's Republic of Korea's (hereafter North Korea) foreign policy orientation has evolved in pursuing its systematic objectives of national security, national identity, and economic prosperity. North Korea does not use the term "national security." Since "national security" is the most familiar term with many readers, however, this chapter uses the term "national security." In official documents and state-sponsored media in North Korea, national

7

security is expressed in terms like "defending the sovereignty," "territorial integrity," and "fundamental interests of the state." The three goals are also stipulated in North Korea as the three main principles of *Juche* ideology: military self-defense (*chawi*), political independence (*chaju*), and economic self-sustenance (*charip*). By focusing on these three policy goals, one can understand the logic of North Korea's foreign policy decision-making strategy toward the United States.

There is no doubt that assurance of national security is the most important consideration of foreign policy for any country. Needless to say, security that may be defined as territorial integrity and political independence is a significant domestic factor in shaping North Korea's foreign policy decision making. When a small country like North Korea is confronted with a threat from enemies that are perceived to be hostile and militarily superior, the importance of national security cannot be overstated. The goal of assuring national security has been the most significant and underlying force formulating North Korea's foreign policies toward the United States.

North Korea has had an intense adversarial relationship with the United States since its creation on September 9, 1948. After the Japanese surrendered in World War II, the United States and Soviet forces remained in Korea. These two superpowers were supposed to remain in Korea until an independent Korean government could be established. Each occupied a side of the 38th parallel, the United States to the South and the Soviet Union to the North.

Both the Soviet Union and the United States, however, used the Korean peninsula as a means to assert their hegemonic aspiration and ideological stances. This tension led to a prolonged occupation of the peninsula by both powers and culminated in the establishment of two separate governments with leaders handpicked by Washington and Moscow: Rhee Syngman in the South and Kim Il-sung in the North. North Korea's tense relationship with the United States worsened during the Korean War, continued through the Cold War, and has deepened due to North Korea's pursuit of nuclear weapons programs in the last thirty years.

Since the Korean War, North Korea has feared a military attack from the United States. North Korea's supreme policy goal toward the United States has been to protect the regime from a military attack. Even though tension on the Korean peninsula was always high, the regime survival of North Korea was relatively secure during the Cold War. North Korea was protected under the Communist Bloc. And during the Cold war era, the military power of Pyongyang and Seoul maintained a relative balance.

Since the demise of the Soviet Union and the Communist Bloc along with the diplomatic normalizations between South Korea and the two Communist giants Russia and China in 1991 and 1992 respectively, however, ensuring national security and regime survival has been the most essential missions for North Korea. Furthermore, since the post–Cold War era, the maintenance of the military balance between the two Koreas has tilted away from Pyongyang's side. The strengthened U.S.-South Korea military alliance is perceived as a formidable security threat to North Korea. It was at this moment that North Korea started pushing forward its nuclear weapons ambition on a full scale by withdrawing from the Treaty on the Non-Proliferation of Nuclear Weapons (hereafter referred to as NPT).[1]

Pyongyang leadership has endeavored to pursue national security to maintain regime survival against what it perceives to be hostile countries. North Korea is extremely suspicious of U.S. goals, wary of U.S. motivations, and fearful of ever-impending American aggression. Some scholars of North Korea argue that North Korea's imminent threat from the United States is probably overblown because the United States did not directly attack North Korea for the seventy years since the Korean War stopped with the signing of an armistice. If their argument holds true, it is true as well that North Korea has not attacked the United States since the end of the Korean War. Why does the United States view North Korea as a serious threat to its national security?

If one looks at the map, however, one would be surprised if North Korea did not feel insecure and threatened by external powers, in particular the United States, which would result in developing nuclear weapons. As Sukhoon Hong analyzes in chapter 3, there has been a constant legitimacy competition between the two Koreas. And North Korea is still very much haunted by the Japanese colonial rule over Korea between 1910 and 1945 and is suspicious of Japan's ambitions to reemerge as an aggressive power as Anand Rao puts it in chapter 4.

Of course, South Korea and Japan have their own security concerns over North Korean threats. Therefore, it can be said that in some sense the United States serves as a stabilizer in the region by mitigating the potential aggressive actions they might take against North Korea. Given the disparities of power and status between the United States and its two allies in East Asia, however, it is very unlikely that either South Korea or Japan would take unilateral actions against North Korea without the consent or permission of the United States[2] Considering that fact that American troops have undertaken several rounds of joint military exercises with South Korea and Japan annually, on the contrary, both U.S. regional allies would be drawn into a much bigger conflict to assist a U.S.-led war if the United States wanted to carry out military actions against North Korea.

In referring to its fear over a U.S. invasion, the Korean Central News Agency published an official commentary after its nuclear test in 2016: "History proves that powerful nuclear deterrence serves as the strongest treasured sword for frustrating outsiders' aggression."[3] The agency went on to say, "The Saddam Hussein regime in Iraq and the Qaddafi regime in Libya could not escape the fate of destruction after being deprived of their foundations for nuclear development and giving up nuclear programs of their own accord."[4]

In this sense, North Korea's nuclear preoccupations are the direct result of its perception of the endless siege by the United States. Thus, North Korea has been driven by a deep-seated fear of regime collapse caused by the threat of a U.S. military attack; that is, the core motivation behind the nuclear saber-rattling is "regime survival."[5]

The Threat of the United States toward North Korea

The United States has never veered from its position that North Korea (whether it is a nuclear power or not) is very dangerous and is a grave security threat to the U.S. national interest. The United States claims that North Korean foreign policies are and will be more emboldened and aggressive because North Korea believes that the possession of nuclear weapons will provide a shield from any outside attacks including a U.S. invasion. In relation to aggressive postures, North Korea could directly threaten others unless certain demands were not met.

The United States also worries about the possibility that North Korea could simply attack South Korea or Japan, both of which are important allies with the United States. Even if there were no direct nuclear attacks by North Korea against the United States and its Asian allies, the United States is concerned about the likelihood that the North Korean nuclear weapons could trigger a regional nuclear arms race causing regional instability. If the North Korean nuclear conundrum is not resolved, countries in Asia may want to pursue their own nuclear armament. South Korea once tried to develop its nuclear weapons and Japan has enough technological and financial resources to achieve its nuclear weapons in a short period of time. A nuclear Japan would be a headache for China and even Taiwan is interested in arming itself with nuclear weapons.

The backbone of the NPT regime is composed of two main pillars: (1) nuclear-weapon states commit to eliminating their arsenals and agree to not spread nuclear weapons, and (2) non-nuclear weapon states pledge not to seek them. Since the treaty entered into force in 1970, only two states, India and Pakistan, have developed nuclear weapons and have been recognized as nuclear states in addition to the five nuclear weapons states recognized by the treaty—the United States, Russia, China, France, and the United Kingdom. It shows that the NPT regime has been well honored and respected in terms of controlling the proliferation of nuclear weapons in world politics. The nuclear North Korea, however, could further damage the NPT regime and might encourage other states to follow in its footsteps, which could bring forth rapid proliferation of nuclear weapons like wildfire in world politics.

Another concern of the United States regarding North Korea's nuclear weapons is that it could give or sell nuclear weapons and nuclear technology to other states as well as non-state actors, in particular terrorist organizations.[6] Having suffered from severe economic sanctions, North Korea may want to capitalize on its nuclear weapons to alleviate its economic hardship.

Considering its capability and intention, however, do North Korea and its nuclear weapons really pose a threat to the United States in a way that the United States worries? Is the U.S. security concern about North Korea legitimate? North Korea's nuclear weapons are driven by its actual fear of American invasion, and Pyongyang has made it clear that it will not use nuclear weapons unless it is attacked by outside forces. In addition, North Korea knows well that initiating military conflicts against the United States would be a suicidal act.

North Korea, however, is designated and demonized as a rogue or enemy state to the United States. Traditionally speaking, large states tend to latch that title on a competitor of similar size and caliber, such as China and Russia in the twenty-first century. The United States has not done so and in fact, has given that title to states that pose no real de facto threat to American security or economic concerns. The question that one has to ask is why the United States chooses to create more tension over what seems to be states that cannot in any credible way affect the United States. This question is especially important considering that the United States is still considered a hegemonic power militarily speaking, and therefore theoretically continues to hold unilateral power over all other states.

In Mearsheimer's *The Great Tragedy of Great Power Politics*, the traditional argument is that great powers compete against one another for dominance in the global system.[7] Through this logic, one can assume that Mearsheimer argues that powers of the same caliber compete against one another rather than those from different levels of power. This is generally observed well as the main competitors of the United States in the twenty-first century are Russia and China, which seem to have aligned to counterbalance the United States.

The problem, however, arises when considering the case of North Korea. In comparing North Korea's power against the United States, one can see that the United States' military and economic capabilities far outclass North Korean powers. While North Korea has successfully advanced its nuclear weapons programs, the American military has vastly superior nuclear weapons technology that is capable of containing the threats from North Korea. The influences of North Korea are also severely limited being contained only to its region as compared to the United States' global outreach. Hence, the question that has to be asked is why does the United States seek to attach the label of enemy state and to put unimaginable pressure on North Korea?

The framework through which the United States has undertaken its hostile policies and then military interventions in other sovereign countries has always had a pattern with three necessary conditions. A typical pattern of hostile U.S. behaviors leading up to the military interventions is characterized by a biblically driven mandate to defeat evil, preoccupation with maintaining hegemonic power, and pressure from the alliance partners to show its security commitments.

Human Rights and Demonization

One of the most conspicuous themes that affects how the United States conducts its foreign policy is human rights. The United States government has been integral in pushing for international recognition of human rights as a core concern for conducting its foreign policy for all states.[8] From the Western tradition of natural rights, Western powers have always believed that the legitimacy of a state comes from its ability to dutifully protect and maintain its people's rights.[9] This has most likely arisen because of the Cold War structure where the struggle between the United States and the Soviet Union was ideological in nature where individual freedoms were more respected in the Western hemisphere.

While the United States government has issued statements about the protection and upholding of human rights, the push for human rights also came from the American public as revelations about human rights came to light in the free press.[10] Thus, the issue of human rights is a key ideological struggle between the values of individual and natural rights in the United States against the powers that do not follow suit.

Considering that human rights are generally more respected in democracies than in non-democratic regimes, the United States has traditionally preferred to be in the presence of democracies rather than non-democratic states if they are not aligned against them. The preference for democracies is due to liberal ideas of Democratic Peace Theory and constructivism.[11]

From a constructivist point of view, nation-states that share a commonality in identity with one another will be more likely in getting along with one another. The United States also has a stake to see the world become more democratic as democratic powers prefer to engage in peaceful diplomacy rather than war. This preference for diplomacy is in line with American interests as it provides stability in the international system through which the United States as a hegemon benefits greatly, especially when there is trade involved.[12] From this we see that powers that the United States is closest to are the Western European powers of Britain, France, and Germany, as these three powers have strong democratic foundations that have been well institutionalized.

Ever since the 1990s, Responsibility-to-Protect (R2P) has arisen as a new norm where the international community is expected to play a role in correcting violations of human rights.[13] R2P allows for a means to bypass sovereignty in cases where there are gross violations of human rights due to another state's inability or refusal to protect the human rights of its own citizens. Furthermore, R2P requires members of the international community not only to "intervene in cases of human rights violations but also to prevent such actions from happening.[14]

Considering North Korea's well-documented violations of human rights, the United States has good moral reason not only to pressure these governments to change, cause regime collapse, or intervene, but also to protect the human rights of neighboring states too. As seen, R2P is another factor that contributes to American animosity toward North Korea.

American exceptionalism further exacerbates the views that the United States has toward North Korea. Despite this exceptionalism being mainly focused on the American domestic political arena early on, it has evolved to become more global with Wilson's structure.[15] As this exceptionalism is based on the creeds that American actions are justified by moral principles and that the United States is exemplary to other states, actions hearkening to R2P are very much expected.[16]

In addition, the United States has extended human rights themes to demonize North Korean leadership. North Korea has been portrayed as a part of an "axis of evil" along with Iraq and Iran in the American public and media that the Kim regime develops nuclear weapons and slaughters innocent civilians including Americans. A recent case mentioned by Washington to demonize North Korea is the death of Otto Warmbier who had been detained in North Korea for seventeen months as a prisoner and who was returned to the United States in a coma and died. Otto's death among the American people and policymakers in Washington was viewed as an evil and despicable act that could be conducted only by a monster like the Kim regime.

The United States has persuaded the American people as well as the international community that the maximum pressure against the North Korean regime is driven and should be justified by the moral responsibility of the United States to subjugate the evil perpetrator. It is imperative that the economic sanctions and possible military actions are absolutely necessary both by the U.S. unilateral action and by the collective action through the United Nations. The U.S. pressure on North Korea is clearly driven by American exceptionalism, a belief that the United States should play a special role as a defender of goodness.

The majority of states that the United States considers adversarial have controversial human rights records. States that are prime examples of this are China, Russia, North Korea, and Iran. However, aside from the Western European powers, many allies of the United States are violators of human rights as well. Israel, a key ally of the United States, has been a key violator of human rights when considering the issue of the Palestinian people. Similarly, Saudi Arabia has a well-known record of gender-based discrimination where women hold little political power and are unable to drive. As such, it is important to note that human rights violations alone are not a sufficient condition for the United States to consider another power like North Korea an enemy or rogue state.

Preoccupation with Maintaining Hegemonic Power

Since the bipolar global structure that existed during the Cold War came to an end, the United States has been preoccupied with maintaining its hegemonic power in every corner of the world. Even though it seems that almost four decades after the end of the Cold War, any meaningful alliance has not developed to counter U.S. hegemony, there are clear signs that the American predominance has been noticeably challenged.

With its growing power, China demands changes to reshape the international order, which has been underpinned by the United States over the last two decades. Russia under the slogan of "Strong Russia" has reemerged to regain the status as a global power. In particular, the United States has struggled to perpetuate its hegemonic power and influence in Asia due to the challenges posed by China and North Korea. The United States has maintained its hegemony using military prowess and the propagation of American ideology. Giving prominence to a story of the existence of North Korean threat in Asia has contributed to the maintenance of the U.S. preponderance and justified the stay of the troops in South Korea and Japan. Reinforcement of the alliances with South Korea and Japan is crucial for the United States to check and balance the rise of China as well.

Another consideration for hostile U.S. policies is related to the world economic order. Looking from a Marxist perspective, the American hegemony is maintained through a global capitalistic order.[17] The United States sits in the very core of the global capitalist system that it has set up with its closest allies having the most links to the United States such as the European powers, whereas those who are exploited the most are on the periphery of this. As Marxist theory is only concerned about capital and the exploitation of labor, American hegemony maintains its strength because of the United States' ability to appease the needs of other states directly below it while at the same time being able to oppress and control those at the periphery. This method of thinking is very much in line with the World-Systems theory by Immanuel Wallerstein.[18] In examining the evidence for this, the states that have the closest relations to the United States are Britain, Germany, and Japan; these three states are prime examples of core states in Wallerstein's World-Systems theory.

However, it must be noted that volume of trade in international trade does not equate to closeness of relationship between a periphery state and the core state in the system. It is simply one necessary condition rather than a sufficient condition that would dictate a peripheral state's opinion on the capitalist hegemon. One could argue that China, despite hugely benefiting from American trade, has less-than-friendly intentions toward American influence in its region. This can be due to China's hegemonic desires.

Nevertheless, Marxists should point out that a huge portion of the Chinese population, its non-bourgeois class of factory workers and manufacturers, are being exploited in the United States' favor where goods are sold cheaper and profits are maximized for American corporations. Ultimately, one could say that from the Marxist perspective, powers that are closest to the United States act in a similar fashion when it comes to international capitalist exploitation, and those that the United States perceives as hostile may have the necessary condition of being a state that has undergone international capitalist exploitation.

The World-Systems theory is based on the world liberal economic order where the United States uses is economic power to coerce world powers to comply with its demands and preferences. Institutions such as the International Monetary Fund and the World Bank are prime examples of the United States' established liberal economic order. Furthermore, ever since Bretton Woods, the United States dollar has been the currency to conduct international trade giving the United States political leverage against any possible adversaries.[19]

Considering the advantage that the United States has in the global economy and the ability to manipulate it domestically with the treasury, states that have not complied to the United States political demands generally suffer from American economic sanctions. However, despite economic sanctions from the United States, North Korea has remained defiant and has continued its activities. North Korea has continued testing nuclear weapons and missile technology despite sanctions from the United States and the United Nations. Considering that all diplomatic and economic pressures have already been used have failed to discourage North Korea from continuing with such nuclear and military activity, North Korea, armed with the *Juche* (self-reliance) doctrine and faced with economic isolation, can be said one of the most tenaciously defiant states challenging the American global hegemonic power. As such, the second necessary condition for a state to be

considered an enemy of the United States would be its deviance or defiance
to the American capitalist world order.

Commitments to Alliance Partners

Another variable to explain the hostile U.S. policies toward North Korea is
the relationship that North Korea has with regional American allies in Asia.
While security concerns have always been an important factor in American
foreign policy, the 9/11 terrorist attacks on American soil play an even bigger
role. In order to maintain hegemony, the United States must give a reason to
other powers to allow its dominance, which can be summarized as stability,
peace, and trade.

Much like Pax Britannica where free trade on the high seas was protected by Britain, the United States is doing the same thing.[20] The success of
American dominance in certain regions of the world can be credited to the
United States' military backing to protect the international order should there
be cracks. During the Cold War, American military protection may have been
seen as necessary for the core states with the Soviet Union around the corner;
however, in the new unipolar world, the United States continues to maintain
troops in Japan and Germany despite the nonexistence of a Soviet threat.
American military protection is contingent upon any threats that can damage
its international capitalistic order, regardless of where it comes from. This
feeling of heightened security concern has only amplified post-9/11 where
real unpredictable threats to the United States' global hegemony come from
non-state actors that do not follow the norms of state-based diplomacy. As
such, aside from possible state aggressors against American allies, non-state
aggressors and their backers are now of concern too.[21]

As such, one can see that the United States acts on behalf of its regional
allies from around the world, designating their adversaries as enemies to ease
their security concerns. This is evidently seen in North Korea. It is important
to note that American designation of certain small powers as enemy states
can sometimes be an American-led initiative, or due to the influence of their
concerned regional allies.

To explain South Korea and Japan's reliance on the United States, Walt's
theory on the balance of threat must be taken into consideration. In looking
at one of the original questions of this chapter in regard to Mearsheimer's
balance-of-power theory, the balance-of-threat considers the perception of
threat as the defining reason behind the formation of alliances between these
powers and the United States.[22]

The subjective perception of the threat that arose from North Korea's
nuclear weapons programs as well as its belligerence to the liberal economic
world order has caused much consternation in these states. Alternatively, the

United States, despite being more powerful than North Korea in every single dimension, has been led into these alliances partly because of the perceived threats from North Korea to the global hegemonic order.

While it is important to consider that the third necessary condition that allows for the United States to designate North Korea as an enemy with very aggressive policies toward it, North Korea is a clear and present threat to the American allies in Asia. The root cause of it lies in the balance-of-threat theory. As such, the third necessary condition for a small state to be considered an enemy state in the eyes of the United States is that they have to be enemies of the American allies in the region.

Thus, the United States has always come under great pressure from its alliance partners to show its commitment to their security. Given the fact that North Korea's nuclear activities are expanding, it surely poses a grave threat to South Korea and Japan, which are crucial allies of the United States in the region. Both the U.S. alliance partners are constantly anxious about North Korea becoming a powerful regional actor with nuclear capabilities and malicious intentions. It appears that South Korea and Japan have been demanding that the United States should contain and hold North Korea's growing power in check. The hostile U.S. policies and possible military actions against North Korea are highly expected to take place whenever and wherever the three aforementioned conditions are satisfied.

Reverse Effect and Illegitimacy of Economic Sanctions

Economic sanctions are deemed effective tools to change states' behaviors in international politics. North Korean nuclear ambitions have been punished by economic sanctions in the international community. The severity of economic sanctions toward North Korea has been elevated since its first nuclear test in 2006.

Main economic sanctions toward North Korea are imposed by the international community through the United Nations Security Council.[23] However, sanctions are a major source of North Korea's perceptions of hostile U.S. attitudes and policies for two reasons. The United States has implemented unilateral sanctions toward North Korea restricting more economic activities and targeting a much larger list of North Korean government officials and businesses than the UN sanctions.[24] Furthermore, the United States has increased sanctions of the secondary boycott targeting Chinese people and firms helping North Korea. The United States in particular may want to use trade cards to press China to impose economic sanctions on North Korea in a more meaningful way. In addition, in North Korea's view, it is the United States who has taken lead in initiating sanctions, mobilizing support at the United Nations, and getting resolutions passed at the UN Security Council.

However, North Korea has defied years of sanctions and they have failed to alter its nuclear behaviors. Economic sanctions are predicated upon two assumptions: (1) North Korea will give up its aggressive military ambitions including nuclear weapons if economic conditions become bad enough; and (2) revolutionary activities will occur to lead to regime collapse when there is widespread discontent and frustration among people. If people in North Korea view that the government is responsible for their aggravating economic plight, they will be likely to rise up against the Kim regime. Questions about regime security in North Korea become more interesting as the Kim regime persists despite predictions that it could and should not. Kim Jong-un has been in power for almost ten years now since his father died in 2011. It appears to be clear that he has consolidated his firm power and his power is very secure from the fear of forced removal without major challenges to his authority.

What has really been going on inside North Korea may also have something to do with the inability of economic sanctions to produce the changes that the United States wishes in the North Korean nuclear conundrum. The North Korean regime's legitimacy is not founded on economic performance but on ideological grounds. In other words, the Kim regime is maintained by what may be termed "pathological nationalism," not its ability to satisfy people's material needs. Standing up against the sole superpower in the world is an enormous source of national pride. One should recognize that external threats (actual or perceived) might empower a regime that otherwise might experience a legitimacy crisis.

Regime change or regime collapse comes in mainly three forms: (1) from the inside of the ruling coalition in the form of a military coup, (2) from the bottom by people who are close to a mass revolution, and (3) foreign imposition through military conquest. None of the three models of regime change is likely to take place in North Korea.

What are the secrets to regime persistence in North Korea? Drawing from the literature on authoritarian persistence, many observers have identified how dictators survive and stay in power. A large literature, however, has centered on only coercive measures and censorship of the flow of information.[25] It has missed one crucial variable "regime legitimacy" to understand regime survival and regime change.

Regime legitimacy may be defined as "right to rule" or "the belief in the rightfulness of a regime, in its authority to issue commands so that the commands are obeyed not simply out of fear or self-interest, but because they are believed to have moral authority and because subjects believe that they ought to obey."[26] If a regime fails to generate and maintain legitimacy, then the regime will collapse. This is a simple and empirically very practical concept.

When the regime lacks and loses legitimacy, then there is a crisis and the regime collapses. Every political system attempts to establish and cultivate the belief in its legitimacy in order to have orders obeyed willingly rather than the threat of force. All political systems try to legitimize their exercise of power from only one source, that is, the support or consent of the people. This is only one source of legitimacy. Even in very authoritarian countries like North Korea, the regime tries to support itself by getting legitimacy from the people. Without people's consent, leadership will lose its base forever. This commonsensical premise is best manifested in Jean-Jacques Rousseau's *The Social Contract* that "the strongest man is never strong enough to maintain his mastery at all times unless he transforms his strength into right and obedience into duty."[27]

In theory, there are two strategies that the ruling elite utilize for generating political legitimacy: their performance in satisfying people's needs and the promotion of a belief system through an ideology. The first strategy with which a regime pursues legitimacy is performance-based, which usually refers to the regime's capability to achieve economic development. Performance here, however, is defined to encompass the security, welfare, and justice functions of government and not just economic performance.

This premise suggests that the state and the ruling class are able to justify the exercise of power by satisfying people's economic needs and prosperity. In other words, the concentration of power in the state cannot be justified except in terms of its use in pursuit of the collective will of the political community and enhancement of people's need satisfaction. Thus, proper and effective use of power to promote the collective well-being of the political community can generate regime legitimacy. Poor performance is frequently advanced by those contesting the incumbent's right to rule.

As opposed to the performance basis of regime legitimacy, the second strategy with which a regime pursues legitimacy is governing ideology. The ideological foundation of legitimacy is related to psychology and mass value and belief system whereas the performance basis is more of a question of utilitarian and material perception.[28] According to Max Weber, the "basis of every system of authority, and correspondingly of every kind of willingness to obey, is a belief, a belief by virtue of which persons exercising authority are lent prestige."[29]

Based on these two statements, the key component of regime legitimacy is the belief by the governed in the rulers' moral right to issue commands and the people's corresponding consent to obey such commands. In other words, when regime legitimacy is created and maximized on the basis of inculcating a belief system, the leadership's survival is not directly linked to its performance to satisfy people's needs. In this vein, North Korea is the most striking example of a regime that uses values and beliefs as the basis of power and authority.

Thus, a regime makes effort to persuade the masses and seeks to institutionalize a belief system (a system of values) in the populace upon which people's consent and loyalty to the regime are built. This belief system, then, is "propagated by means of the various agents of [political] socialization (some people call it negatively as indoctrination or brainwashing), especially those over which the regime can exercise some direct control, such as the mass media and the educational system."[30] It is at this institutionalization stage of a belief system that ideology appears to play a very important role in providing and spelling out the nature and contents of a common political belief system. In the ideology instigated by the political leadership, the nature of the current political system and the ultimate goals of the regime are spelled out, which permits the justification of current policies and the current regime.

As Han S. Park argues, "an ideology presents the populace with a comprehensive political belief system enumerating the ultimate goals of the society and the legitimate means by which these goals can be achieved. As such, it provides the individual with a vision of his political society, his place in it, and a set of reasons why this system is worthy of his loyalty."[31] In other words, the belief system as "a set of values" advanced by the ruling elites becomes internalized and embedded among the members of the society, and a sense of the consent and loyalty to the regime is generated on the basis of this shared belief system.

As aforementioned, governing ideology can be defined as a system of beliefs, norms, and values held by the people that cannot readily be compromised or changed. In this sense, it gives a nation its character and, thus, identity. A governing ideology, then, has both its utility function as an agent of regime legitimization and the provider of system (national) identity. Having been elevated to the position of North Korea's official ruling ideology, *Juche* ideology gives North Korea a national identity as "Koreanistic Socialism" (*Josonsik Sahwhejui*).

In conclusion, Kim's regime has been successful in "persuading" the masses and institutionalizing a belief system (a system of values) of nationalism in the populace upon which people's consent and loyalty to the regime are built. This belief system of pathological nationalism, then, is propagated by means of the various agents of political socialization, especially those over which the regime can exercise some direct control, such as the mass media and the educational system.

The ruling elites of North Korea cite the hostile policy of the United States as the primary reason for their economic misfortune. They propagate that standing up against the sole superpower, the United States, is an enormous source of national pride. The external threat (actual and perceived) from the

United States has empowered Kim's regime so that it is able to mobilize and unify its people with anti-American sentiment and strong nationalism. In this regard, the United States has been complicit in keeping Kim and his associates in power.

Economic sanctions also hurt not the Kim leadership but people of North Korea. The economic plight that North Korean citizens have been suffering from is beyond our imagination. News of people being starved to death due to food shortages and the lack of medical supplies now become very familiar stories. And the night images of North Korea from satellites that are almost completely dark are not surprising any more. A recent image of Russian diplomat families escaping North Korea on a hand-pushed railcar clearly epitomizes how dire the economic situation in North Korea has been.[32] Simply speaking, economic sanctions have left millions of average North Koreans in life-and-death situations.

Article 507 of the Compendium of the Social Doctrine of the Church published by the Holy See clearly stipulates that "[t]he true objective of such measures is open to the way to negotiation and dialogue. Sanctions must never be used as a means for the direct punishment of an entire population: it is not licit that entire populations, and above all their most vulnerable members, be made to suffer because of such sanctions. Economic sanctions in particular are an instrument to be used with great discernment and must be subjected to strict legal and ethical criteria. An economic embargo must be of limited duration and cannot be justified when the resulting effects are indiscriminate."[33]

Considering that the most vulnerable members of the North Korean community suffer from sanctions that have been imposed for many years with no end in sight, sanctions toward North Korea cannot be justified. In addition, given the reverse effect and injustice of economic sanctions, it is about time for the United States and the international community to reconsider sanctions toward North Korea, which is one of the preconditions for solving the issue of North Korean nuclear weapons.

Nuclear Conundrum

At the center of the adversarial interdependence between North Korea and the United States is North Korea's nuclear weapons. As of now, North Korea appears not to give up its nuclear weapons, which are cherished as "treasure swords" unless the United States completely abandons its hostile policies toward North Korea. Pyongyang's nuclear ambition is viewed as a grave threat from the U.S. standpoint. The United States also is determined to maintain its pressure including economic sanctions until North Korea stops its nuclear weapons. It appears to be certain that the adversarial relationship between the United States and North Korea will not be improved anytime soon—or ended.

It is not to say that both countries had some opportunities to reconcile their relationship with agreements over North Korean nuclear weapons. During the Clinton administration, Pyongyang gestured to cooperate with Washington, which promised to support economic aid and to provide formal security assurance to North Korea in the 1994 Geneva Agreed Framework. This agreement affirmed that both the United States and North Korea would "work together for peace and security on a nuclear-free Korean peninsula (Article 3, Geneva Agreed Framework in 1994)."[34] In the 2000 US-DPRK Joint Communiqué, Washington and Pyongyang reaffirmed to accept mutual respect and sovereignty to improve peace and security in the Asia-Pacific region.

However, during the first term of the Bush administration, President Bush proclaimed North Korea an "axis of evil," and the Hawks of Washington persisted in the U.S. right to launch preemptive attacks against the terrorist countries. As a result, North Korea, on January 10, 2003, announced its withdrawal from the NPT and stopped demanding bilateral talks with the United States. Pyongyang became extremely hostile to Washington and tried to develop and advance nuclear technologies. The United States missed this golden opportunity to solve the North Korean nuclear conundrum.

Another golden chance was the recent effort of the two summit meetings that took place in 2018 and 2019 respectively between Donald Trump and Kim Jong-un. Both meetings, however, ended with no breakthrough agreement. Considering the symbolic success of the first summit in Singapore, the lack of a concrete conclusion of the second summit reminded us that both sides repeated their own stances once again.

Even though the two summit meetings failed to produce any meaningful and tangible outcomes in the denuclearization and peace on the Korean Peninsula, did the summits indicate that North Korea wanted to be pro-American at the time? The two submit meetings appeared to be clear signs that Kim Jong-un wanted to improve the relationship with the United States. Since he ascended to power after his father's death in 2011, China is the only country that he had visited before the two summit meetings with President Trump. It was certain that he would not want to travel to Hanoi, Vietnam, for the second summit by a sixty-hour train ride unless he was very much interested in improving North Korea's relationship with the United States.

His grandfather originated and advanced *Juche* ideology to integrate North Korea (and *Juche* gives North Korea its national identity) and his father secured the means of national self-defense by obtaining nuclear weapons. With these two goals achieved by his predecessors, Kim Jong-un has been striving to enhance economic situations to satisfy people's economic needs.

Rather than being pro-American, all of a sudden, Kim Jong-un was motivated by his desperate need to enhance his people's livelihood. His rare admission of the economic failure to build a "great socialist country by 2020" at the Central Committee of the Workers' Party in January 2021 clearly showed how difficult the North Korean economy had been going through. He said that the five-year economic plan from 2016 and 2020 to improve the national economy has been "seriously delayed by severe internal and external situations and unexpected manifold challenges."[35] It looks like a usual condemnation of North Korea against the United States for its economic failure, but it was something very unusual that North Korean leaders openly admitted some policy failures.

There is no doubt that no country has been more severely punished by economic sanctions than North Korea. Sanctions have been imposed by the United States unilaterally and by the United Nations collectively. As Weiqi Zhang extensively examines in chapter 2, China is the only country to provide North Korea with an economic lifeline. But since China has joined the international community to cast affirmative votes for various sanctions at the United Nations Security Council, North Korea is aware of the clear limitation on economic cooperation with China through trade and assistance.

And North Korea knows very well that it would not be able to resuscitate its catastrophically crippled economy without improving its relationship with the United States because it is only the United States that has the power to alleviate and lift sanctions of the United Nations. North Korea believes that the lifting of sanctions (even partial lifting) by the United States is key to improving the national economy. Although North Korea never dismissed all doubts about the U.S. intention to invade and pursue regime change in North Korea, it would view the lifting of sanctions as a signal of the United States to assuage its hostile policies against North Korea. The lifting of sanctions is also viewed by North Korea as a sign of the U.S. sincerity to abandon its hostile policies and to build mutual confidence.

Despite many expectations of the second summit between President Trump and Chairman Kim in Hanoi, the lack of a concrete conclusion left many questions on what happened and why it happened. Much of the confusion over what happened in the second summit and why it failed comes from the contradicting accounts of both parties after the summit. According to Trump, the reason the United States walked away from the negotiations in this instance is that the DPRK (Democratic People's Republic of Korea) wanted "sanctions lifted in their entirety" and that "they were willing to denuclearize a large portion of the areas that we wanted, but we couldn't give up all of the sanctions for that."[36]

However, in a statement released by the DPRK minister Ri, this was not the case. He stated that the DPRK's demands were to lift five out of the eleven UN sanctions on DPRK from 2016 to 2017 that "hamper the civilian economy and the livelihood of our people"[37] in exchange for the permanent and complete destruction of the Yongbyon nuclear facility in the DPRK under U.S. supervision. He further stated that the United States wanted the DPRK to have further denuclearization steps as part of this summit; however, he did not specify what those steps were.

Despite North Korea's claim that it showed willingness and actions of goodwill, the United States has proven unwilling to change its position on complete, verifiable, and irreversible dismantlement (CVID). The United States has never veered from its adamant position that CVID is a precondition for the removal of any sanctions. The United States has demanded that North Korea completely give up all its nuclear weapons and programs, have the dismantling of them verified by a team of international inspectors, and should not return to rebuild the nuclear program. The United States has also insisted that North Korea should demonstrate sincere and concrete steps toward CVID through meaningful actions before any meaningful talks take place.

On the contrary, North Korea views CVID as a possible outcome that the United States and North Korea can work together to achieve through talks and negotiations. North Korea's focus has always been placed on CVIG which means "Complete, Verifiable, and Irreversible Guarantee of regime survival." Chairman Kim has made it clear that he is committed to denuclearization and to the halt of further nuclear or missile tests only if and when the United States guarantees it would not try to overthrow the regime by force. North Korea has been consistent in that it wishes to denuclearize a step-by-step process where each action of dismantlement on the North Korean side is followed by an action of concession on the American side.

North Korea keeps demanding that the United States provide security guarantees through the suspension of the annual U.S.–South Korean joint military drills, a lifting of sanctions, the official end of the Korean War, and the Peace Treaty before it takes further steps toward denuclearization. On the contrary, the United States still requires that North Korea should show rapid and genuine dismantlement of nuclear weapons through rigorous inspection and verification before any rewards are granted. It seems that a well-known gap between the United States and North Korea still remains very difficult to be bridged.

However, it is highly likely that North Korea is genuinely and eventually willing to give up its nuclear weapons *if and only if* the very reason that drove it to develop nuclear weapons is eliminated, that is the fear of regime survival created by hostile U.S. attitudes and policies against North Korea. The denuclearization of the Korean peninsula was also reportedly "the dying wish of Chairman Kim Il-sung and General Secretary Kim Jong-il."[38]

As of this writing, the U.S.–North Korean relations (and the inter-Korean relations as well) return to the era of "fire and fury" and childish nuclear button exchange between Trump and Kim Jung-un in January 2018. As the U.S.–South Korean joint military drills are resumed in 2022, North Korea is about to conduct its seventh nuclear testing soon. It has been almost two years since Biden administration was sworn in. It is reported that a major policy review toward North Korea has been completed in Washington. According to several media reports and Press Secretary Jen Psaki's news conference in April 2021, the Biden administration appears to have considered all policy options to deal with North Korea. It is clear, however, that the Biden administration is not willing to maintain the strategic impatience toward North Korea that was an official policy under the Obama administration. It seems that the Biden administration has learned that the strategic impatience toward North Korea not only failed but also made it possible for North Korea to buy more time to advance its nuclear capabilities. Nor does it appear to pursue President Trump's style of grand bargaining. As Press Secretary Jen Psaki's comments indicate, the United States seems to intend to adopt a middle-ground policy option of the bottom-up approach that "calls for a calibrated, practical approach that is open to and will explore diplomacy with the DPRK."[39]

Even though the policy review toward North Korea laid out by the Biden administration sounds positive, stressing diplomacy and dialogue, it does not contain any concrete and substantive measures to induce North Korea to return to the negotiating table. It is time for the new administration of the United States to consider and implement new radical approaches with the immediate return to the diplomatic negotiations to solve the North Korean nuclear conundrum.

It has been clear that different perspectives and approaches between different U.S. administrations toward Pyongyang are not the main decisive variable. North Korea may have preferred President Trump's style of grand bargaining, but during the Clinton administration, Pyongyang signed in the 1994 Geneva Agreed Framework. North Korea does not adhere to nor is it constrained by any particular negotiation styles or formats. It means that regardless of the different positions and approaches of the U.S. government toward North Korea's nuclear weapons ambitions, what Pyongyang wants to see as a precondition to resuming negotiations is the abandonment of the three aforementioned hostile U.S. policies and attitudes toward North Korea: economic sanctions by the United States and the United Nations, the U.S.–South Korean joint military exercises, and demonization of North Korea.

In order for there to be tangible progress over the nuclear negotiations, some considerations should be reexamined and reemphasized along with the fact that North Korea will not collapse, nor will it change its system to the Western style of capitalism. And the military option should be ruled out from consideration even as the last resort. It is evident that any aggressive military action by the United States will surely turn the Korean Peninsula into a blazing inferno.

The immediate cause of the North Korean security fear is the annual U.S.–South Korean joint military drills around the Korean Peninsula. The annual military drills are always viewed as invasion simulations of the United States and South Korea against North Korea aimed at pursuing regime change and the absorption of North Korea into South Korea. President Trump gave orders to suspend the joint U.S.–South Korea military exercises while he was at the White House. The halt to major military exercises by American and South Korean forces in exchange for North Korea to freeze nuclear activities need to be continued. It would be conducive to temporarily diffusing the tensions and the hostile atmosphere around the Korean Peninsula, but it can't be a permanent solution to the North Korea problem.

Denuclearization is still a difficult process as the approaches that North Korea and the United States have in their minds are in conflict with one another. The traditional methods that the United States has used to denuclearize North Korea such as the comprehensive verifiable irreversible dismantlement (CVID) of nuclear weapons prior to the lifting of sanctions have failed in the past. If the United States wishes to succeed in successfully creating an agreement with North Korea, it may have to pursue the denuclearization of North Korea through step-by-step diplomacy where North Korea would disarm and denuclearize bit by bit in exchange for the gradual lifting of sanctions and security guarantees. If the United States continues with its CVID approach, it is likely that the conclusion of any future negotiations will be similar to the previous failures without any meaningful results.

It is important to note that a partial lifting of the sanctions would be the first step in a long process to denuclearize North Korea. The removal of sanctions needs to be followed by several further steps including diplomatic normalization and the turning of an armistice between the United States and North Korea into a genuine peace treaty to plant stability and peace on the Korean peninsula. Given the fact that the North Korean issue is one that has been ongoing for seventy years with little breakthrough, it is likely that there would be bumps along the way to the denuclearization of North Korea and permanent peace on the Korean Peninsula. The United States must approach the issue of North Korea with the mindset of more engagement, a long-term process where concessions are made between the two parties. The North Korean nuclear issue is a complicated issue that is core to the survival of the regime. The Biden administration's most difficult task would be to convince North Korea that its regime survival is intact and guaranteed after denuclearization, something much more difficult than the Iran Nuclear Deal.

NOTES

1. North Korea announced its decision to withdraw from the NPT on March 12, 1993, but in June 1993 "suspended the effectuation" of that withdrawal. North Korea officially announced its withdrawal from the NPT effective as of January 11, 2003. https://www.iaea.org/newscenter/focus/dprk/fact-sheet-on-dprk-nuclear-safeguards.

2. Wartime Operational Control Authority (OPCON) over South Korean military currently belongs to the United States Forces Korea (USFK). The U.S. and South Korean militaries have discussed the schedule for the transfer of wartime operational control authority in 2022.

3. Megan Specia and David E. Sanger, "How the 'Libya Model' Became a Sticking Point in North Korea Nuclear Talks," *New York Times*, May 16, 2018, https://www.nytimes.com/2018/05/16/world/asia/north-korea-libya-model.html.

4. Ibid.

5. Sico Van der Meer, "States' Motivations to Acquire or Forgo Nuclear Weapons: Four Factors of Influence," *Journal of Military and Strategic Studies* 17, no. 1 (2016).

6. Matthijs M. Maas, "How Viable Is International Arms Control for Military Artificial Intelligence? Three Lessons from Nuclear Weapons," *Contemporary Security Policy* 40, no. 3 (2019): 285–311; Stephen J. Cimbala, "Nuclear Proliferation in the Twenty-First Century: Realism, Rationality, or Uncertainty?" *Strategic Studies Quarterly* 11, no. 1 (2017): 129–46.

7. John J. Mearsheimer, *The Tragedy of Great Power Politics* (W.W. Norton & Company, 2001).

8. Adarsh Mathur and Naresh Kumar, "Human Rights Issues in American Foreign Policy," *The Indian Journal of Political Science* 67 (October 2006): 745.

9. Ibid., 747.

10. Ibid., 750 and 752.

11. Sarah M. Burns and Chad Van Schoelandt, "Democratic Peace Theory, Montesquieu, and Public Choice," in *Reclaiming Liberalism*, edited by David F. Hardwick and Leslie Marsh (London: Palgrave Macmillan, Cham, 2020), 247–79; Elena Dück, "Identity Makes the World Go Round: Social Constructivist Foreign Policy Analysis" (PhD diss., 2020).

12. Spyros Sakellaropoulos and Panagiotis Sotiris, "American Foreign Policy as Modern Imperialism: From Armed Humanitarianism to Preemptive War," *Science & Society* 72 (April 2008): 208.

13. Gareth Evans and Mohamed Sahnoun, "The Responsibility to Protect," *Foreign Affairs* 81 (2002): 99.

14. Ibid., 101.

15. Meghana V. Nayak and Christopher Malone, "American Orientalism and American Exceptionalism: A Critical Rethinking of U.S. Hegemony," *International Studies Review* 11 (June 2009): 256.

16. Robert G. Patman, "Globalisation, the New U.S. Exceptionalism and the War on Terror," *Third World Quarterly* 27 (September 2006): 965.

17. Sakellaropoulos and Sotiris, "American Foreign Policy," 208.

18. Immanuel Wallerstein, *World-Systems Analysis: An Introduction* (Durham, NC: Duke University Press, 2006), 12.

19. Michael Mastanduno, "System Maker and Privilege Taker: U.S. Power and the International Political Economy," *World Politics* 61 (January 2009): 130.

20. Thomas P. M. Barnett, "The Pentagon's New Map," in Phil Williams, Donald M. Goldstein, and Jay M. Shafritz (eds.), *Classic and Contemporary Debates in International Relations* (Belmont, CA: Thomson Wadsworth, 2006), 542.

21. G. John Ikenberry, "From Liberal Leviathan: The Origins, Crisis, and Transformation of the American World Order," in Phil Williams, Donald M. Goldstein, and Jay M. Shafritz (eds.), *Classic and Contemporary Debates in International Relations* (Belmont, CA: Thomson Wadsworth, 2006), 141.

22. Kenneth N. Waltz, *Theory of International Politics* (Long Grove, IL: Waveland Press, 2010); Stephen M. Walt, *The Origins of Alliances* (Ithaca, NY: Cornell University Press, 1987).

23. Arms Control Association, "UN Security Council Resolutions on North Korea, Fact Sheets and Briefs," January 2022, https://www.armscontrol.org/factsheets/UN -Security-Council-Resolutions-on-North-Korea; Yong Suk Lee, "International Isolation and Regional Inequality: Evidence from Sanctions on North Korea." *Journal of Urban Economics* 103 (2018): 34–51.

24. U.S. Department of the Treasury, "Sanctions Programs and Country Information," https://home.treasury.gov/policy-issues/financial-sanctions/sanctions-programs -and-country-information.

25. Daniel Byman and Jennifer Lind, "Pyongyang's Survival Strategy: Tools of Authoritarian Control in North Korea," *International Security* 35, no. 1 (2010): 44–74.; Young Whan Kihl and Hong Nack Kim, *North Korea: The Politics of Regime Survival* (New York: Routledge, 2014); David Reese, *The Prospects for North Korea Survival* (New York: Routledge, 2020).

26. Rodney S. Barker, *Political Legitimacy and the State* (Oxford; New York: Clarendon Press; Oxford University Press, 1990), 11.

27. Muthiah Alagappa, *Political Legitimacy in Southeast Asia: The Quest for Moral Authority* (Redwood City, CA: Stanford University Press, 1995), 1.

28. Han S. Park, *Human Needs and Political Development: A Dissent to Utopian Solutions* (Cambridge: Schenkman Publishing Company, 1984).

29. "Political Legitimacy," Stanford Encyclopedia of Philosophy, April 24, 2017, at https://plato.stanford.edu/entries/legitimacy/#:~:text=According%20to%20Weber %2C%20that%20a,virtue%20of%20which%20persons%20exercising.

30. Park, *Human Needs and Political Development*, 70.

31. Ibid., 145.

32. Iva Nechepurenko and Mike Ives, "Russians Escape North Korea on a Hand-Pushed Railcar," *New York Times*, February 26, 2021, https://www.nytimes .com/2021/02/26/world/europe/north-korea-russia-covid-railcar-trolley.html.

33. "Compendium of the Social Doctrine of the Church," in *Pontifical Council for Justice and Peace*, The Holy See, http://www.vatican.va/roman_curia/pontifical _councils/justpeace/documents/rc_pc_justpeace_doc_20060526_compendio-dott-soc _en.html.

34. The Agreed Framework between the United States of America and the Democratic People's Republic of Korea was signed on October 21, 1994, between North Korea (DPRK) and the United States. See https://media.nti.org/pdfs/aptagframe.pdf.

35. North Korean *Rodong Newspaper*, January 6, 2021.

36. John Hudson, Anne Gearan, and Simon Denver, "Abrupt End of Summit May Have Exposed Limits of Trump's Strategy on Kim," *Washington Post*, February 28, 2019, https://www.washingtonpost.com/world/national-security/dispute-over-sanctions-leaves-trump-and-north-koreans-in-free-fall/2019/02/28/f701b450-c805-4e25-af11-fbdf4e0a79bc_story.html.

37. Ibid.

38. "The denuclearization of the Korean Peninsula was the dying wish of Chairman Kim Il-sung and General Secretary Kim Jong-il," First Vice Foreign Minister Kim Kye Gwan told a meeting with Chinese officials in Beijing, according to a statement. Geoffrey Cain, "Denuclearized North Korea Was Kim Jong-il's 'Dying Wish,'" Says Diplomat," TheWorld, June 20, 2013, https://www.pri.org/stories/2013-06-20/denuclearized-north-korea-was-kim-jong-ils-dying-wish-says-diplomat.

39. Press Secretary Jen Psaki's news conference on April 30, 2021, at https://www.whitehouse.gov/briefing-room/press-briefings/2021/04/30/press-gaggle-by-press-secretary-jen-psaki-aboard-air-force-one-en-route-philadelphia-pa/.

Chapter 2

Pursuing Interdependence and Independence

North Korea's Foreign Policy on China

Weiqi Zhang

North Korea's foreign policy serves regime preservation internationally and domestically. One crucial piece of its international survival strategy is China who not only rescued the Kim regime during the Korean War and supported it militarily and economically during the Cold War but also has shielded it from international sanctions and political pressure since the end of the Cold War. While the Kims need China's support and protection for national security and economic stability at the international level, domestic survival requires them to keep China at arm's length from domestic politics. And the strategic dilemma worsened due to North Korea's nuclear program.

The first section of this chapter describes the political logic behind North Korea's survival strategy. The next two sections apply the logic to analyze the China policies under the three generations of Kims regimes. The analysis shows that, even though Kim Il-sung and Kim Jong-il managed to balance their international and domestic strategies and retained China's support even when their policies hurt Chinese interests, the inexperienced Kim Jong-un mistakenly followed his predecessors' strategies, which are unfit for the domestic and international political conditions he faces.

POLITICAL LOGIC BEHIND NORTH
KOREA'S SURVIVAL STRATEGY

The survival of a North Korean leader means not only the preservation of the regime in international politics but also that of his political status as the supreme leader in domestic politics. Therefore, foreign policy is not only a key piece of a North Korean leader's survival strategy but also firmly controlled and often directly implemented by the leader with little involvement of the foreign services or social factors such as public opinion.[1]

International survival strategy responds to perceived external threats, which are affected by the capability gap between North Korea and other states and its perceived intention of the latter.[2] From North Korea's perspective, the major external threat has come from the United States, a superpower that has openly demonstrated aggressive intentions toward the North Korean regime. For instance, the United States is technically still at war with North Korea due to the lack of a peace treaty on the Korean War, imposed sanctions and diplomatic isolation on the country, and designated it a "state sponsor of terrorism" and "axis of evil." Consequently, the United States is considered by North Korean leaders as the enemy of the state and the culprit behind its economic and diplomatic difficulties.

Among the strategic options for small powers to deal with the threat from major powers, the best option for North Korean leaders is balancing, externally and internally.[3] Externally, North Korea formed security alliances with Russia (former Soviet Union) and China who shared interests in containing the expansion of the U.S. sphere of influence. In the security arrangements, North Korea serves as a buffer zone while the other two keep the North Korean regime stable with economic and military assistance. Nonetheless, the heavy reliance of the Kims regimes on the two big powers does not give them much leverage.[4] For instance, the North Korea–China relationship has been described as one of "lips and teeth," meaning if lips are gone then teeth will be cold, because if North Korea collapses then not only would it affect northeastern China but also it could take 20 percent of the Chinese military to secure its 1,420 kilometers (880 miles) border with North Korea.[5] For that reason, in order to secure Chinese assistance, North Korean leaders could hijack Chinese foreign policy by escalating regional crises and putting itself in danger, driving wedges between China and its partners, or even playing off between China and its adversaries.[6]

Internally, to insure against the potential abandonment by China, North Korean leaders have stressed on improving domestic defensive capabilities.[7] For example, North Korea has maintained one of the world's largest militaries, and its military expenditure accounts for on average more than 20 percent of its GDP.[8] Another pillar of North Korean defensive capability is nuclear weapons. North Korean leaders have always been interested in this cost-effective way to achieve deterrence.[9] Not only did Kim Il-sung witness how nuclear weapons easily defeated Japan during World War II but also his successors are convinced that nuclear weapon is key to regime survival. For example, the Korean Central News Agency (KCNA) said that "history proves that powerful nuclear deterrence serves as the strongest treasured sword for frustrating outsiders' aggression" and that "the Saddam Hussein regime in Iraq and the Qaddafi regime in Libya could not escape the fate of destruction after being deprived of their foundations for nuclear development and giving up nuclear programs of their own accord."[10]

In addition to international security threats, North Korean leaders face domestic political challenges. To them, national security is important only if they remain the supreme leader of the country. From the perspective of the selectorate theory, leaders face the selectorate (a group of people who have the power to choose leaders and receive privileged benefits from them) and need support from the winning coalition (a subgroup of the selectorate that is essential for the leaders to stay in power).[11] The sizes of selectorate and winning coalition in a political system affect how leaders govern. The North Korean political system has a small selectorate and an even smaller winning coalition, approximately three hundred officials mostly from the military.[12] A small winning coalition strongly motivates the leader to buy their loyalty with public resources. However, a small selectorate also means that the members in the winning coalition of one leader are likely to remain in the winning coalition of the next leader. Thus, their loyalty to the incumbent leader is not guaranteed. Because of this, North Korean leaders seek to nip domestic challengers in the bud at all costs. In particular, since North Korea's actions such as pursuing nuclear weapons would trigger a security dilemma in northeast Asia and potentially free it from serving as the buffer zone for Russia and China, North Korean leaders are wary of being overpowered by their patrons who have access to and influence among the winning coalition and may collaborate with foreign powers.

Lastly, North Korean leaders have to cope with the threat of the ejectorate, the unenfranchised masses who can collectively overturn the regime via uprising or revolution.[13] The leaders could either rely on the winning coalition to suppress the masses, appease the ejectorate with economic development, or control them with ideological assimilation.

North Korean policy on China under Kim Il-sung and Kim Jong-il

North Korea's founding father, Kim Il-sung, rose to power thanks to his successful experience as a guerrilla field commander in northeastern China and then the commander of the Korean battalion in the Soviet Union Army and promises to give the Korean people a future of "eat[ing] rice and meat soup, dress[ing] in silk and liv[ing] in house with tile roof."[14] Despite the domestic and international support, as a leader of a newly established, poor, and weak country, Kim Il-sung considered his position vulnerable not only due to the U.S. threat but also domestic challengers. In particular, he was wary of China's influence in North Korean politics.

Kim's wariness can be partly attributed to the *Minsaengdan Incident*. In 1928, the Korean communists in northeast China merged with the Chinese Communist Party (CCP) under the directive of the Communist International. It was at that time when Kim Il-sung became a CCP member. After the Japanese invasion of Manchuria in 1931, the anti-communist Koreans formed the *Minsaengdan* to seek Japanese protection from the communists. Fearing the infiltration of the *Minsaengdan*, the local CCP leaders initiated a series of purges of Korean communists. Even though Kim Il-sung dodged the executions, he was expelled from the CCP and became suspicious of the CCP.

After Kim Il-sung became the leader of the Korean Workers' Party (KWP), his wariness was extended to the Yan'an faction, a pro-China faction in the KWP. Despite the purge of the Korean communists in Manchuria, many Korean communists joined forces with the CCP in the Yan'an, Shaanxi, province in western China and helped Chinese communists fight the Japanese and later the Nationalist Party. By the end of the war, there were over one hundred thousand ethnic Koreans in the Chinese Army and many of them became officers and developed close relations with the Chinese communist leaders.[15] When they returned to Korea after the Chinese Civil War and joined the KWP, they were referred to as the "Yan'an faction" because of their experience in and connections with China.[16]

The Yan'an faction on the one hand significantly strengthened the North Korean military. On the other hand, due to his suspicion about the CCP, Kim Il-sung was concerned that the Yan'an faction might pursue policies in favor of Chinese interests and deemed them a major challenger with Chinese support. For instance, to keep the Yan'an faction and China at bay, Kim Il-sung excluded the Yan'an faction and China from the planning and early conduct of the Korean War until his regime was on the brink of losing the war and requested China to intervene.[17] Even though China's intervention rescued Kim's regime, he ended up facing a more influential Yan'an faction in the regime. To contain the Chinese influence, during the negotiation of the

Korean Armistice Agreement, Kim Il-sung requested all foreign forces to withdraw from the Korean Peninsula.[18] Since the Soviet Union did not have its military stationed in North Korea and the United States and South Korean forces were not expected to abide by North Korea's request, Kim's message essentially asked the Chinese military to leave Korea.

In the meantime, a de-Stalinization movement started in the Soviet Union. Fearing that this movement could be used by the increasingly powerful Yan'an faction to jeopardize his position, Kim Il-sung announced in 1955 the *Juche* ideology, which emphasizes self-reliance, independence from foreign interference, and "the need to give primacy to one's own national interest and peculiarities."[19] However, what Kim Il-sung feared still happened. In February 1956, encouraged by Khrushchev's criticism of Stalin's personality cult and leadership, the Yan'an faction, who were already under political attack from Kim, decided to remove him from power. In August, they staged in vain a coup by openly challenging Kim's authority at a KWP Central Committee meeting and were subsequently purged from the regime by Kim Il-sung. Believing that China was behind the coup, Kim Il-sung suspended military exchange with China and eliminated Chinese influence in North Korea throughout the rest of the Cold War.[20]

After taking care of the domestic threat, Kim Il-sung focused on the external threat. Even though North Korea started its nuclear program in the 1950s,[21] its progress was stagnant due to the constraint of the Soviet Union. Therefore, before acquiring sufficient nuclear deterrent capabilities, North Korea needs the Soviet Union and China to balance against the United States. In 1961, North Korea signed the Mutual Aid and Cooperation Friendship Treaties with the Soviet Union and China, respectively. The treaty with China has often been referred to as proof of the China–North Korea alliance. Nonetheless, it also reflects Kim's wariness about Chinese influence in North Korea. For instance, comparing the treaties with the Soviet Union and China, the one with China stresses more on the signatories not interfering in each other's domestic affairs. It should also be noted that even though North Korea has used a variety of positive words to describe its relationship with China, "alliance" is not one of them.[22] Rather, North Korean leaders consider their role as a protector of China from Western influence and U.S. invasion, which deserves compensation from China.[23]

In the 1960s, North Korea-China relations deteriorated because of the breakdown of the China-Soviet Union relations. One reason for Kim Il-sung to side with the Soviet Union was that it was more capable and could offer more military and economic support than China. Another reason was that Kim Il-sung embraced the replacement of Khrushchev with the more conservative Brezhnev in the Soviet Union, and he wanted to prevent the Chinese Cultural Revolution from spilling over to North Korea and damaging his winning coalition. Additionally, Kim was displeased at the fact that the Chinese government did not stop the Red Guards from criticizing him for not recognizing Mao's leadership in the international communist revolution.

Motivated by the Soviet Union and North Korea's marginalization, China normalized relations with the United States and Japan and conducted market reform, all of which were considered by Kim Il-sung a betrayal of North Korea and communism. However, the North Korean economy fell into stagnation in the 1970s. Knowing that China and the Soviet Union needed North Korea to be on their respective sides, Kim took advantage of his strategic position and played them off to extract resources. Despite heavy reliance on foreign aid, North Korean media rarely reported about foreign aid to minimize its impact on the public perception of the regime.[24]

Several significant changes in the 1990s disrupted Kim Il-sung's survival strategy. Internationally, the collapse of the Soviet Union and the U.S. victory in the Gulf War exacerbated Kim Il-sung's security concerns. Even though China whose economic and military capabilities had significantly improved by then was the only country that North Korea had to balance against the United States, Kim Il-sung questioned its reliability and willingness to help. One reason is that China's need for North Korea as a buffer zone declined because of its improving relations with the United States and its allies. Also, the Chinese government directly or indirectly claimed on multiple occasions that the treaty with North Korea did not commit Chinese military protection.[25]

Domestically, Kim Il-sung died in July 1994 and the throne was passed on to Kim Jong-il. Despite decades of governing experience along with his father, the then Kim Jong-il did not have Kim Il-sung's godlike status or a winning coalition as loyal as that of his father. For instance, in the early 1990s, Kim Il-sung was addressed as "Great Leader" while Kim Jong-il was "Dear Leader" or simply "Leader." A more serious challenge for Kim Jong-il was economic. Besides the disruption of Soviet economic aid, the heavy floods in 1995 and 1996 and the subsequent great famine crippled the Public Distribution System that North Koreans had relied on for decades for food and other necessities (North Koreans refer to the period as the Arduous March of Suffering). To alleviate the economic burden on the regime, Kim Jong-il relaxed economic control and allowed economic activities in the black market. According to North Korean defectors who survived the period, 90 percent of their income came from trading in the black market.[26] Nonetheless, the relaxation of government control was a temporary solution to the economic downturn and not economic reform. Once the economy showed signs of recovery, the black market was cracked down and the government reclaimed control.

The economic collapse affected the interest and loyalty of Kim's winning coalition. To ensure political survival, one year after the death of his father,

Kim Jong-il replaced his father's KWP-centered winning coalition with the military and adopted the "military first" policy. One key piece of the military first policy is nuclear weapons even though North Korea signed the Non-Proliferation of Nuclear Weapons treaty (NPT) in 1985. The long-term goal of developing nuclear weapons is to boost security even without reliable protection from Russia or China and improve regime legitimacy.

In the short term, the pursuit of nuclear weapons can also be used to conduct tension diplomacy, that is, escalating regional tension to bargain for foreign aid. The main goal of this strategy is to secure China's support, which was increasingly crucial to the Kim regime but dwindling in the early 1990s. Even though China then had less concern about its security, it sought regional stability for the sake of its economic development. If another war breaks out in the Korean Peninsula or the Kim regime collapses, then huge waves of North Korean refugees would flow into China's northeastern regions and crush the regional economy there. Therefore, China would go to great lengths to avoid economic and political instability in North Korea.

China's need for stability was taken advantage of by Kim Jong-il. When North Korea's nuclear program was discovered (it is also plausible that the information could be leaked by the North Korean government on purpose), it threatened to withdraw from the NPT and attack South Korea. The provocation successfully brought significant aid from China. Between 1996 and 2001, China provided 1.3 million metric tons of food to North Korea and kept providing necessities to North Korea for humanitarian reasons in the coming years of international sanctions.[27]

Kim Jong-il's tension diplomacy also attracted U.S. attention and resulted in the bilateral negotiation of the Agreed Framework of 1994. Based on the agreement, North Korea would freeze its nuclear program and subject it to international monitoring. In return, the United States would provide North Korea economic aid including five hundred thousand tons of heavy oil every year, two light-water reactors, and "formal assurance against the U.S. threat or use of nuclear weapon."[28] However, the agreement soon fell apart as the U.S. Congress failed to approve the spending for the programs. As a result, the U.S. oil shipments were delayed, and the light-water reactors were never built. In fact, the U.S. policy makers reportedly were not serious about the agreement because they expected the Kim regime to soon collapse.[29]

The failure of the Agreed Framework and the breakout of the second Iraq War worsened Kim Jong-il's security concerns and motivated him to escalate the tension further to keep China close. In January 2003, North Korea announced to withdraw from the NPT and reportedly revealed its highly enriched uranium stockpile. The United States in response halted its aid to North Korea. China transferred border security from local police to the military and immediately increased economic assistance to North Korea.[30]

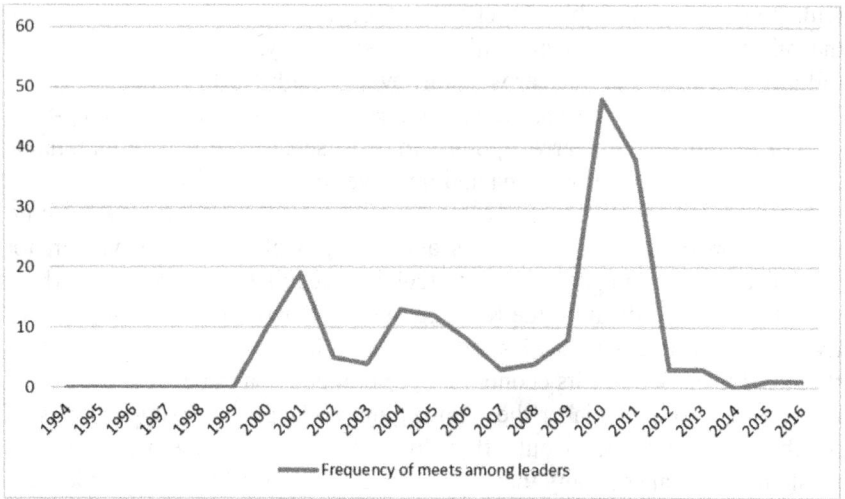

Figure 2.1: Number of Meetings between Chinese and North Korean Leaders.
Source: Data collected from NK News Leadership Tracker database. NK News. "NK Leadership Tracker," 2017. www.nknews.org.

For instance, between 2001 and 2005, China's total exports to North Korea rose from 0.57 to 1.08 billion U.S. dollars, and its imports from North Korea from 0.17 to 0.5 billion U.S. dollars.[31] Consequently, China–North Korea trade since then has accounted for more than 80 percent of North Korean total trade.[32] In the meantime, the booming trade was facilitated by the increase in the frequency of meetings between the leaders of the two countries (figure 2.1).

Internationally, Kim Jong-il's tension diplomacy also compelled China to intervene to de-escalate the tension. In 2003, China hosted the Six-Party Talk. While China and the other four countries sought the eventual denuclearization of the Korean peninsula, North Korea joined the talk reluctantly because Kim Jong-il had little faith in multilateralism and considered the nuclear issue as something between North Korea and the United States.[33] He agreed to join the talk with the expectation to have bilateral negotiations with the United States. Additionally, although China sought a multilateral solution, North Korea viewed the talk as a "five against one" plot to force it to give up nuclear weapons.[34] The Six-Party Talk reached a breakthrough in 2005 when North Korea agreed to return to NPT and IAEA and expressed commitment to denuclearization in exchange for energy aid. However, tension escalated again in November 2005 when the United States sanctioned Banco Delta Asia, a bank in Macao that managed finance for North Korea, and then North Korea boycotted the talk.

The failure of the negotiation pushed Kim Jong-il to return to tension diplomacy even though it defies China's request. Kim Jong-il was confident that his tension diplomacy would continue to work on China because if China was willing to protect the Kim regime for the sake of regional stability before it had nuclear weapons, then it will have more reasons to keep a nuclear-capable North Korea stable. In October 2006, North Korea conducted its first nuclear test. The United Nations Security Council (UNSC) immediately passed Resolution 1718 to condemn North Korea. Although China supported the resolution, it managed to soften the tone of condemnation and severity of the sanction. In terms of implementation of the sanctions, China restricted imports from North Korea on the one hand and increased economic aid and exports to North Korea for humanitarian causes on the other hand. The former policy cut foreign currency that the Kim regime can spend on the nuclear program or the winning coalition, while the latter alleviates the pressure for North Koreans to flee to China.[35]

Partly surprised by China's negative reaction and partly because of greater bargaining chips in hand, North Korea return to the Six-Party Talk in 2007. After the United States expressed commitment to normalizing relations with North Korea and agreed to remove North Korea from the list of state sponsors of terrorism, lift sanctions, and provide energy aid along with its allies, North Korea shut down five nuclear reactors in Yongbyon. Then the negotiation halted again as North Korea and the United States disagreed on the pace and extent of inspection. North Korea subsequently declared that it would not

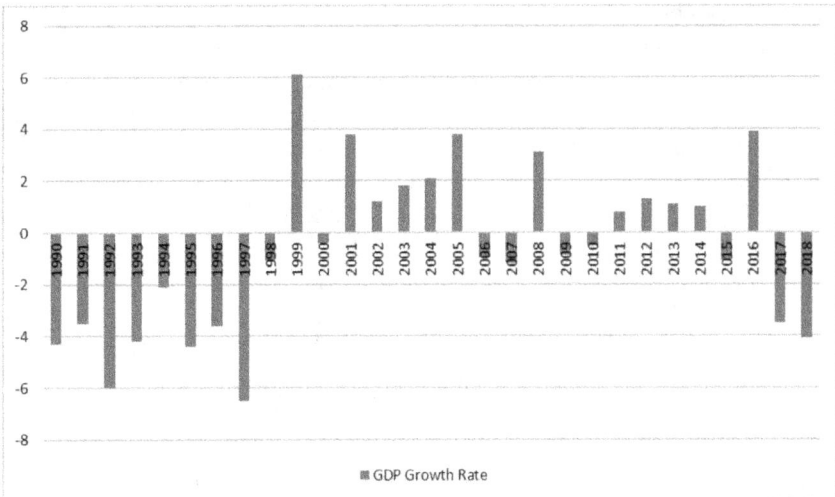

Figure 2.2: North Korean GDP Growth.

Source: Data collected from Trading Economics Trading Economics. "North Korea GDP Annual Growth Rate," 2020. https://tradingeconomics.com/north-korea/gdp-annual-growth-rate.

participate in the Six-Party Talk or be bound by the previous agreements, and returned to tension diplomacy again. In May 2009, North Korea conducted its second nuclear test. The UNSC responded by expanding the list of sanctions on North Korea. China, frustrated about North Korea's defiance, decreased its fuels exports to North Korea by 44 percent.[36] Nonetheless, Chinese leaders understood that they had little leverage over North Korea and that it was unlikely for North Korea to give up nuclear weapons. When the North Korean economy turned into chaos under the currency reform at the end of 2009, China prioritized regional stability and boosted bilateral trade to prevent the economy from collapsing (figure 2.2).

As the tension diplomacy succeeded at the international level, Kim Jong-il became increasingly concerned about North Korea's trade reliance on China and sought trade diversification. One reason is that, despite positive relations, North Korea has been overcharged for goods from China.[37] A more important reason for Kim's desire to be less reliant on China was the fact that not only had Chinese leaders encouraged North Korea to adopt Chinese-style economic reform but also China's economic success had attracted much interest among North Korean elites and the population after they tasted the benefits of market economy when the government allowed private market activities during the Arduous March. Government and military officials who had access to public resources profited from doing business with private entrepreneurs in and outside North Korea. Those who grew up during the Arduous March are often referred to as the "*Jangmadang* (market) generation." Compared with the older generations, they are used to market activities, more entrepreneurial, and willing to break rules to pursue self-interest.[38]

Afraid of losing authority and control, Kim Jong-il was reluctant to implement economic liberalization. For instance, the Rason Special Economic Zone (SEZ), envisioned by Kim Il-sung to become the "Singapore of the East," was established in 1992 to take advantage of its proximity to China and Russia and access to a warm water port. Nonetheless, the economic activities in Rason had been mostly stagnant under Kim Jong-il because not only must foreign businesses be invited by the North Korean government to invest in the SEZ, but also the government was not serious enough about it to even pave a road to the Chinese border, or invest in power plants or the port itself.[39] When the economy recovered in the 2000s thanks to market relaxation policies and Chinese economic aid, Kim decided to recentralize economic authority. On November 30, 2009, the North Korean government announced a currency reform without advance notice to replace the old currency with a new one at a ratio of 100 to 1 and imposed a limit on the amount of money each person could exchange. This policy effectively wiped out the illegal savings that private entrepreneurs had accumulated from years of market activities. To appease his winning coalition, the government offered public employees the same wage in the new currency, which means a one hundred times increase in their buying power. However, the reform quickly turned into a disaster as such a sudden and significant increase in purchasing power in the society drove up inflation so quickly and so high that the government had to impose price control on goods. Consequently, as sellers refused to sell at below-market prices, the supply of goods plummeted so much that even the elites in Pyongyang could not guarantee stable food supplies for their families.[40]

The failed currency reform incurred domestic criticism and tremendous political challenges. Kim Jong-il's declining health since February 2010 added new urgency to securing Chinese resources.[41] To ensure China's support, North Korea significantly escalated tension in the Korean Peninsula. For instance, North Korea sank a South Korean warship in March 2010 and bombed Yeonpyeong Island in November. As China needed to keep the Kim regime stable, its trade with North Korea skyrocketed after the incidents. In the meantime, Kim Jong-il sped up communication with China. From 2010 to 2011, Kim Jong-il and other senior North Korean officials had eighty-six meetings with their Chinese counterparts (figure 2.1). One main reason for such frequent meetings with China was that Kim needed the Chinese leader's blessing on his successor, Kim Jong-un, as 2011 turned out to be the last year of Kim Jong-il.

Kim Jong-un Era

Kim Jong-un pursues the same political goal as his predecessors: national security, a loyal winning coalition, and supportive masses. In March 2013, he announced his *byungjin* policy, parallel development of nuclear weapons and economy, slightly different from Kim Il-sung's *byungjin*, which stressed on conventional military and economic growth. Kim Jong-un also follows Kim Jong-il's international strategy. Not only is he dedicated to developing nuclear weapons, but he is also determined to hold on to them after witnessing the fate of Libyan and Iraqi leaders. For example, he amended the North Korean Constitution to declare North Korea a "nuclear-armed" state.

Kim Jong-un also used nuclear weapons to continue the tension diplomacy. He ordered more nuclear and missile (mostly short-range ballistic missiles) tests in his first few years than Kim Jong-il did during his entire era.[42] Nonetheless, the international environment that Kim Jong-un faces is different from that of his father and unsuitable for tension diplomacy. First, international attention on North Korea has waned. After years of fruitless negotiations, the United States and its allies shifted from engagement to "strategic patience" and became disinterested in rewarding North Korea's provocations. In China, a "generational" leadership transition took place in

November 2012, where most of the key officials in the Politburo Standing Committee, State Council, and Central Military Committee were replaced.[43] To extract resources from and shape the foreign policy of the new Chinese administration on North Korea, Kim Jong-un ordered a missile test one month after Xi Jinping was elected the general secretary of the CCP. And in February 2013, one week before the Chinese New Year and one month before Xi became the president of China, North Korea ordered its third nuclear test.

The tension diplomacy backfired this time. Unlike previous Chinese administrations that followed the long-time foreign policy principle of "keep a low profile (*taoguang yanghui*), never take leadership (*yongbu chengba*) and do some good (*yousuo zuowei*)," the Xi administration is more ambitious and seeks to "do lots of good" or "make difference actively (*dayou kewei*)," which contradicts North Korea's nuclear ambition when the international community looked to China to contain North Korea's behavior. So, to Xi Jinping, Kim Jong-un's defiance and provocation was unacceptable or even hostile. After the 2013 nuclear test, China officially protested North Korea,[44] a rare occasion between the two countries, voted for new UN sanctions, and imposed its own ban on exports of dual-use goods to North Korea.[45]

China's change in attitude and policy on North Korea also affected Kim Jong-un's domestic survival strategy. Domestically, Kim Jong-un's leadership position then was insecure due to his lack of legitimacy. Unlike Kim Jong-il who grew up in North Korea and had years of experience governing along with Kim Il-sung, Kim Jong-un spent most of his life abroad, had no publicity in North Korea and had little time to prepare for governing. When he was announced the heir apparent to Kim Jong-il in 2010, few North Koreans even knew who he was. Kim Jong-un saw the similarities between his situation and that of Kim Il-sung at the inception of North Korea and followed his grandfather's domestic survival strategy. For instance, Kim Jong-un mimics Kim Il-sung's appearance to improve his image among the people. Thanks to North Korea's nuclear deterrence capability (though limited), the regime is safe enough from external threats for Kim Jong-un to shift from Kim Jong-il's "military first" policy to focus more on economic development. He said, "[I]n the past, it was fine if we didn't have food as long as we had bullets. But now we must have food, but not necessarily bullets,"[46] and reiterated to his subjects Kim Il-sung's early promise of a future of "white rice and meat soup."

The failure of tension diplomacy on the Xi administration made Kim's economic plan uncertain. With a new, young, inexperienced leader, the Kim regime needs a loyal winning coalition more than ever to survive in case of popular unrest. However, a more serious challenge Kim Jong-un faced was his lack of legitimacy among North Korean elites. To the political elites, Kim Jong-un was a young, inexperienced, and Western-educated playboy who shared with them few connections. Being appointed by Kim Jong-il alone does not necessarily give Kim Jong-un legitimacy. Given the Chinese leaders' increasing disappointment about his behavior, Kim Jong-un was worried that another August Faction Incident with Chinese support could be looming. Like what Kim Il-sung did in the 1950s, Kim Jong-un quickly formed his own winning coalition and eliminated his political challengers. For example, Kim Jong-un shifted from the "military first" policy to weaken the power of senior military leaders, separated the nuclear force from the other three branches of the military, and put it under his sole and direct control.[47]

One of Kim Jong-un's key helpers was Jang Song-taek, his uncle and mentor designated by Kim Jong-il.[48] As part of the Kim family, Jang was the second most powerful person in the Kim Jong-il regime. He also developed good relations with Chinese leaders from years of working with the Chinese on economic cooperation such as special economic zones and pushed for Chinese-style economic reforms in North Korea. By helping Kim Jong-un contain the military, Jang created political space in North Korea for his pro-China faction to revive and grow. Given Jang's close connections with North Korean elites and quick expansion in power, he became de facto the most powerful person in Kim Jong-un's North Korea. Consequently, Kim Jong-un considered Jang a serious threat because he could be easily overthrown if Jang and China worked together.

Kim preempted this threat first. In December 2013, two years after Kim Jong-il died, Jang was accused of and executed for forming a faction against Kim Jong-un and sacrificing sovereignty to "a foreign country" (implying China). To cleanse the rest of the pro-China faction, Kim Jong-un suspended all governmental interaction with China and recalled all North Korean business agents in China.[49] By the end of the cleansing, Kim Jong-un purged approximately 340 people (140 of them were senior officials), sending an unequivocal message to other elites about to whom they should pay loyalty.[50] With the pro-China faction gone, Kim Jong-un restructured his selectorate. In the 2014 Supreme People's Assembly election, 55 percent of the assembly members were replaced.[51] In the meantime, Kim Jong-un tightened the ideological control. For example, watching foreign media was considered a more serious crime during Kim Jong-un era than Kim Jong-il era.[52]

The cleansing of senior officials shook the loyalty of Kim Jong-un's winning coalition as no one is safe under him. Without a loyal winning coalition to suppress the masses, Kim Jong-un tried to improve his legitimacy among the people with economic growth and claim credit for it, a practice adopted by Kim Il-sung during the Cold War. An analysis of the KCNA reports about China between 1997 and 2018 shows that the reports have been centered around economic cooperation and revolutionary friendship.[53] Comparing the two Kim regimes, it is found that the KCNA during the Kim Jong-un era published fewer quarterly reports about China than during the Kim Jong-il era, signaling cooling relations. It is also found that, whereas the frequency of economic topics about China during the Kim Jong-il era increased when the North Korea–China trade volume rose, the KCNA published fewer economic reports during the Kim Jong-un era even when the trade volume rose. To maintain a nominally positive relationship with China, the frequency of friendship topics rose in 2014 after a sharp plummet during the Jang Song-taek incident.

Kim Jong-un's lip service did not work on China. Disappointed in Kim Jong-un's defiance and purge of Jang's pro-China faction, the Xi administration distanced itself from North Korea and improved relations with South Korea. For instance, in September 2015, South Korean President Park Geun-hye was invited to attend the seventieth anniversary of the victory against Japan and seated close to Xi whereas the North Korean delegate was sidelined. Sensing the frustration of China, Kim Jong-un assured China that he would stop nuclear tests before China sent a senior official delegation to attend the seventieth anniversary of the KWP in October. However, knowing that he could not afford to give up nuclear weapons or worsen relations with China, Kim Jong-un switched to a new form of tension diplomacy. Unlike the previous tension diplomacy that aimed to trigger China's need to protect North Korean stability, the new tactic seeks to drive a wedge between China and the United States and its allies, making China an enemy of North Korea's enemy and thus forcing China to stand with North Korea. In January 2016, North Korea conducted a fourth nuclear test. Not only was China not notified of the test in advance for the first time but also the test location was so close to China that several counties in the Chinese Jilin province could feel the tremor from the test.[54] And the provocation continued. In September, North Korea conducted a second nuclear test of the year. China condemned North Korea's behavior and supported UNSC economic sanctions on North Korea, but it also claimed that the sanctions "were not intended to produce negative consequences on North Korea's humanitarian situation."[55]

In South Korea, however, North Korea's provocations successfully motivated President Park to decide to deploy the U.S. Thermal High Altitude Area Defense (THAAD) anti-ballistic missile system, which she had shown great interest since 2013. The THAAD decision triggered strong opposition and an economic boycott from Chinese leaders who were concerned about the ramification of THAAD on Chinese national security. However, unlike what happened in the 2000s, the deterioration of relations between China and South Korea and the United States did not improve North Korea–China relations. After all, it was North Korea who started the unwelcome chain reaction. When North Korea tested a nuclear-capable intermediate-range missile during a meeting between U.S. President Trump and Japanese Prime Minister Abe in February 2017, China responded with a ban on all coal imports from

North Korea, which account for approximately 40 percent of North Korea's total exports.[56] The KCNA subsequently harshly criticized China for its "mean behavior" and "dancing to the tune of the US."[57] In September 2017, Kim Jong-un escalated tension further and tested another hydrogen bomb.

Determined to protect bilateral relations, China and South Korea reached an agreement where South Korea promised not to hurt Chinese national interest with THAAD and China allowed South Korea time to "appropriately handle the issue." The failure of Kim Jong-un's tension tactics to improve North Korea-China relations affected his domestic and international survival strategy. Domestically, China's economic punishment crippled the North Korean economy and worsened the political condition of Kim Jong-un. Concerned that China might find someone to replace him, Kim Jong-un resumed his challenger elimination campaign. His second victim was Kim Jong-nam, his half-brother. As Kim Jong-il's eldest son, Kim Jong-nam was the heir apparent until he was arrested in Japan in 2001 for using a fake passport. Since then, he had lived in Macau, a special administrative district of China. To Kim Jong-un, his half-brother who in the Korean political culture had more legitimacy to the throne could be used by China and his domestic challengers to overthrow him. Even though Kim Jong-nam repeatedly announced that he was not interested in the leadership position, Kim Jong-un still ordered multiple assassination attempts on his brother and eventually succeeded in February 2017. With all the possible challengers gone, Kim Jong-un felt safe enough to visit China one year after Kim Jong-nam's death. At his first meeting with Kim Jong-un, Chinese President Xi told Kim that he "expects political stability" in North Korea.[58]

Internationally, due to the failure of the tension diplomacy on China, Kim Jong-un reversed the strategy and sought to improve relations with China's competitor, the United States, in order to keep China close, an approach similar to what Kim Il-sung adopted during the Cold War on China and the Soviet Union. The election of Donald Trump to the White House and the subsequent deterioration of U.S.-China relations offered Kim Jong-un a great window of opportunity to de-escalate tension with the United States. To break the ice, Kim Jong-un surprisingly proposed to participate in the 2018 PyeongChang Winter Olympics and agreed that the North Korean team and the South Korean team would march under one pro-unification flag. Kim's successful charm offensive during the Olympics paved way for a summit with South Korean President Moon and two summits with U.S. President Trump, one in Singapore in May 2018 and the other in Hanoi in February 2019. During the summits, Kim Jong-un expressed his willingness to denuclearize in exchange for the lift of sanctions and a security guarantee from the United States.

China's attitude toward North Korea quickly changed as it did not want to be left out of the solution to the nuclear issue or see North Korea becoming too close to the United States and its allies. For instance, shortly after the announcement of the Singapore summit in June 2018, China loosened its restrictions on trade with North Korea.[59] Moreover, prior to Kim's trip to the Singapore summit with Trump, Xi invited Kim to China for an unofficial visit in March, during which Xi proposed to continue high-level communications and frequent in-depth exchanges and improve trade ties between the two countries. Xi also expressed China's support for the Kim regime.[60] Kim and Xi met two more times in 2018, once before and once after the Singapore summit, to discuss the bilateral relations and the nuclear issue.

After the Hanoi summit in 2019, Xi paid a state visit to North Korea, during which he said that China "seeks to join Pyongyang in turning the blueprint of the bilateral ties for a new era into reality," and "will firmly support the DPRK's [Democratic People's Republic of Korea] socialist enterprise, the implementation of its new strategic line and a political solution to solving the nuclear issue and materializing lasting peace and security in the peninsula."[61]

The deterioration of the U.S.-China relations could have given Kim Jong-un opportunities to play off between the two great powers. However, the stagnation of the North Korea–U.S. negotiation after the Hanoi summit dampens China's urge to consolidate its relations with North Korea, especially when its own economy is hit by the trade war with the United States and the breakout of the COVID-19 pandemic. Without good options, in December 2019, Kim Jong-un ended the negotiation with the United States and returned to tension diplomacy, announcing that denuclearization is not up for negotiation. Nonetheless, given the negative response of the Xi administration to Pyongyang's previous nuclear provocations, this time Kim Jong-un could only escalate tension with lower intensity. In June 2020, North Korea cut all communication with South Korea and demolished the joint liaison office between the two. Such provocation by North Korea will most likely continue in the near future. However, the pattern of Kim Jong-un's foreign policy implies that he is running out of options in the long term. At the time of writing, Mr. Biden has won the 2020 U.S. presidential election. Despite many differences between President Biden and his predecessor, they share a similarly "tough" position on China. To North Korea, this means that its low-intensity provocation policy probably needs to continue in the near future.

CONCLUSION

North Korea's foreign policy on China is key to its leader's domestic and international survival. Internationally, on the one hand, the Kims have taken advantage of North Korea's geopolitical importance to China to secure the latter's economic and political support. The review of North Korea's policy on China shows that the Kims regimes were willing to go to great lengths, such as improving relations with China's adversaries, escalating regional instability, or even sabotaging China's relations with neighboring countries, to ensure the continuation of Chinese support. On the other hand, to maintain control over domestic politics, the Kims have spared no effort to root out Chinese influence in the country.

In retrospect, the path of political survival has narrowed down since Kim Jong-un came into power. One important reason is Kim Jong-Un's inexperience in foreign policy strategy. Failing to sense the ambition of the Xi administration, Kim Jong-un mistakenly followed his father's nuclear escalation strategy, which backfired on him politically and economically. Then he shifted to his grandfather's strategy to eliminate political challengers and improve relations with China's competitor, the United States. However, the political cleansing undermined the loyalty of the elites in the regime. Negotiations with the United States and its allies have reached a deadlock. And even though China is willing to maintain economic and political stability in North Korea for the sake of a stable regional political environment, the Xi administration has been increasingly impatient with North Korea's tension diplomacy and has shown its willingness to punish North Korea for it.

Since the Chinese leadership may not change any time soon, the number of options for North Korea will be very limited in the near future. One option for Kim Jong-un is to continue the tension diplomacy but keep it not too provocative so as to keep China's support. A better option is to play off between China and the United States without compromising too much of his leverage too quickly and that would require superb political wisdom from the Kim Jong-un regime.

NOTES

1. K. D. Oh and R. C Hassig. *North Korea through the Looking Glass* (Washington, DC: Brookings Institute Press, 2000); Han Park, *North Korea: The Politics of Unconventional Wisdoml* (Boulder, CO: Lynne Rienner Publishers, Inc, 2002); Margaret Hermann and Charles Hermann, "Who Makes Foreign Policy Decisions and How?" *International Studies Quarterly* 33, no. 4 (1989): 361–88.

2. Hermann and Hermann, "Who Makes Foreign Policy Decisions and How?"; Walt, Stephen. *The Origins of Alliances* (Ithaca, NY: Cornell University Press, 1987).

3. Weiqi Zhang and Ginger Denton, "The North Korean Nuclear Dilemma: Does China Have Leverage?" *Journal of Asian Security and International Affairs* 6, no. 2 (2019): 107–35.

4. Ibid.

5. Hong Nack Kim, "China-North Korea Relations after Kim Jong-Il," *International Journal of Korean Studies* XVII, no. 1 (2013): 21–49.

6. Balázs Szalontai, "North Korea between China, Japan and the ROK, 2012–2016." *Korea Journal* 58, no. 3 (2018): 156–83.

7. Dong Sun Lee and Iordanka Alexandrova, "North Korean Nuclear Strategy: Envisioning Assured Retaliation," *International Relations of the Asia-Pacific* 21, no. 3 (December 10, 2019): 1–30. doi:10.1093/irap/lcz028.

8. Eleanor Albert, "North Korea's Military Capabilities," *Council on Foreign Relations*, 2019. https://www.cfr.org/backgrounder/north-koreas-military-capabilities.

9. Stephen Schwartz, "The Costs of U.S. Nuclear Weapons," *Nuclear Threat Initiative*, 2008. http://www.nti.org/analysis/articles/costs-us-nuclear-weapons/; Kenneth N. Waltz, "Nuclear Myths and Political Realities," *The American Political Science Review* 84, no. 3 (September 1990): 731. doi:10.2307/1962764.

10. Megan Specia and David Sanger, "How the 'Libya Model' Became a Sticking Point in North Korea Nuclear Talks," *New York Times*, May 16, 2018. https://www.nytimes.com/2018/05/16/world/asia/north-korea-libya-model.html.

11. Bruce Bueno de Mesquita, Alastair Smith, Randolph M Siverson, and James D Morrow, *The Logic of Political Survival* (Cambridge, MA: MIT Press, 2003).

12. Ministry of Unification of South Korea, "2011 Key Figures of North Korea," Seoul, 2011; Daekwon Son, "Bringing North Korea to the Negotiating Table: Unstable Foundations of Kim Jong-Un's North Korean Regime," *International Relations of the Asia-Pacific* 21, no. 2 (October 30, 2019): 1–31. doi:10.1093/irap/lcz024.

13. William Zimmerman, *Ruling Russia: Authoritarianism from the Revolution to Putin* (Princeton, NJ: Princeton University Press, 2014); Bruce Bueno de Mesquita and Alastair Smith, "Political Succession: A Model of Coups, Revolution, Purges, and Everyday Politics," *Journal of Conflict Resolution* 61, no. 4 (2017): 707–43.

14. Andrei Lankov, *The Real North Korea: Life and Politics in the Failed Stalinist Utopia* (Oxford University Press, 2013), chapter 1.

15. Daniel Wertz, "Issue Brief: China-North Korea Relations," *The National Committee on North Korea*, 2019. https://www.ncnk.org/resources/briefing-papers/all-briefing-papers/china-north-korea-relations.

16. Lankov, *Real North Korea*; Adrian Buzo, *The Making of Modern Korea*. 3rd ed. (New York: Routledge, 2016).

17. J. Shen, "'Weihu Dongbeiya Anquan de Dangwu Zhi Ji' [The Urgent Task in Safe- Guarding Northeast Asian Security]," *Shijie Jingji Yu Zhengzhi [World Economy and Politics]* 9 (2003): 55–60; D. Suh, D., *Bukhan Munhon Yongu [Studies of North Korean Documents]*, edited by D. Suh (Seoul: Institute for Far Eastern Studies, 2004).

18. Jae Ho Chung and Myung-hae Choi, "Uncertain Allies or Uncomfortable Neighbors? Making Sense of China–North Korea Relations, 1949–2010." *The Pacific Review* 26, no. 3 (2013): 243–64. doi:10.1080/09512748.2012.759262.

19. Lankov, *Real North Korea*.

20. Dick K. Nanto and Mark E. Manyin, "China–North Korea Relations." *North Korean Review* 7, no. 2 (2011): 94–101. doi:10.3172/NKR.7.2.94.

21. Hans M. Kristensen and Robert S. Norris, "A History of U.S. Nuclear Weapons in South Korea," *Bulletin of the Atomic Scientists* 73, no. 6 (November 2, 2017): 349–57. doi:10.1080/00963402.2017.1388656.

22. Weiqi Zhang and Dmitry Zinoviev, "How North Korea Views China: Quantitative Analysis of Korean Central News Agency Reports," *The Korean Journal of Defense Analysis* 30, no. 3 (2018): 377–96.

23. Chol Kim, "Commentary on DPRK-China Relations," *Korean Central News Agency*. May 3, 2017, http://www.kcna.kp/kcna.user.article.retrieveNewsViewInfoList .kcmsf#this.

24. Lankov, *Real North Korea.*

25. Samuel Kim, "Sino-North Korea Relations in the Post-Cold War World," In *North Korea: The Politics of Regime Survival*, edited by Young Whan Kihl and Hong Nack Kim (New York: Routledge, 2015), 188; M. R. Chambers, "Dealing with a Truculent Ally: A Comparative per- Spective on China's Handling of North Korea," *Journal of East Asia Studies* 5, no. 1 (2005): 35–75; J. D. Pollack, *No Exit: North Korea, Nuclear Weapons, and International Security* (New York, NY: Routledge), 2011.

26. N. Kretchun, C. Lee, and S. Tuohy, *Information Penetration and Government Control in North Korea* (Baltimore, MD: The Paul H. Nitze School of Advanced International Studies (SAIS) at Johns Hopkins University), 2017.

27. Lankov, *Real North Korea*

28. Agreed Framework, "Agreed Framework of 21 October 1994 between the United States of America and the Democratic People's Republic of Korea," International Atomic Energy Agency, 1994. https://www.iaea.org/publications/documents /infcircs/agreed-framework-21-october-1994-between-united-states-america-and -democratic-peoples-republic-korea.

29. Kessler, Glenn. "South Korea Offers To Supply Energy If North Gives Up Arms." *Washington Post*, July 13, 2005. https://www.washingtonpost.com/wp-dyn/ content/article/2005/07/12/AR2005071200220.html.

30. Dick K. Nanto and Mark E. Manyin, "CRS Report for Congress: China-North Korea Relations," 2010, http://www.crs.gov; Lankov, *Real North Korea.*

31. Trade Map, International Trade Centre, "Trade Map," 2020, http://www .intracen.org/marketanalysis.

32. Zhang and Denton, "The North Korean Nuclear Dilemma."

33. Dean J. Ouellette, "North Korea's Perception of Multilateralism," *Hyundai North Korea Research* 16, no. 3 (2013): 145–213.

34. Ibid.

35. Zhang and Denton, "The North Korean Nuclear Dilemma."

36. Ibid.

37. Nanto and Manyin, "CRS Report for Congress."

38. Hyun-bi Park, "Jangmadang Teaches North Koreans to Break Rules," *NK News*, October 7, 2015.

39. Andray Abrahamian, "A Convergence of Interests: Progress for Rason Special Economic Zone," *Korea Economic Institute Academic Paper Series*, February 2 (2012).

40. Lankov, *Real North Korea.*

41. "Kim Jong Il 'Has 3 Years to Live.'" *Chosun Ilbo*, March 17, 2010, http:// english.chosun.com/site/data/html_dir/2010/03/17/2010031700811.html.

42. Missile Defense Project, "North Korean Missile Launches and Nuclear Tests: 1984–Present," Center for Strategic and International Studies, December 19, 2020, https://missilethreat.csis.org/north-korea-missile-launches-1984-present/.

43. Cheng Li, "The 2012 Chinese Leadership Transition," Brookings Institute, December 1, 2011, https://www.brookings.edu/on-the-record/the-2012-chinese -leadership-transition/.

44. Kristin Huang, "How China Responded to Previous North Korean Nuclear Tests," *South China Morning Post*, September 4, 2017, https://www.scmp.com/news /china/diplomacy-defence/article/2109692/how-china-responded-previous-north -korean-nuclear-tests.

45. Megha Rajagopalan, "China Releases List of Goods Banned from Export to North Korea," Reuters, September 23, 2013, https://www.reuters.com/article/ us-china-north-korea-ban/china-releases-list-of-goods-banned-from-export-to-north -korea-idUSBRE98M0E420130923.

46. *Chosun Ilbo*, "Kim Jong-Un Adopts Grandfather's Old Slogan," December 7, 2010, http://english.chosun.com/site/data/html_dir/2010/12/07/2010120700297.html.

47. Shane Smith, *North Korea's Evolving Nuclear Strategy* (Washington, DC: US-Korea Institute at SAIS, 2015), 16.

48. Chico Harlan, "North Korea Succession: Kim Jong Il Appoints Jang Song Taek Caretaker for Kim Jong Eun," *Washington Post*, August 16, 2010, http://www .washingtonpost.com/wp-dyn/content/article/2010/08/15/AR2010081503356.html ?sid=ST2010083105101.

49. "N.K. Businessmen in China Summoned Back after Jang's Execution," *Yonhap News*, December 14, 2013, https://en.yna.co.kr/view/AEN20131214001400315.

50. Institute for National Security Strategy, "White Book on Kim Jong-Un's Five-Year Misrule," Seoul, 2016.

51. Alexandre Mansourov, "North Korea's July 19 Local Elections Dispel ROK Alle-Gations of Public Unrest," 38 North, 2015.

52. Joe McDonald, "China Trade with North Korea Up But Imports Off," Associated Press, July 6, 2017, https://www.apnews.com/0e6c59c30aaf483bba441d9bdbe4 757b/China-trade-with-North-Korea-up-but-imports-off.

53. Weiqi Zhang, and Dmitry Zinoviev, "How North Korea Views China: Quantitative Analysis of Korean Central News Agency Reports," *The Korean Journal of Defense Analysis* 30, no. 3 (2018): 377–96.

54. Huang, "How China Responded to Previous North Korean Nuclear Tests."

55. Ibid.

56. Sang-Hun Choe, "China Suspends All Coal Imports from North Korea," *New York Times*, February 19, 2017, https://www.nytimes.com/2017/02/18/world/asia/ north-korea-china-coal-imports-suspended.html?_r=0.

57. Kanga Kong, "North Korea Says China 'Dancing to U.S. Tune' in Rare Spat," Bloomberg Politics, February 23, 2017, https://www.bloomberg.com/politics/articles /2017-02-24/north-korea-says-china-dancing-to-u-s-tune-in-rare-criticism.

58. Xinhua News, "Xi Jinping, Kim Jong Un Hold Talks in Beijing," People.cn, 2018, http://en.people.cn/n3/2018/0328/c90000-9442453.html.

59. Dan De Luce and Ken Dilanian, "China Eases Economic Pressure on North Korea, Undercutting the Trump Admin," NBC News, September 5, 2018, https://www.nbcnews.com/news/north-korea/china-eases-economic-pressure-north-korea -undercutting-trump-admin-n906166.

60. Xinhua News, "Xi Jinping, Kim Jong Un Hold Talks in Beijing."

61. Xinhua News, "China Ready to Join DPRK in Turning Blueprint of Bilateral Ties into Reality: Xi," Xinhua Net, June 21, 2019, http://www.xinhuanet.com/english /2019-06/21/c_138162516.htm.

Chapter 3

North Korean Policy on South Korea

Development Strategy and Regime Competition

Sukhoon Hong

Some moves initiated the improvement of inter-Korean relations thanks to the Pyeongchang Winter Olympics in 2018, enlarging the mood of peace. The Panmunjeom Declaration in April and the Pyongyang Joint Declaration in September of the same year led to mitigating military tensions between the two Koreas. The two leaders agreed to transform the demilitarized zone (DMZ) into a peace zone in the Panmunjeom Declaration, marking a significant step toward a peace regime. In September, they agreed to implement the terms agreed to in previous inter-Korean summits and establish a west coast joint special economic zone and an east coast joint special tourism zone, expanding inter-Korean economic cooperation. However, since the collapse of the summit in Hanoi in February 2019, talks have been halted, even social and cultural exchanges have lacked progress, and the issues such as denuclearizing North Korea and establishing a peace regime on the Korean Peninsula have been in troubled waters. In addition, the Korean Peninsula has been at a standstill with the pandemic escalating U.S-China tensions and North Korea's demolition of the inter-Korean liaison office in Kaesong on the pretense of anti-regime flyers from the South. In addition, the two Koreas cannot go alone with the discussion on North Korea's denuclearization and the peace regime on the Korean Peninsula. The decisions and cooperation of the neighboring countries, including the United States, serve as core determinants of the issues. The Kim Jong-un regime's credibility and resolve for denuclearization are the preconditions for peace and prosperity of the Korean Peninsula. Here lies the question. Why is North Korea, which heightened military tensions—declaring the "completion of state nuclear force" on November 29, 2017, based on the *byungjin* (development of the economy and nuclear capabilities in parallel)—attempting to alter its foreign policy on South Korea, such as agreeing to ameliorate its relations with the South in 2018, all of a sudden, taking part in summit talks with South Korea and the United States? One can observe that Pyongyang's foreign policy behaviors have vacillated between confrontation and engagement as opposed to a consistent pattern of brinkmanship. However, we can reduce its uncertainty and lack of prediction in Pyongyang's foreign policy through increasing understanding of its leaders' perceptions and preferences as well as historical contexts. This chapter will analyze not only the influence of North Korea's transition to an "economy-first" strategy from 2018 to 2019 but also the strategy to strengthen defense capabilities and strive for "self-reliance" since 2022. The chapter will also discuss the South Korean government's strategy regarding North Korea for peace on the Korean Peninsula in the future.

NORTH KOREA AND THE THEORY OF BASIC NEEDS AND POLITICAL DEVELOPMENT

North Korea's policy analysis tends to be based on domestic policy determinants. Herbert Simon argues that one needs to know where preferences originate.[1] In this research, domestic priorities of policies are based on three basic human motives (power, achievement, and social affiliation) that organize what individuals know about foreign policy and should also shape how they make their decisions. In North Korea, decision makers have sought to develop state policies based on their relative preferences (i.e., regime survival, and economic benefits), rather than by structural determinants such as balance of power and national interests.[2]

In his research, domestic priorities of policies are drawn from a theory of human needs and development.[3] This paradigm relies on three basic assumptions regarding the relationship between human needs and development. First, humans will work to satisfy their most immediate needs to the greatest extent possible. Second, the most immediate needs within a given society will determine that society's course of political development. Finally, governments and political systems are legitimate insofar as they can enhance a population's ability to satisfy these immediate needs.[4]

Corresponding to the first assumption, this paradigm explains the foundation of the development theory on a set of four hierarchical structured human needs: (1) the need to "survive," (2) the need to interact and to share psychological attachments with others ("belongingness"), (3) the need to enjoy a leisurely mode of living ("leisure"), and (4) to attain superior quality of life relative to others by securing superfluous material goods and social status ("control or relative gratification").[5] In this hierarchical human needs theory, physical survival is the most essential and basic requirement for human beings. It is universal that all of humankind wants and needs to survive.

The survival need is defined simply as the desire of all living beings to stay alive and notes that the high value placed on survival transfers a high value onto anything that is essential for survival. People want to obtain basic necessities such as food, shelter, and safety. When the need for survival has been sufficiently satisfied, human beings will begin to seek others with whom they can identify and share the day-to-day experiences of life. In this stage, the need to belong supplants the now-satisfied need to "survive."

Once the need to survive and the need to belong have been satisfied, humans will seek fulfillment of the need for leisure. "Leisure" is defined as a desire for material consumption beyond what is required for survival and belongingness. The need for leisure can include the desire for vacation time, the decision to seek out faster means of transportation, or the acquisition of time-saving appliances. As man possesses the time and material resources necessary for a leisurely life, he will become preoccupied with the desire to maintain a superior life relative to other individuals. At this point, social status will become a salient consideration in an individual's life. This desire may manifest itself as a drive to win fixed-sum competitions. Social status is a relative value, thus, winning by some necessitates losing by others.

In the second and third assumptions, the structure of the process of political development corresponds to the four human needs. That is, for each set of human needs, there is a corresponding stage of political development designed to meet that need. For survival, there is the political process of "regime formation." For social interaction and belonging, there is the goal of "political integration." For the enjoyment of leisure, there is the goal of "resource expansion," and for the need to secure superfluous goods over others, there is the political goal of "conflict management."[6]

These stages appear to represent much of the process of developmental political change, regardless of the regime type (ideological and structural) directing the process in any given instance. In this regard, North Korea is not abnormal or atypical, that is to say, the policy goals of North Korea are not drastically different from any other country. The North Korean regime must constantly strive to satisfy people's material needs to the greatest possible extent to maintain and reinforce its legitimacy. Congruent with the outlined stages of human needs, the North Korean regime establishes policy goals that fit its political system and situation. In order of importance, these are

(1) national security, (2) political integration, (3) resource expansion, and (4) conflict management.

The goal of national security remains paramount to all other policy goals, followed by political integration and resource. In North Korea, first and foremost, the regime wishes to ensure its own survival. Once survival is assured, then, it is expected to pursue a system identity. Furthermore, North Korea seeks prosperity on the basis of the establishment of survival and identity.[7]

North Korea's Policy Goals: Kim Il-sung and Kim Jong-il Era

The pattern of Pyongyang's policy strategy has been one of "brinkmanship,"[8] yet, at times, North Korea has shown a willingness to negotiate with the outside (i.e., the United States, South Korea, and Japan). For the nuclear controversy, North Korea has used its nuclear program as a bargaining chip in its effort to secure concessions from the United States, Japan, and South Korea.[9] In fact, on October 21, 1994, North Korea consented to the Geneva Agreed Framework and began the Six-Party Talks leading to the September 19th Joint Statement of 2005,[10] and the February 29, 2012, nutrition aid agreement with Washington. In order to engage with Japan, Kim Jong-il even admitted to the abduction of Japanese citizens and in 2005 apologized to the visiting Japanese prime minister Junichiro Koizumi for these previous covert actions.[11] Regarding inter-Korea relations, Pyongyang adopted the June 15th Declaration of 2000 and the October 4th Agreements of 2006. Regarding economic benefits, Pyongyang agreed to open and operate "the Mount Kumkang Tourism (1998)" and "the Kaesong Industrial Complex (2000)" with the South. These events illustrate Pyongyang's serious interest in engaging itself in fruitful negotiations with the West and the Asian community at large.

In North Korea's policy patterns and decision-making processes, "brinkmanship" is commonly regarded as being irrational, and defies any systematic explanation. In other words, to the outside observer, it seems that the North Korean government is a black hole. Some scholars mention that North Korea's irrational, violent, and unpredictable style increases the danger of North Korea acting as a rogue state. Furthermore, the opacity of its internal policy process has raised many questions about this mysterious and isolated regime.[12]

However, some scholars have seen in the actions of North Korea a unique internal logic and motivation.[13] They suggest that North Korea's brinkmanship is based, not on irrationality or roguish madness but on its version of rational calculation.[14] In terms of North Korea's nuclear provocation, specifically, Pyongyang has also seen its possession of such capabilities as a means to improve its bargaining power in the international community and as a means to address domestic political and economic challenges.

Although they acknowledge the importance of external variables, their primary explanations are the internal variables, such as North Korea's domestic political stability, leadership, history, and culture.[15] This focus on domestic politics implies that Pyongyang's policy may appear to be a response to changes in other powerful states' foreign policies, but they reflect the domestic environment in several areas.

Nominal Goals in National Policy

In 1980, Kim Il-sung announced at the Sixth Congress of the Korean Workers' Party that North Korea would seek a foreign policy based upon "military strength, self-reliance, revolution, and liberation," or *Juche*. Further, he stressed that North Korea would seek a friendly relationship with other states (implying the United States and South Korea) only if such states would not employ strong-arm tactics and fully respect North Korean sovereignty.[16]

Regime survival has remained paramount for North Korea even during its continued periods of isolation following the end of the Cold War. In 1992, the regime's New Year's address warned against "imperialists and enemies . . . concentrated on attacking our country" and proclaimed North Korea as "the last fortress of socialism."[17] In 1993, Kim Il-sung made it clear that the Democratic People's Republic of Korea's (DPRK) foreign policy would remain focused on "independence, peace, and emphasizing friendly ties with socialist countries, non-aligned countries, and capitalist countries that respect North Korea."[18] In 1998, Kim Jong-il reiterated that stance, stating that the goals of "independence, friendly relations, and peace" mentioned in the North Korean constitution and by his predecessor were compatible with other foreign policy goals such as "military strength, self-reliance, revolution, and liberation." After Kim Jong-il assumed power in 1995, North Korea held to a "military–first (*Songun Jeongchi*)" ideology. It is important, however, for regimes to concentrate on internal economic difficulties as well as external threats since regime survival as a lone ideology cannot serve as a basis for legitimacy.[19] In 1998 North Korea put forth that economic development (*Kangsong Daekuk)* was fundamental to achieving a strong and prosperous nation.[20]

In 2012, North Korea's New Year's Joint Editorial focused on strengthening internal solidarity around Kim Jong-un. It did so by emphasizing the legacy of Kim Jong-il and concentrating on building a "strong and prosperous nation (*Kangsong Kukka*)." Further, it reiterated that Pyongyang's foreign policy goals are based on the fundamentals of "independence, friendly relations, and peace." The same editorial, however, takes a strong political stance.

Specifically, Pyongyang stated an intention to proceed with its pro-China position. The editorial also demanded the removal of U.S. troops from South Korea and condemned the Lee Myung-bak government of South Korea as traitors.[21]

Salient Goals and Strategies in the DPRK's Policy

The first strategy is performance-based and usually refers to the regime's capability to achieve economic development. This premise suggests that the ruling elite can legitimize their policy-making power so long as they are facilitating the population's progression through the hierarchy of needs.[22]

As shown before, regimes must strive to satisfy people's material needs to the greatest possible extent to maintain and reinforce legitimacy. Ruling elites generate political legitimacy to meet basic needs and promote "the prosperity of the people' and promote 'a belief system through an ideology.' According to the 'Human needs and development theory," social institutions are invented to provide a regularized mechanism for the satisfaction of a particular human need. Institutions such as the family, religious groups, mass media, and educational systems are made for meeting the need for belonging. Institutions are human inventions designed to foster and maintain a belonging need. In this need stage, ideology as the foundation of regime legitimacy is "trivial and largely irrelevant."[23] In this vein, ideology is also a means by which to inculcate into the population a belief system favorable to the regime's goals and strategies. He also describes the belief system as "a set of values" advanced by the ruling elites that becomes internalized and embedded among the members of the society, fortifying consent and loyalty to the regime based on this shared belief system.[24] Therefore, the regime responds to satisfy the belonging need of people by developing a political ideology that generates a common belief system for the populace to embrace. Regime legitimacy is formed from an ideology.

In the process of making the DPRK's policy, there are three levels to the internal structure of a policy: design-objective, strategy, and tactics. Policy legitimacy is an inescapable and necessary requirement for achieving the consensus that leaders need.[25] Therefore, policy legitimacy is a prerequisite for an administration to gain the national consensus required to transmit a leader's policy preferences in actionable policy for the state as a whole. At this juncture, the most pressing policy concern for the North Korean leadership is system survival. The primary conditions of system survival are the defense against military provocation, the preservation of national legitimacy relative to South Korea, and the preservation of culture against perceived western influence. To these ends, North Korean leadership has endeavored to create an ideological environment in which the population will share and thus, grant consensus to these policy goals.

Strategies under the DPRK's Priorities

Korea has responded with policy objective strategies and tactics that are consistent with its political system. North Korea requires specific set conditions such as a strong military for defense, the preservation of legitimacy over that of South Korea, and the protection of its ideologies from the corrupted capitalist culture. Economically, Pyongyang maintains a "closed door" policy that includes protecting against outside mass media and interaction with the outside world as an extension of its "information control" policy. From the perception of Pyongyang's leaders, the demise of the Soviet Union and the socialist bloc in Eastern Europe created a need to protect the population and political system from the same adversarial forces that induced these collapses.[26] For North Korea, the economic reform and democratization resulting from western influence would lessen the chances of regime survival. According to *Rodong Sinmun*, Pyongyang insists, "if one defends socialism, it is victorious and if one discards socialism, it is death."[27] Therefore, the North Korean regime prevents its citizens from being exposed to the outside world. In order to reduce the possibility of regime collapse, Pyongyang maintains strict policies of information control.

Secondly, North Korea borrows various policies from the Chinese economic development model designed to alleviate its devastating economic reality. While many Western observers claim that the food shortage is due to the failed government system, several reasons contribute to this difficulty. In 1996, heavy rainfall and floods ruined most of its arable land. In addition, many farming areas have suffered an erosion of the topsoil, which affects the production of food.[28] Also, the reduction of trade relations, particularly with China, causes difficulties. Since there is a difficult balance between receiving humanitarian aid without being too dependent on foreign powers, North Korea has tried to localize its agricultural productivity through Yon Hyong-muk's model of regional self-help. Initially, in May 1990, Kim Il-sung reiterated North Korea would trade with capitalist countries while maintaining the commitment to *Juche* and socialism. Kim proposed that "the DPRK would establish friendly economic and cultural relations with capitalist countries which respect our sovereignty."

As a part of improving and rebuilding their economy, Chung suggests focusing on collective cooperatives that would improve the general manner of economic management. It would allow for "unprofitable enterprises to be closed down and reorganized into specialty-based enterprises"[29] and these changes would strengthen the cabinet's role in the economy. Another aspect of economic rebuilding includes the emphasis on the advancement of scientific technology. This strategy would encourage economic and technological efficiency and promote better planning. North Korea also pursues a dualist strategy with its reform systems. Chung emphasizes the difference between a dual economy and how it emerges mostly during a transitional period of gradual reforms and market liberalization with a dual strategy, where a set of economic structures with different methodological characteristics follows a long-term goal.[30] There can be a shift from reforms within the system to a reform of the system, where the strength of autonomy remains while allowing and involving partial marketization. With the *Juche* philosophy still so deeply rooted, there may be ways to move the course of the policies for better economic benefit without changing the system altogether.

After the death of Kim Il-sung in 1994, the Kim Jong-il regime adopted more pragmatic foreign policy strategies in economic relations with politically adversarial countries such as South Korea and the United States. Despite the *Juche* ideology's emphasis on a self-reliant system, North Korea has embraced economic assistance from the South and even the United States. In the Agreed Framework signed by the United States and North Korea in October 1994, the United States agreed to provide North Korea with heavy oil, new light-water nuclear reactors, and eventual diplomatic and economic normalization in exchange for a freeze in the North's nuclear weapons program. North Korea accepted the engagement policy of South Korea through the June 15th summit talks in 2000 between Kim Dae Jung, the president of the Republic of Korea (ROK), and Kim Jong-il, the chairman of the defense committee of the DPRK.

Thirdly, during the Kim Jong-il era, Pyongyang incorporated "ultra-nationalism" into its general foreign policy strategy on South Korea. North Korea's national memory of the oppressive Japanese colonial rule, the partitioning of the peninsula, and the ongoing legitimacy competition with South Korea fueled this streak of nationalism. The nationalism of Kim Il-sung solidified Pyongyang's legitimacy against competing factions in the formative stages of the DPRK. After the death of Kim Il-sung, Kim Jong-il used his father's nationalism to ensure regime survival and integrate the political system. The DPRK's leadership advocates the people's respect and reverence for Kim Jong-il, the people's adherence to *Jaju* (national independence), and, most importantly, the North's policy toward inter-Korean unification without any intervention of countries such as the United States.

North Korea's nationalist sentiment strongly affects its militarism. The Kim Jong-il regime has advanced military capabilities along with "Military-first (*Songun*)" politics. At the beginning of the 1990s, North Korea discerned former allies, China and USSR, as betrayers because both countries established diplomatic relations and economic cooperation with South Korea and supported the simultaneous entry of the North and South to the United Nations (UN).[31] This provides further context for the desperate manner in which North Korea handled its policies of military preparedness and general isolation.

In terms of the importance of *Songun* politics, Pyongyang asserts that "*Songun* politics of the Workers' Party of Korea is the noblest patriotic politics as it helps reliably protect the dignity and sovereignty of the country and nation and achieve their prosperity."[32] Also, *Rodong Sinmun* supports that

> Songun politics of the WPK (the Workers' Party of Korea) is the only genuine political mode as it most fully reflects the popular masses' desire and aspiration and helps most successfully achieve the independence of the country and nation., But for the invincible military power built up under the banner of Songun, the U.S. imperialists would have forced a nuclear war upon the Korean nation long ago, and the territory of Korea would have suffered from the thermonuclear war ignited by them.[33]

Considering North Korea's militaristic leanings, it is not surprising that Pyongyang's leaders insisted on continuing to develop nuclear deterrence at any price. After the Iraq war and events in Libya, the North Korean regime felt its security was threatened by the United States. The turmoil in the Arab world brought about by U.S. and Western military intervention directed Pyongyang's leadership to work toward a nuclear arsenal to deter U.S. military attacks. The DPRK's leaders believe that nuclear armament is imperative to deterring a preemptive military attack led by the United States.[34] In 2012, Kim Jong-un, the new leader of the DPRK, spoke at a military parade that "the time has gone forever when the enemies threatened and intimidated us with atomic bombs."[35] The North Korean leadership appears to have made efforts toward these goals in its own way, all the while claiming to seek a nuclear resolution and attain security assurances from the United States. For North Korea, it was never an easy task to procure both national security and economic interests under the circumstances of its hostile relationship and confrontation with South Korea and the United States over the state of its nuclear program.

Moreover, North Korean leaders have depended on the rejection of South Korean values as the basis of regime legitimacy.[36] In terms of establishing national identity in the course of inter-Korean relations, North Korea depends on the legitimacy competition, which explains the fundamental orientation and policy priority toward South Korea. Pyongyang felt security threats from the South in each March of 2007, 2008, and 2009, since these seasons used to bring the Joint U.S.-ROK military exercises in the disputed territorial areas. On this point, Pyongyang sees the Joint U.S.-ROK military exercises as a substantial security threat. It illustrates that for the DPRK, the U.S.-ROK military alliance is one of the primary threats to its regime's safety. Therefore, North Korea condemned the Joint U.S.-ROK military exercises as "to all intents and purposes, maneuvers for a nuclear war" and "to seize the DPRK by force of arms," and claimed that the training "threatens the sovereignty of the DPRK and take necessary countermeasures including those to further bolster up all its deterrent forces (a spokesman for the DPRK Foreign Ministry, KCNA, March 3, 2008)." During the Joint US-ROK military exercise ("Key Resolve"), just before North Korea tested a long-range missile (North Korea declared it is a "satellite"), Pyongyang asserted maximal "security" needs toward Seoul from 2006 to 2009.

Indeed, after the second nuclear test, the Lee administration in South Korea pushed for support for United Nations Security Council (UNSC) Resolution 1874 and the UNSC Presidential Statement (Ministry of Foreign Affairs and Trade [MOFAT], 2010). Under UNSC Resolution 1874 in June 2009, Pyongyang sharply expressed its regime legitimacy preference toward the South. In this relationship, the North Korean leadership tends to promote its national identity and the legitimacy of the Pyongyang regime toward the South Korean government regarding justifying its nuclear armament.

Under the Lee Myung-bak government's hardline policy toward the North and continued economic sanctions from western countries, Pyongyang's leadership's policy toward South Korea has significantly relied on the policy orientation of establishing "national identity" more than the Roh government's policy preference of economic engagement. Also, we can observe that the "security" needs of Pyongyang's policy increased sharply in the Joint U.S.-ROK military drill period.

New Stage of Economic Development: Kim Jong-un Era

In its December 24, 2017, issue, the *Washington Post* evaluated that Chairman Kim Jong-un managed a successful year in 2017. As Kim Jong-un declared that the state "entered the final stage of preparation for the test launch of an intercontinental ballistic missile" in his 2017 New Year's address, the *Post* analyzed that North Korea proved its missile capabilities by launching an intercontinental ballistic missile (ICBM) that could reach up to 12,874 kilometers in distance, putting the continental United States within its range, and it completed the hydrogen bomb test that had a seventeen-fold magnitude of the atomic bomb dropped in Hiroshima.[37] Viewing these details, North Korea could celebrate the completion of its state nuclear force. However, while North Korea developed nuclear capabilities to the degree it longed for, it is obvious that it will have to bear more cost and pressure to mass-produce and deploy nuclear warheads and ballistic missiles. Even in the 2018 New Year's address, Chairman Kim, while encouraging that 2017 had been "a year when we set up an indestructible milestone in the history of building a powerful socialist country with the spirit of self-reliance and self-development as the dynamic force," emphasized the self-sustaining socialist economy.[38] This is due to the fact that the North Korean regime estimated the severity of the forthcoming international sanctions regime against North Korea. North Korea's enhancement of nuclear and missile capabilities was achieved without a sufficient level of economic development even though the North Korean regime proclaimed the "byungjin" as its foreign policy in 2013.

Unlike his father's regime, the Kim Jong-un regime desperately requires a foundation as a strong socialist country through economic development to safely secure the regime. Chairman Kim cannot maintain his legitimacy only through "*Juche* ideology" and "*Songun* (military-first) politics" based on his predecessors' charisma. The North Korean leadership desires a "party-centered system" running the state—a more stable leadership. Being a leader at a young age, Chairman Kim especially needs a political slogan that he could highlight. The new political slogans of North Korea concentrate on a "young and powerful socialist country" based on economic development. Some analysts indicate that this signals a transition of North Korea's national policy orientation based on its recently improving economic growth and the stage of political development, unlike the rule under Kim Jong-il.

Kim Jong-un's surprise visit to China in March 2018 (the 25th to the 28th) was evaluated as Pyongyang's move to restore the strained relations with Beijing, and thus, to strengthen its hand ahead of the summits with South Korea and the United States. Accompanied by his wife and major political figures such as Vice Chairman Choe Ryong-hae of the Central Committee of the Workers' Party of Korea (WPK) on his visit to China, Chairman Kim portrayed himself as a rational leader of a normal country on his first debut in international diplomacy. Foreign media outlets such as the *New York Times* and the *Wall Street Journal* commented that Chairman Kim had enhanced his initiative for the nuclear talks and engaged in global diplomacy, which his predecessors had failed to do, through the visit to China. Moreover, Kim Jong-un met President Xi Jinping again on May 7, 2018, flying over to Dalian on his jet. While several speculations hovered over the visit before the summit with the United States, Kim's visit on a plane manifests a change in North Korea's diplomacy, breaking away from the conventional behaviors of previous North Korean leaders. This reiterates North Korea's intention to publicize its image as a normal state through the summit talks with China, as Kim declared to build a young socialist country and a strategic state.

This reminds one of "the one big leap" that North Korea introduced before. On his visit to China during a normal diplomatic engagement with his Chinese counterpart, Kim Jong-un induced a change in the perception of North Korea from a reclusive state with egregious human rights records and nuclear development to a normal state solving international issues with rational and diplomatic negotiations. North Korea seems to boast its ability to carry out diplomatic negotiations by manifesting an image of international leadership, departing from the closed image of the past.

Viewing the North Korean economy over the six years under Chairman Kim, the real economic growth rate between 2012 and 2016 was recorded at 1.2 percent per annum, and the gross domestic product (GDP) growth rate in 2016 was recorded at 3.9 percent, according to the Bank of Korea (See figures 3.1. and 3.2). This was the fastest growth rate in seventeen years since 1999 when it marked 6.1 percent and the year 2017 was predicted to pick up with positive economic growth. Inflation and exchange rates have remained stable since 2013, indicating that the economy has coped well despite the sanctions regime against North Korea. North Korea's food shortage also has reduced from 1 million tons under Kim Jong-il to 0.4–0.7 million tons under Kim Jong-un. This is understood to be mainly the result of the increase in the mobilization of the labor force and resources into the agricultural sector, the May 30 Measure (referred to as the "field responsibility system") and the creation of additional income due to the invigoration of the market system. Even in the industrial sector, North Korea has increased investment in light industries and consumer goods, reducing investment in the heavy industry sector. While expanding sectors such as energy, light industry, agriculture, fisheries, and science and technology, North Korea vowed to strengthen its electricity and energy sector at the seventh WPK Party Congress in 2016, differentiating from four "leading sectors" (electricity, coal, metallurgical sector, and train and logistics).

Furthermore, the North Korean economy has structurally deepened trade dependence on China under the sanctions' regime. As South Korea

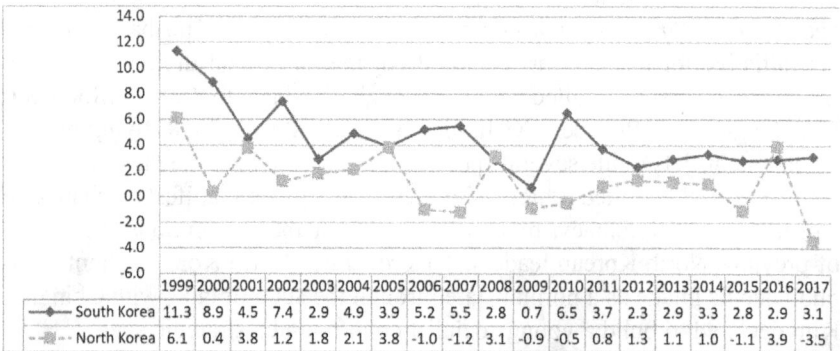

	1999	2000	2001	2002	2003	2004	2005	2006	2007	2008	2009	2010	2011	2012	2013	2014	2015	2016	2017
South Korea	11.3	8.9	4.5	7.4	2.9	4.9	3.9	5.2	5.5	2.8	0.7	6.5	3.7	2.3	2.9	3.3	2.8	2.9	3.1
North Korea	6.1	0.4	3.8	1.2	1.8	2.1	3.8	-1.0	-1.2	3.1	-0.9	-0.5	0.8	1.3	1.1	1.0	-1.1	3.9	-3.5

Figure 3.1: ROK and DPRK: The Rate of Economic Growth (Unit: %).

Source: The Bank of Korea. http://kosis.kr/statHtml/statHtml.do?orgId=101&tblId=DT_1ZGA31&conn_path =I3 (assessed July 24, 2018).

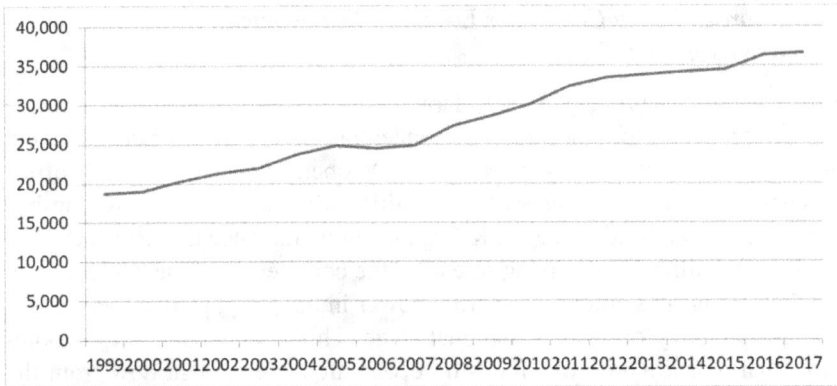

Figure 3.2: DPRK Norminal GNI (Unit: billions of won (ROK)).

Source: The Bank of Korea. http://kosis.kr/statHtml/statHtml.do?orgId=101&tblId=DT_1ZGA31&conn_path =I3 (assessed July 24, 2018).

introduced the May 24 Measures in 2010 and the inter-Korean exchanges severely diminished, dependence on trade with China has skyrocketed and trade with China accounted for 92.5 percent of North Korea's total trade in 2016.[39] Even the type of Chinese imports has changed: the proportion of raw materials plummeted, and the imports of intermediate and final goods increased. Also, the interconnection with the sanctions regime is augmented.

North Korea's growing dependence on the global economy and the pressure of the international sanctions regime will likely inhibit the economy from 2018 onward. Especially with the implementation of UN Security Council Resolution 2375 and the addition of U.S. unilateral sanctions among others will cause North Korea to incur severe economic costs. With the main exports of North Korea such as minerals, fishery goods, and processing trade blocked and the foreign currency from North Korean workers overseas reduced, the North Korean economy suffers a fatal blow. Additional provocations using nuclear weapons or missiles will lead to further sanctions. Crucially, after the ballistic missile launch on November 28, 2016, UNSCR 2397, adopted on December 22, 2017, prohibits the direct or indirect supply, sale, or transfer to the DPRK of crude oil, refined petroleum products, and various types of equipment and raw materials, and allows a country to capture and look into a vessel suspected of engaging in illicit activities with North Korea. Moreover, this resolution requires countries to expel all North Korean laborers earning income abroad immediately but no later than twenty-four months later.[40]

While the Kim Jong-un regime still stresses the "self-development first spirit" for the self-supporting economy, the economic sanctions on North Korea will *de facto* thwart the economic development and improvement of people's livelihoods, engendering a huge obstacle to regime survival.

North Korea's Policy Change for Economic Development:
Resource Expansion Stage

Subsequently, Chairman Kim's declaration of the completion of nuclear force enabled prospects for North Korea's concentration on economic development in 2018. The WPK plenary meeting last October, saw Kim Jong-un's affiliates and new political figures fill the Political Bureau (like Choe Ryong-hae confirmed as the head of the WPK Organization Guidance Department). This hints at the military's shrinking role after the completion of the nuclear force and Kim Jong-un's entourage sharing power in the party, paving the way for active diplomacy on the international stage. This allows pundits to hypothesize that North Korea will focus on economic development now from the byungjin, which was heavily tilted toward nuclear development.

Additionally, this could be explicated with the "state political development theory" in North Korea's stage of national strategy. North Korea under Kim Il-sung established the regime through the *Juche* ideology centered on security. During Kim Jong-il's rule, it weathered the storm of the "Arduous March," maintaining political legitimacy through *Songun* (military-first) politics. Nevertheless, unlike his father and grandfather, Kim Jong-un seems to face a changing situation where the regime and his leadership cannot sustain its legitimacy unless economic development follows. This is the reason why North Korea is asserting the idea of a young powerful socialist state.

China similarly focused on an economic opening policy and economic diplomacy with the United States when the state reached a phase of economic expansion. Other socialist latecomers like Vietnam and Laos followed the same route—an economic development strategy through the normalization of diplomatic relations with the United States (see figure 3.3.). Likewise, North Korea appears to have met such a situation, unable to solely depend on a closed economic policy based on national security and regime legitimacy. The completion of the nuclear force is the chain that links with harsher economic sanctions. The incumbent administrations in Washington and Seoul have three and four years remaining respectively, and North Korea cannot return to the previous economic system of an "isolated North Korean system" as it has seized the opportunity to advance relations with its southern neighbor. The changes within North Korean society and the marketization could jeopardize the *Suryong* leadership in the future.

Therefore, we can assume that Pyongyang would pursue economic prosperity based on the establishment of survival and identity recently in terms of the process of political development. There is the goal of "resource expansion" for its political system and situation Responding to this "resource expansion" stage, Pyongyang would seek a new economic development policy beyond "*Songun* Politics and *Juche* ideology" and "nuclear armament."

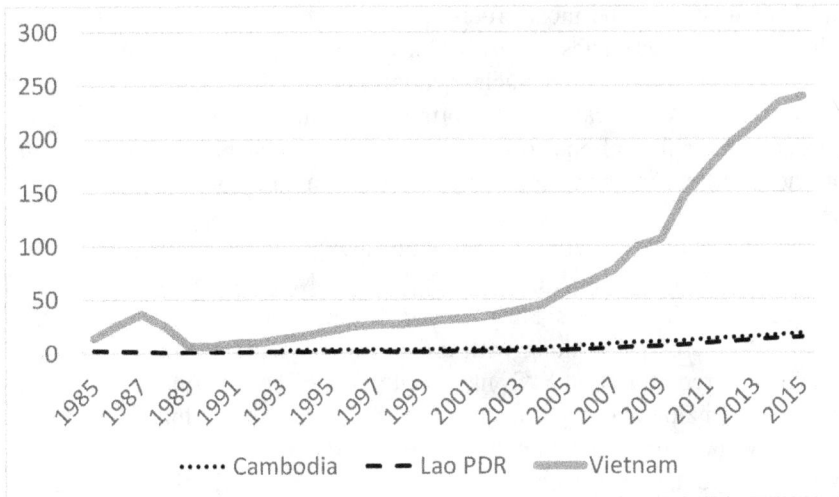

Figure 3.3: Vietnam, Cambodia, and Laos: GDP (Unit: Billion USD).
Source: World Bank National Accounts Data and OECD National Account Data File.

In this vein, on April 20, 2018, North Korea decided to close the Punggye-ri nuclear test site and suspend missile tests at the third plenary meeting of the seventh Central Committee of the WPK.[41] In addition, Director Pak Kwang Ho of WPK Propaganda and Agitation Department wrote in the *Rodong Sinmun* that as the party's byungjin concluded successfully, it is certain that we will succeed in carrying out the new strategic line focusing on economic construction.[42] At the meeting, the North Korean leadership declared that the byungjin had been successfully carried out and announced that the state will focus on "economic construction." North Korea steadily stressed that

[i]t is the WPK's firm will to open an avenue towards prosperity and shape a bright future in the spirit of self-reliance and fortitude as it has done, and the DPRK will undoubtedly achieve another image before long as a nation with a modern socialist economy and knowledge-based economy.[43]

Eventually, North Korea is assumed to have declared a new national strategy, adopting an economic development policy on the South. It is worth noting that this step was a policy decision from the party and not a personal declaration by Kim Jong-un. It implies that North Korea operates like any other "normal state"—establishing and executing a national strategy through the party system—and pursues a peace regime on the Korean Peninsula through diplomatic negotiations. North Korea suggested the summit talks with the United States as a gesture of claiming to be a "normal state" and seems to strive to develop as a strategic state by negotiating with South Korea and the United States. The most crucial points in the DPRK–U.S. summit are whether the United States can trust North Korea and the agreement reached on the method to achieve denuclearization of North Korea. If the two states agree on a "package deal" on the North Korean nuclear issue, the discussions on declaring a formal end to the Korean War, establishing a peace regime on the Korean Peninsula, and carrying out economic cooperation will proceed swiftly.

Unfortunately, instead of the traditional New Year's address in 2020, North Korea issued the "Report on the 5th Plenary Meeting of the 7th Central Committee of the Workers' Party of Korea" addressing the impending issues that North Korea faces along with the changes in national strategy ("a new way"). This report hints at a "frontal breakthrough" considering that the sanctions will remain for a long time, thus, North Korea will continue to pursue an aggressive military policy into the future. The report blamed the U.S. "hostile policy toward the DPRK" for the difficulties in denuclearization negotiations and the uncertainty surrounding the Korean peninsula. The North Korean negotiation strategy toward the United States was about lifting sanctions first, then resuming negotiations on denuclearization. While there is a hiatus in the security environment because of the pandemic, the political landscape surrounding the peninsula is highly likely to experience turmoil due to the North Korean nuclear issue and sanctions on North Korea among others.

North Korea's Shift to a Strategy of Strengthening Defense Capabilities: The Yoon Suk-yeol Administration's North Korea Policy and North Korea's Policy on South Korea

At the Eighth Congress of the Workers' Party of Korea (WPK) in January 2021, North Korea proclaimed a "principle of power for power and goodwill for goodwill" toward the United States and South Korea, highlighting an aggressive posture—enhancement of nuclear capabilities—until Washington withdraws its hostility against Pyongyang. It dismissed the inter-Korean cooperation and exchanges as nonessential issues and attributed the deterioration of inter-Korean relations to the South Korean government. The preceding Moon Jae-in administration's pursuit of a peace process on the Korean Peninsula has been forced into an impasse due to problems such as North Korea's denuclearization, Pyongyang's policy considerations, and the COVID-19 pandemic.

South Korea's new administration, appearing to introduce a hawkish approach toward North Korea, was sworn in on May 10, 2022. As his end goal for the North Korea policy, President Yoon Suk-yeol pledged to "achieve sustainable peace on the Korean Peninsula through complete and verifiable denuclearization of North Korea" in his inaugural address. He expressed that the administration would, in close coordination with the United States, present a "predictable roadmap for North Korea's denuclearization based on 'principles and consistency.'" On inter-Korean relations, the key tenet of the Yoon administration is "to build the bilateral relations with a harmonious blend of pragmatism and flexibility based on principles while leaving a door open for dialogue." To this end, the administration has set forth and implemented a vision for economic cooperation in line with the denuclearization process. Rather than taking steps unilaterally without North Korea's responsible behavior, the government planned to arrange economic development plans for various sectors such as infrastructure, investment, finance, industry, and technology per the steps in North Korea's denuclearization process. In the event of substantial progress in denuclearization, the Yoon government elucidated that it will engage in negotiations for a peace agreement. Particularly, it asserted that it would encourage constructive roles from Beijing and Moscow for North Korea's denuclearization and step up to embark on a cooperative initiative for North Korea's economic development along with the international community. On August 15, 2022, President Yoon articulated an "audacious initiative" on North Korean policy at his Liberation Day address. He elaborated that it will "significantly improve North Korea's economy and its people's livelihoods in stages if the North ceases the development of its nuclear program and embarks on a genuine and substantive process for denuclearization."

Nevertheless, South Korea's new administration aims to strengthen its alliance with the United States, restore cooperative ties with Japan, and respond in principle to North Korea's provocations. As for North Korea's nuclear capability sophistication, corresponding measures such as ROK-U.S. joint military drills and strategic asset deployment are expected. President Yoon and Biden, in a summit in May 2022, agreed to deploy the U.S. military's strategic assets in a timely and coordinated fashion and to pursue relevant further measures. This followed on the grounds that the extended deterrence at the current level seems insufficient and South Korea requires more effective measures of deterrence from the United States in the future. Moreover, the two countries resumed Ulchi Freedom Shield, a ROK-U.S. joint military exercise, for the first time in four years in August 2022.

From the early days of 2022, the North Korean regime carried out several military provocations until recently such as test-firings of hypersonic missiles and long-range missiles. South Korean and U.S. intelligence believe that North Korea finished its preparations to conduct a seventh nuclear test. Stressing the advancement of nuclear force since the 8th WPK Congress in 2021, the regime has maximized the strategy to shore up its nuclear and missile capabilities and severed ties with its southern neighbor despite the new South Korean government's proposal of humanitarian aid and calls for inter-Korean dialogue. According to a report from the Korean Central News Agency on March 25, 2022, North Korea, under the guidance of President

Kim Jong-un of the State Affairs Commission, test-launched a new intercontinental ballistic missile, "Hwasong-17," and officially scrapped its moratorium on testing nuclear weapons and long-range missiles. Amid North Korea's termination of this moratorium, intensifying competition between the United States and China over values, and the ongoing Russian invasion of Ukraine, the uncertainty in the international political landscape and inter-Korean relations have escalated.

On April 4, in a statement, North Korea's First Deputy Director Kim Yo-jong mentioned the possibility of using nuclear weapons against South Korea. On September 29, 2022, WPK general secretary Kim Jong-un markedly reiterated the continuation of developing strategic weapons, claiming that the "neighboring countries should drop their double standards" on developing weapons systems. A series of missile tests in 2022 seems to entail North Korea's motivations to maximize its strategy to further its nuclear and missile development and the preparations for a seventh nuclear test imply a groundwork for a closed foreign policy of self-reliance while having no intention to improve relations with Seoul and Washington. North Korea's policies to prioritize the development of military capabilities appear to hint at North Korea's focus on the policy of self-reliance through strengthening the military instead of a policy of negotiations with the international community in consideration of the U.S.-China rivalry, prolongation of the COVID-19 pandemic, and suspension of inter-Korean ties, among others.

CONCLUSION

In this chapter, the DPRK's domestic priorities behind foreign policies on South Korea are analyzed within the framework of the human needs development theory. Despite external pressures and economic difficulties, Pyongyang has increased North Korea's reliance on its overly nationalistic ideology of *Juche* and *Songun*. The *Juche* and *Songun* ideologies have even guided North Korea's foreign strategies and maneuverings with surrounding countries. The DPRK's foreign policy is determined primarily by the demands of "identity need" relative to South Korea.

North Korea's preference for South Korea is defined by the desire for "national identity." In historical context, the legacy of the Korean War shaped the strong nationalism under *Juche* and the emotional perception of the legitimacy competition with the South's democratic capitalism. To win a war over legitimacy against the South, the Pyongyang regime has maintained its "Korean-style socialist system (*urisiksahoejui*)" with "*Juche* (self-reliance)" ideology against Seoul. Both *Juche* and *Songun*'s ideologies are tied to Pyongyang's policy strategy toward Seoul.

In this sense, in terms of Pyongyang's national identity orientation, North Korea adopted *"Jaju* (national independence)" for its policy strategy toward the South government. Pyongyang demands the withdrawal of U.S. forces from the South and tries to stir anti-American sentiment in South Korean society. With the success of the Seoul Olympic Games in 1988, South Korea's economy rapidly developed and surpassed the North, creating the perception of an economic threat from the South. The Pyongyang regime adopted a pragmatic policy (*silli*) as a new strategy for dealing with the South Korean government after the establishment of the Kim Jong-il regime in 1998. South Korea's engagement policy (Sunshine Policy) toward North Korea is a strategy designed to mitigate military tensions on the Korean Peninsula and democratize the North through commercial exchanges and cooperation.

From this economic openness policy, North Korea has derived certain benefits for regime survival, such as economic aid and some relief from Western sanctions. This engagement policy itself will not be enough to bring about a resolution of military tensions between the two Koreas. North Korea has continued to pursue its aggressive "military first" policy, resulting in numerous armed conflicts illustrating that the legitimacy competition is intact. North Korea proposes talks to alleviate tensions whenever a progressive party assumes power in the South but increases the level of criticism against the ruling party whenever a conservative party is in power.

In this vein, we infer that Pyongyang tends to stand in a hostile position whenever the South government is willing to infringe on Pyongyang's legitimacy and dignity regardless of the South's economic assistance. North Korea also gets intimidated militarily by the U.S.-ROK joint military exercises. During the U.S.-ROK military exercises, Pyongyang pursues security rather than legitimacy relative to Seoul's policy. However, this paper confirmed that the Pyongyang leadership's policy priority has mostly depended on "identity need" in the context of history.

According to the human needs and development theory, Pyongyang has to adopt a new development policy for responding to the "resource expansion" stage of its political system and situation. It is absolutely clear that North Korea's change in attitude is the utmost priority to drive the virtuous cycle of improved inter-Korean relations and advancing DPRK-U.S. relations after the PyeongChang Olympics forward. North Korea's recent proclamation to transform its strategy to "economic development" at the plenary meeting of the WPK on April 20, 2018 appears to be a positive sign in improving relations with the United States. North Korea seems to have reached the limit in maintaining political legitimacy through the byungjin focused on nuclear development. The North Korean *suryong* leadership needs economic development to secure its rule. Moreover, North Korea is predicted to enter a new phase in its national strategy to ensure confidence domestically in the

Kim Jong-un regime's political stability and to develop the country into a "strategic state" based on a party-centered system. Unfortunately, in showing economic performance under the sanctions, North Korea is not likely to seek a dramatic change on the economic front. It reveals a limitation of the independence and self-reliance of the people's economy in North Korea.

Primarily, the South Korean government should assess North Korea's intentions closely, establish a negotiation strategy against North Korea, and resolve the North Korean issue in coordination with the United States. While the rapprochement with North Korea is important, it is essentially difficult to discuss the North Korean denuclearization issue and the peace regime on the peninsula without U.S. cooperation. In other words, it is imperative to firmly grasp Pyongyang's intent and sufficiently coordinate with the United States, formulating a strategy regarding North Korea and exchanging opinions with the United States after the U.S.-DPRK summit in Singapore. Eventually, the long-term resolution between the two Koreas and the United States will begin in earnest only when the peaceful resolution to the North Korean nuclear issue between North Korea and the United States is guaranteed, along with the South Korean government's lead.

After the breakdown of the North Korean–American summit in Hanoi in 2019, the issue of North Korea's denuclearization and agreement on a peace regime on the Korean Peninsula is going through a difficult process. To elaborate, consultation and cooperation with the United States are necessary to discuss the peace regime on the peninsula. Seoul should continuously reiterate the risk of a military option to disentangle the North Korean nuclear issue and assert that the sanctions have been in place to resolve the North Korean nuclear issue through peaceful and diplomatic means. The South Korean government should endeavor to aid the United States in systematically focusing on the peaceful resolution of the North Korean nuclear issue and the settlement of peace on the peninsula and in the process, the two sides should share frank views by enhancing bilateral networks.

Provided that the South Korean government hopes to lead the inter-Korean rapprochement and the political environment on the Korean Peninsula, it should pursue a "two-track" strategy, separating the North Korean nuclear issue. In other words, it should undergo a shift to a "peace paradigm" as a constructive alternative mentioned earlier. Inter-Korean relations need a "reset in policy regarding the North" focused on sociocultural exchanges, apart from the nuclear issue. For a perpetual peace regime, social exchanges and cultural understandings should precede at the civilian level. South Korea's policy on North Korea requires a focus on the constituents of the society through social and cultural integration rather than concentrating solely on state-centered institutional integration. To this end, Seoul should encourage Pyongyang's policy change, and the inter-Korean exchanges and cooperation in apolitical fields should expand further. Additionally, the pursuit of peace on the peninsula and the North Korean policy calls for cooperation and understanding from the international community. That is to say, international cooperation is necessary for the peace and prosperity of the Korean peninsula and this requires establishing networks globally and striving for diplomatic engagement for support.

The previous Moon Jae-in administration's peace process on the Korean Peninsula was significant and necessary to advance inter-Korean relations and institutionalize a peace regime. However, the negotiations on North Korea's denuclearization have unfortunately been in deadlock since the collapse of the Hanoi summit between the United States and North Korea in 2019; and it has drawn criticisms for weakening South Korea's diplomatic prowess toward its neighbors. North Korea has pressed ahead with developing its nuclear and strategic weapons and the absence of inter-Korean talks and the United States' and North Korea's confrontational policy against one another have strained inter-Korean relations. The international security threats caused by events such as Russia's attack on Ukraine pose serious challenges to South Korea in establishing policies on North Korea and fostering cooperation in Northeast Asia.

Against this backdrop, the newly inaugurated Yoon government's foreign policy is predicted to orient toward the consolidation of the alliance with the United States based on shared democratic values and a composed North Korean policy based on the principle of reciprocity. We will likely see the sanctions regime imposed on North Korea, instability surrounding the Korean Peninsula, and a low possibility for inter-Korean/U.S.-DPRK dialogue remain unchanged. In conclusion, it is high time for South Korea to address solutions for survival, formulating a sustainable North Korean policy and approaches to prepare for Korean unification—keeping an eye on fundamental shifts in international politics while putting domestic political differences aside.

Overall, the South Korean government should comprehend North Korea's transition of the national strategy to disentangle the intricacy of foreign variables and to shore up inter-Korean ties. The South Korean government would assume a proactive role in the Korean Peninsula issue and pursue the "initiative of peace on the Korean Peninsula." Consequently, it should settle the peace regime on the peninsula, seeking a peaceful resolution to the North Korean nuclear issue by the virtuous cycle of the advancement of inter-Korean relations and improvement of DPRK-U.S. relations. Finally, Korean unification should be based on peaceful means. Thus, it is necessary to contemplate the most appropriate approach to peaceful unification, abandoning the idea of war. In the end, both South and North Koreans should be able to enjoy peaceful coexistence and prosperity. To this end, it is mandatory to foster a social and national atmosphere to entice North Korea to adopt reform and opening-up measures. From a framework of "peace paradigm," peace and unification will only be possible under a long-term strategy, proceeding with social and normative understanding and integration while the system centered on "democratic peace" and universal "human rights" and social constituents with common interests are guaranteed.

NOTES

1. See Herbert A. Simon, "Human Nature in Politics: The Dialogue of Psychology with Political Science," *The American Political Science Review* 79, no. 2 (June 1985): 293–304.

2. Suk-Hoon Hong and Yun-Young Cho, "Consistent Pattern of DPRK's Policy on ROK: What Shapes North Korea's Foreign Policy?," *International Area Studies Review* 20, no. 1 (2017): 58–59.

3. See Han S. Park, *Human Needs and Political Development: A Dissent to Utopian Solution* (Cambridge: Schenkman Publishing Company, 1984); and Han S. Park, *Globalization: Blessing or Curse?* (Sentia Publishing Company, 2017).

4. Han S. Park, *Human Needs and Political Development*, 59.

5. Conforming to most of the basic premises underlying Maslow's conception of the "hierarchy of human needs," as well as the psychological perspectives of cognitive development, I suggest here a fourfold hierarchical structure of human needs. They are (1) survival, (2) belongingness, (3) leisure, and (4) control. Abraham H. Maslow, *Motivation and Personality* (New York, NY: Harper and Row Publishers Inc., 1954).

6. Han S. Park suggested that "development has common objectives at any level of social complexity: individual, group, state, and the global community itself" and "one universal and important objective of development is need satisfaction. Need satisfaction is a concept that is applicable universally, and thus, a definition of development as the process in which members of the political system (country) pursue and obtain need–satisfaction. This conception of development is so universal that it will defy ideological and cultural barriers." Han S. Park, *North Korea Demystified* (New York, NY: Cambria Press, 2012), 3.

7. Some goals are more urgent than others, and we can expect these to be pursued prior to the pursuit of other, less urgent goals. The concept of preference ordering is a more formal version of this idea. Milton Friedman, *Essays in Positive Economics* (Chicago, IL: University of Chicago Press, 1953); and Park, *North Korea Demystified.*

8. Dixit and Skeath define brinkmanship as "a threat that creates a risk but not certainty of a mutually bad outcome." Avinash Dixit and Susan Skeath, *Games of Strategies* (New York: W.W. Norton and Company, 1999), 302. According to Scoot Snyder, brinkmanship is "a unilateral strategy in negotiation which involves mixing aggressive and provocative tactics, including issuing unconditional demands, blustering, bluffing, threatening, stalling, manufacturing deadlines, and even walking out of

the negotiation." Scott Snyder, *Negotiating on the Edge: North Korean Negotiating Behavior* (Washington, DC: United States Institute of Peace Press, 1999), 76.

9. Selig Harrison, *Korean Endgame: A Strategy for Reunification and U.S. Disengagement* (Princeton, NJ: Princeton University Press, 2002).

10. The United States and North Korea came to the brink of war in June 1994. But the visit of former U.S. President Jimmy Carter to Pyongyang and negotiations with Kim Il-sung averted war and led to the U.S.–DPRK Agreed Framework of October 1994.

11. Han S. Park, *North Korea Demystified* (New York, NY: Cambria Press, 2012).

12. Victor D. Cha, "Hawk Engagement and Preventive Defense on the Korean Peninsula," *International Security* 27, no. 1 (2002): 46–50.

13. David C. Kang, "International Relations Theory and the Second Korean War," *International Studies Quarterly* 47, no. 3 (2003); Scott Snyder, *Negotiating on the Edge. North Korean Negotiating Behavior* (Washington, DC: United States Institute of Peace Press, 1999); and Kyung-Ae Park, "Explaining North Korea's Negotiated Cooperation with the U.S.," *Asian Survey* 37, no. 7 (1997).

14. Specifically, some indicated that the U.S. policy toward North Korea is based on the mistaken conceptualization of and assumptions about North Korea's capabilities and intentions. Kang, "International Relations Theory and the Second Korean War," 310.

15. Han S. Park, *North Korea: The Politics of Unconventional Wisdom* (Boulder, CO: Lynne Rienner Publishers, 2002).

16. Report of "The Sixth Congress of the Worker's Party of Korea on the Work of the Central Committee" (Pyongyang: Korean Workers' Party Publishing House, 1980), 1.

17. "New Year's Address," *Rodong Sinmun*, January 1, 1992 [in Korean].

18. "New Year's Address," *Rodong Sinmun*, January 1, 1993 [in Korean].

19. Park, *North Korea: The Politics of Unconventional Wisdom*, 159.

20. *Rodong Sinmun*, September 9, 1998 [in Korean].

21. *Rodong Sinmun*, January 1, 2012 [in Korean].

22. Park, *Human Needs and Political Development: A Dissent to Utopian Solution*, 118.

23. Ibid., 70–138.

24. Ibid., 78; Alexander L. George (1969) argues that "a political actor's belief system about the nature of politics is shaped particularly by his orientation to other political actors." He insists that this approach should be useful for studying an actor's decision-making type and its application in specific situations. He explains that "the operational code is a particularly significant portion of the actor's entire set of beliefs about political life. These beliefs are associated with the concept of operational code control as guides for political decision-making and leadership type. Alexander L. George, "The 'Operational Code': A Neglected Approach to the Study of Political Leaders and Decision-Making," *International Studies Quarterly* 13, no. 2 (June 1969): 190–222.

25. Richard Smoke, "On the Importance of Policy Legitimacy," *Political Psychology* 15, no. 1 (1994): 101.

26. Park, *Human Needs and Political Development: A Dissent to Utopian Solution*, 150.

27. *Rodong Sinmun,* January 13, 1999 [in Korean].

28. Han S. Park, "North Korean Perception of Self and Others: Implications for Policy Choices," *Pacific Affairs* 73, no. 4 (2000/2001): 507.

29. Young Chul Chung, "North Korean Reform and Opening: Dual Strategy and *Silli* (Practical) Socialism," *Pacific Affairs* 77, no. 2 (2004): 289.

30. Ibid., 286.

31. Alexander Zhebin, "The Foreign Policy of the DPRK," in *North Korea Demystified*, ed. Han S. Park (New York, NY: Cambria Press, 2012), 205.

32. *Korean Central News Agency*, March 3, 2008 [in Korean].

33. Ibid.

34. Park, *North Korea Demystified*.

35. Korean Central News Agency, April 15, 2012 [in Korean].

36. Han S. Park, *North Korea: The Politics of Unconventional Wisdom* (Boulder, CO: Lynne Rienner Publishers, 2002).

37. *The Washington Post*, December 24, 2017.

38. "New Year's Address," *Rodong Sinmun*, January 1, 2018 [in Korean]

39. KOTRA, "In 2016, North Korea's Total Trade Volume: 6.55 billion dollars," July 24, 2017, http://www.kita.net/info/organ/index.jsp?sCmd=VIEW&nPage =1&nPostIndex=12511 (accessed on July 29, 2018).

40. United Nations, http://unscr.com/en/resolutions/2397 (accessed on July 23, 2018).

41. *Rodong Sinmun*, April 21, 2018 [in Korean]

42. Ibid.

43. Chung Guk Won, "Socialist Korea Enters New Stage of Development," *Korea Today* (Pyongyang, DPRK: June 2018), 15.

Chapter 4

Presence of Malice

Japan and North Korea's Non-Relations

Anand Rao

What motivates the foreign policy of the Democratic People's Republic of Korea (DPRK, referred to as "North Korea" hereafter) in general, and toward Japan in particular? The latter will be the focus of this book chapter. In recent years, there have been some big surprises in North Korea's diplomacy. The biggest surprise came in June 2018, when for the first time a sitting United States president met a sitting North Korean dictator. Donald Trump's meeting with Kim Jong-un in Singapore that year was appointment-level television, even if their encounter yielded little in substance. Kim Jong-un, not yet thirty years old and virtually unknown to the outside world when he took power in 2011, achieved in his meeting with Donald Trump a level of validation for his hereditary regime's legitimacy that had eluded both his father and grandfather. The year 2018 also saw Kim meet for the first time President Moon Jae-in of South Korea and China's leader Xi Jinping. In the spring of 2019, Kim then held his first meeting with President Vladimir Putin of Russia. After years of isolation following his rise to power in 2011, Kim Jong-un in the space of a little more than one year held crucial face-to-face meetings with the top political leaders of all three countries that share a land border with North Korea.

Conspicuous in his absence among national leaders meeting Kim Jong-un before the pandemic was then Prime Minister Abe Shinzo of Japan. While Japan does not share a land border with North Korea (or any other country), it remains a vitally important country in the Northeast Asia region despite the perception that it has declined in influence relative to a rapidly rising China. Japan's colonial rule over all of Korea from 1910 to 1945 caused a backlash that inadvertently gave rise to the totalitarian communist ideology that came

77

to dominate North Korea, and through a peculiar turn of events in the early post–World War II era, Japan became home to a small but significant community of North Korean citizens.[1] Japanese influence has arguably been central to state formation and identity in North Korea.

Therefore, the objective of this book chapter is to explain the motivations behind North Korean policy toward Japan and why (among other things) that policy has yet to yield a summit meeting between Kim Jong-un and the prime minister of Japan. A meeting between a North Korean dictator and a sitting Japanese prime minister would not be without precedent. In 2002 and again in 2004, Prime Minister Koizumi Junichiro met Kim Jong-il in Pyongyang. The potential benefits of a diplomatic breakthrough with Japan could be enormous for North Korea. Japan's establishment of diplomatic relations with South Korea in 1965 and mainland China in 1972 played a major role in spurring international trade for the latter two countries and helped fundamentally transform their respective economies into consumer-based powerhouses.

But formidable obstacles remain to achieving such a breakthrough in the case of North Korea. The leaders of North Korea desire greater economic prosperity for their country to shore up the regime's legitimacy, but without the accompanying political change that hardliners in the Japanese government demand. And more significantly, the surprising conclusion I have reached is that North Korea is now a good deal more important to Japan than Japan is to North Korea. For a poor country with apparently little to offer, this has put North Korea in an unusually advantageous position in its dealings with Japan. The first part of this chapter will briefly explain Japan-North Korea interactions before 2011, and then move on to examining the situation since Kim Jong-un took power in December 2011.

JAPAN AND NORTH KOREA UP TO 2011

Key events in three different years prior to 2011 made it exceedingly difficult for Japan and North Korea to advance in any way toward forging closer political ties. This does not mean, however, that economic ties were nonexistent. In fact, for much of the second half of the twentieth century, Japan was one of North Korea's largest trading partners alongside China and the Soviet Union. In 1999, according to IMF data cited by Noland, North Korea's adjusted trade with Japan amounted to US$342 million.[2] This comprised nearly 16 percent of North Korea's total trade that year and was second only to North Korea-China trade at $514 million. These numbers, however, are somewhat misleading since the absolute volume of trade between North Korea and Japan was never especially large and would eventually be dwarfed by Japan's trade with South Korea. Ethnic Koreans in Japan who declared loyalty to North Korea were a key conduit for this trade and also cash remittances sent there.

But politics and threat perceptions would eventually become far more important than economics in North Korea's relations with Japan. Sanctions rather than trade would come to characterize economic interactions between the two countries. In 1965, the United States essentially brokered a deal that led to the establishment of diplomatic relations between Japan and South Korea. The treaty stipulated that the government of the Republic of Korea (aka South Korea) was the only lawful government in Korea, closing off the possibility that Japan could establish diplomatic relations with both Koreas.[3] This made sense at a time when South Korea was ruled by a virulently anti-communist regime under Park Chung-hee, just twelve years removed from the signing of the Korean War armistice. Decades would pass before a rapprochement between South Korea and North Korea was no longer unthinkable.

The next year that saw a significant event shape Japanese attitudes toward North Korea was 1998. On August 31 of that year, North Korea for the first time launched a missile that traveled over Japanese airspace and landed in the Pacific Ocean.[4] This news shocked people in Japan and caused the government to take the security threat from North Korea much more seriously by focusing greater attention on the development of a missile defense system. As hard as it is to believe now, Japanese politicians and bureaucrats did not focus so much on North Korea as a major security threat until this 1998 missile launch. Official Japanese views of extraordinary developments in South Korean politics until that time illustrate this point. The election of avowed leftist and former dissident Kim Dae-jung as president of South Korea in December 1997 was not viewed negatively in Japan, a strong contrast with how the South Korean political left and its inclination toward rapprochement with North Korea would come to be viewed in later decades by Tokyo. In fact, it can be argued that the high point of bilateral relations between Japan and South Korea occurred when Kim Dae-jung and Japanese Prime Minister Obuchi Keizo held a very cordial and successful summit meeting in October 1998. But the mutual goodwill would dissipate after the turn of the century as the perceived North Korean threat began driving a wedge between the two East Asian democracies.

Events in the third critical year of 2002 did the most to damage any chances in the near future of a thawing in relations between the two countries. But in the late summer of that year, there was great hope. For years rumors had persisted that agents sent by Pyongyang in the 1970s and 1980s had kidnapped Japanese citizens from the shores of those areas in Japan located across the sea from North Korea. The leader of North Korea, Kim Jong-il, had been in power since the death of his father Kim Il-sung in 1994. His time in power up to that point had had its ups and downs. His initial few years in power in the middle of the 1990s were marked by a general economic crisis and famine conditions, as North Korea reeled from the loss of support provided by the Soviet Union following that country's dissolution in 1991. While the situation was terrible, his regime survived and the inauguration of Kim Dae-jung as South Korean president in February 1998 presented a new and previously unimaginable opportunity for the two Koreas to resolve their differences.

Perhaps the high point for Kim Jong-il's regime occurred in October 2000, when U.S. Secretary of State Madeline Albright visited Pyongyang in a bid to negotiate a framework for ending the technical state of war between the two Koreas. It was the first visit ever by a sitting U.S. secretary of state to North Korea. History had been made earlier that year in June when Kim Dae-jung flew to Pyongyang and became the first sitting South Korean leader to meet a North Korean dictator. As the last year of the twentieth century came to a close, prospects for the ending of North Korea's isolation appeared better than ever before.

Developments in U.S. politics thwarted such an outcome. The deadlocked presidential election held in November 2000 gave way to victory for the hawkish George W. Bush in December and his inauguration as president in January 2001. Bush exhibited great hostility to all aspects of his predecessor Bill Clinton's foreign policy and sought to reverse almost everything he had accomplished.[5] The U.S. détente with North Korea was abandoned, relations between Bush and Kim Dae-jung were frosty at best, and in his January 2002 State of the Union speech, Bush went so far as to label North Korea as part of an "axis of evil" that also included Iran and Iraq.

In this environment, Kim Jong-il turned to Japan as a potential alternative partner for alleviating North Korea's economic problems and heightened dependence on China in the years since the Soviet Union's dissolution in 1991. Despite the concerns about North Korean missile launches and other provocations, Koizumi Junichiro agreed to become the first sitting Japanese prime minister to meet a North Korean leader when he traveled to Pyongyang in September 2002. His main purpose in traveling there was to find out what had happened to seventeen Japanese citizens who had allegedly been kidnapped by North Korean agents.

In a remarkable display of honesty for a dictatorial regime, Kim Jong-il admitted that such kidnappings had indeed taken place. Five abductees were identified and allowed to meet Koizumi and his entourage. Of the remaining twelve people the Japanese wished to know about, the North Koreans claimed that eight had died and four had never been taken.[6] Among the deceased named was Yokota Megumi, who had been abducted at the age of only thirteen in 1977. Yokota's mother and father, who both became internationally known figures for drawing attention to their daughter, were both still living twenty-five years after her disappearance when they heard this devastating news.

This disclosure by the North Korean government did not have the intended effect of laying the foundation for a possible normalization of relations with Japan. Instead, the revelations shocked people in Japan and led to a public outpouring of extreme anger and grief over Yokota's fate and the realization that other abductees had been living for decades against their will in North Korea. Many Japanese refused to believe that Yokota or the other abductees were dead and assumed the North Korean regime was lying for one reason or another about them. While the North Koreans insisted they had provided a full and honest accounting of what had happened to the abductees, the Japanese side became convinced that the North Koreans had not truly come clean and in the ensuing years would come to demand more information about other missing people.

With such revelations, there was no way the Koizumi government could move forward with any kind of normalization of ties with North Korea. The Bush administration's advocacy of "regime change" for members of the "axis of evil" became a reality six months after the Koizumi-Kim summit when U.S. armed forces invaded Iraq in March 2003 to oust Saddam Hussein from power. U.S. leaders, shocked by the terrorist attacks of September 11, 2001, appeared to be in the grips of a regime change binge that would threaten to topple all governments suspected of aiding and abetting anti-U.S. terrorists in any way. By this point, some hardliners in Japan were more eager to see Kim Jong-il overthrown by U.S. armed forces than to see him talk again with a Japanese politician.

But Kim Jong-il did talk with Prime Minister Koizumi one more time, in the spring of 2004. In exchange for receiving money and thousands of tons of rice from Japan, the North Korean government agreed to let Koizumi fly back from Pyongyang to Tokyo accompanied by the children of those five identified Japanese citizens who had lived for years as abductees in North Korea before moving back to Japan following the first Koizumi-Kim meeting in 2002.[7] But the damage done by the overwhelmingly negative reaction in Japan to the revelation of abductions of Japanese citizens by North Korean agents was too much to overcome. Any further breakthroughs in North Korea's relations with Japan were almost out of the question after the first Koizumi-Kim meeting.

This turned out to be the case despite the landmark Pyongyang Declaration that was concluded between Japan and North Korea at that 2002 meeting. For the first time, North Korea agreed to participate in a multilateral and regional security initiative. Point four of the Declaration in English stated that the two countries would "cooperate with each other in order to maintain and strengthen the peace and stability of Northeast Asia."[8] Such cooperation never came to fruition, but at the time North Korea's willingness to signal such a level of engagement with Japan further illustrated its desire not to remain overly dependent on China.

A significant amount has been written about how the grim fates of Iraqi dictator Saddam Hussein (executed in 2006) and Libyan dictator Muammar al-Qaddafi (killed by a mob in 2011) led Kim Jong-un and those around him to conclude that possession of nuclear weapons deterrent (which neither Hussein nor Qaddafi ever had) would be essential to his regime's survival.[9] I would also argue that Kim Jong-un drew lessons from North Korea's failed bid to achieve a breakthrough in relations with Japan. Kim Jong-il in 2002 acknowledged to the Japanese that North Korean agents had in fact kidnapped Japanese citizens, but that did nothing to improve the situation. On the contrary, it produced a surge of unbridled hostility to North Korea among members of the Japanese public. It seems likely that Kim Jong-un observed this development closely and realized the perils of attempting a rapprochement with Japan.

This background brings us to the present era, which began in December 2011 when Kim Jong-il died and Kim Jong-un replaced him as leader of North Korea. The contours of the present era in relations with Japan were further solidified when Abe Shinzo became prime minister for a second time beginning in December 2012. The rest of this chapter will look at North Korea's strategies for dealing with a Japan that came to be dominated politically by a hawkish revisionist who owed his political ascendance in part to the stances he took against North Korea in the past.

Kim Jong-un Takes Power in 2011

Kim Jong-un became the head of an impoverished, underperforming country after his father died in December 2011. Estimates vary and are uncertain, but per capita gross domestic product (GDP) in North Korea at that time likely stood at less than $1,000 when measured nominally. By 2011, the per capita GDP in South Korea had risen to more than $24,000. Poverty in North Korea was a relatively old story by then, and in fact, so was the economic prosperity in South Korea. What was startlingly new and different at the time of Kim Jong-un's accession compared to the year (1994) when his father took power, however, was the rapid rise of China to near middle-income country status. According to World Bank data, per capita GDP in China rose from just $473 in 1994 to $5,618 in 2011.[10]

Why was China's economic rise important to North Korea, and what if anything did this mean for North Korean policy toward Japan? It is crucial to answer these questions as a way of understanding why North Korea has not opened itself up to greater interactions with the world in a manner similar to fellow communist states in Asia like China and Vietnam. This refusal to open has been a key stumbling block to any real change in North Korea's stance toward Japan.

China has been the essential guarantor of North Korea's existence and legitimacy ever since it chose to intervene in the Korean War in November 1950 and save Pyongyang from what would have been certain destruction. Therefore, China's transformation by 2011 into an economic superpower with an economy that had finally grown large enough to surpass the Japanese economy as the world's second largest appeared to portend inevitable changes for North Korea. It has always been a mistake, however, to assume that North Korea would one day have to follow the Chinese model of reform and opening. In particular, China's move to establish diplomatic relations with Japan in 1972 and strengthen bilateral economic ties after that was carried out as part of a larger grand strategy that was supported by the United States to tilt the balance of power away from the Soviet Union.

North Korea's incentives for cultivating better relations with Japan were never similar. As I wrote earlier, North Korea's short-lived extension of an olive branch to Japan in 2002 was likely rooted in the need to ensure economic survival and boost regime legitimacy rather than being part of any grand strategy on the part of Pyongyang. And for Pyongyang, the extension of that olive branch backfired spectacularly. Therefore, North Korea fell back on attempting to cultivate ties with South Korea while that country (in strong opposition to the wishes of the United States under President Bush) adhered with limited effectiveness to its so-called Sunshine Policy of rapprochement until a change of presidents to the conservative Lee Myung-bak in 2008. So by the time Kim Jong-un assumed power in 2011, China's transformation could not be ignored but at the same time the emulation of China by North Korea in terms of increasing ties with Japan was far-fetched and illogical.

Finally, political developments in Japan during Kim Jong-un's first year in power made a North Korean opening of any kind to Tokyo even more difficult. The next section of this chapter will examine how the political comeback of Abe Shinzo in Japan further hardened North Korean attitudes toward that country after 2012.

Abe Shinzo Stages a Political Comeback in 2012

Abe Shinzo, who was assassinated in July 2022, owed much of his political ascendance in Japan to events related to the Japanese abductee issue. First elected to the Japanese House of Representatives in 1993, Abe was initially little more than one among many hereditary backbenchers who are so commonplace in Japan's conservative and long-ruling Liberal Democratic Party (LDP). Abe's grandfather Kishi Nobusuke was prime minister of Japan from

1957 to 1960, but in the family dynasty-based world of Japanese politics that made him far from unique or special. Abe's situation changed completely when he accompanied Prime Minister Koizumi on his first trip to North Korea in September 2002.

Among politicians taking a hard line against North Korea following Kim Jong-il's acknowledgment of the abductions, Abe was among the most visible and high profile. He appeared on Japanese television news almost nightly in the fall of 2002, often standing with one or more of the five abductees who had been brought back to Japan for what the North Koreans understood would be a brief visit away from their children (who eventually joined them in Japan in 2004). Instead, the abductees remained in Japan and none of them have traveled to North Korea in the years since. The North Koreans viewed this as a betrayal by the Japanese government. There can be little doubt that Abe strongly opposed having the abductees go back to North Korea.

Abe quickly parlayed his newfound political fame into advancing up the ranks of the seniority-based and hierarchical LDP far more rapidly than what is considered normal. In 2003, at the relatively young age of forty-nine, he became secretary general of the LDP. Two years later in 2005, after the LDP won a landslide victory in a general election that September, he obtained the highly coveted position of chief cabinet secretary. In September 2006, after Koizumi stepped down, Abe became at the age of fifty-two the youngest prime minister in the history of post–World War II Japan. His first premiership, however, was marred by perceptions that Abe was elitist and out of touch. He resigned in September 2007 after just one year in office.

Out of the prime minister's office but still a member of the Japanese House of Representatives, Abe kept a relatively low profile and apparently learned some lessons from his disastrous tenure as prime minister. This is because to the surprise of many, he was elected president of the LDP once again in September 2012 while the party was spending a rare period in the opposition. But the LDP got back into power just three months later when it won a landslide victory in the December 2012 general election, putting Abe back into the prime minister's seat on December 26.

Abe's political comeback in Japan was the culmination of the complete failure of non-LDP governance from 2009 to 2012. The now-defunct Democratic Party of Japan (DPJ) governed during that time and did not perform well. Its response to the catastrophic undersea earthquake and tsunami of March 11, 2011 was heavily criticized, and on the foreign policy front the DPJ came across as weak and ineffectual in responding to China's increasingly aggressive claims to sovereignty over the Japan-controlled Senkaku/Diaoyu islets in the East China Sea. Abe's reputation for hawkishness served him well in the midst of growing tensions with China.

For North Korea, Abe's return to power in Japan also meant a return to an intense focus on the abductee issue as the basis for resolving bilateral differences. In the year that elapsed between Kim Jong-il's death in December 2011 and Abe's return as prime minister in December 2012, Kim Jong-un was too focused on consolidating his hold on power to bring about any change in relations with a Japan that was at any rate led by a DPJ government that appeared destined for certain defeat in the next general election. That changed once Abe took office with the strongest mandate of any Japanese prime minister in several years. The next section will analyze how North Korea approached Japan in the era of Abe's second premiership.

North Korea and Japan, 2013–2016

The beginning of Abe's second tenure as Japanese prime minister was followed some two months later in February 2013 by the inauguration of conservative Park Geun-hye as president of South Korea. A consistent theme throughout this chapter is that North Korean governmental attitudes toward Japan should never be viewed in a vacuum. When South Korean overtures to North Korea met strong disapproval by U.S. president Bush in 2001 and 2002 and were thus badly discredited, that pushed North Korea toward attempting a breakthrough in relations with Japan as an alternative. Similarly, the continuation of hostile conservative governance in South Korea from Lee Myung-bak (president from 2008 to 2013) to Park Geun-hye created a rationale for North Korea to at least consider further discussions with Japan.

But Abe's premiership presented obstacles, as did the refusal of the United States to consider making any real concessions to North Korea as long as South Korea was led by hardliners. The impending inauguration of Park Geun-hye as South Korean president may have been a factor in North Korea's decision to conduct a nuclear test on February 12, 2013. Not surprisingly, the test caused alarm in a Japan now led by a hardliner like Abe. On April 5, the Japanese government announced the extension of existing sanctions and the implementation of further sanctions against North Korea.[11] The Japanese government had previously implemented numerous economic sanctions against North Korea during the last few years of Kim Jong-il's reign, in the aftermath of the revelations about the Japanese abductees.

Abe further ratcheted up the pressure on North Korea by utilizing Japan's leverage at the United Nations. On March 21, 2013, the UN General Assembly's Human Rights Council adopted a resolution to establish a Commission of Inquiry tasked with investigating human rights violations in North Korea and determining whether they amounted to crimes against humanity.[12] The primary cosponsors of the resolution were the European Union and Japan. This was a huge embarrassment to North Korea, a UN member since joining that organization together with South Korea in 1991. A desire on the part of the Japanese government to force North Korea to come clean on the abduction issue was a primary motivating factor in Japan's move to sponsor this resolution. Abe owed his initial meteoric political ascendance to taking a hard line against North Korea on the abductee issue. It was not a matter he could afford to ignore in the context of maintaining his political credibility.

For North Korea, it seems clear that extracting economic concessions from Japan is a highly desirable objective to bolster regime survival and legitimacy. In this vein, it makes sense that the hardening of Japan's sanctions regime in the spring of 2013 was followed shortly thereafter by an agreement on the part of North Korea to at least talk. Iijima Isao, a top aide to Abe, made a surprise visit to North Korea in May 2013 for the purpose of once again discussing the fate of the abductees. He visited North Korea again in October. For North Korea, there may have been an ulterior motive in opening up to Japan in this way, because doing so apparently created significant irritation in both South Korea and the United States.[13] Not for the last time would Kim Jong-un have an opportunity to create discord among the democracies opposed to North Korea.

Thus, for some months in 2013 and 2014, North Korea appeared willing to revisit the abduction issue in exchange for economic relief from Japan. The Japanese parents of Yokota Megumi, the deceased abductee, were allowed to meet their North Korea–born granddaughter (the daughter of Megumi) in Mongolia in March 2014. In July 2014, North Korea even went so far as to announce the creation of a special investigative committee to look into the backgrounds of all Japanese citizens residing in the country.[14] This led to the announced relaxation of some sanctions by the Japanese government, such as the lifting or softening of the entry ban on North Korean citizens into Japan and the embargo on North Korean ships in Japanese ports.[15]

But the North Korean opening to Japan coexisted with the imperative to ensure that Kim Jong-un would not suffer the fate of Qaddafi or Hussein. A central problem for the government of Japan is that it demanded from North Korea both a full accounting of the abductees and an indefinite moratorium on missile tests plus full denuclearization. North Korea under Kim Jong-un could not or would not make all of these concessions.

Therefore, all progress toward a North Korea–Japan breakthrough was halted when North Korea conducted another nuclear test in January 2016. Japan announced the reimposition of previously lifted sanctions, and North Korea promptly responded by dissolving the special investigative committee and abandoning any pretenses of sincerely wishing to find out what had happened to any other Japanese abductees.[16] In the end, economic relief from Japan was simply not enticing enough for North Korea to give up its march toward being recognized as a nuclear power. This outcome showed how the abductee and nuclear weapons issues were intertwined for Japan in a way that has never been the case for North Korea. The next section will analyze how and why North Korean policy toward Japan changed in the currently ongoing era of political upheaval worldwide.

North Korean Policy toward Japan since 2017

From 2017, North Korean policy toward Japan was deeply impacted by huge political changes in the United States and South Korea. Donald Trump was inaugurated as U.S. president on January 20 of that year, and in May the left-wing Moon Jae-in became president of South Korea following a special election in the wake of Park Geun-hye's impeachment and removal from office. Overall, the net effect of these political earthquakes has led to an overall significant downgrading of the importance that North Korea places on its policy toward Japan. Since North Korean policy toward Japan should never be viewed in a vacuum, it is important to understand how initiatives pursued by Trump and Moon vis-à-vis North Korea turned Japan into the odd person out.

Although Trump took office in the United States before Moon took office in South Korea, it was the latter man who set into motion the landmark changes for North Korea. Moon's inauguration marked the end of nine years of hawkish conservative control of the Blue House, South Korea's White House equivalent, and the restoration of the Sunshine Policy under Kim Dae-jung and Roh Moo-hyun from 1998 to 2008. The 2018 Winter Olympics held in Pyeongchang, South Korea, and attended by Kim Jong-un's sister laid the groundwork for the first meeting between Moon and Kim in April 2018. They would meet two more times after that. In that first meeting, Kim made history by becoming the first North Korean leader to enter South Korean territory.

If Donald Trump were a conventional Republican like George W. Bush, he likely would have frowned upon the first inter-Korean summit meeting held in eleven years and strongly urged Moon to back away from making such overtures to Kim Jong-un. But of course, Trump was very far from being a conventional Republican and therefore did not exercise any kind of veto power over Moon's diplomacy with North Korea. This is important in the context of North Korean policy toward Japan because George W. Bush's clear expressions of displeasure with Kim Dae-jung's Sunshine Policy in 2001 and 2002 were likely a factor in persuading Kim Jong-il to pursue a path to nor-malization with Japan as an alternative.

In 2018, basking in the glow of his sister's well-received presence at the Pyeongchang Olympics and then his meeting with Moon, there was simply no similar motivation for Kim Jong-un to meet with the Japanese prime minister. Trump's first meeting with Kim in June 2018 only further appeared to marginalize Japan's role in North Korean foreign policy. Trump would meet Kim two more times after that. Trump also departed sharply from Japanese preferences by tacitly tolerating short-range missile launches by North Korea that did not have the ability to reach sovereign U.S. territory.[17]

Therefore, it can be stated that the motivations of North Korean policy toward Japan since the start of 2018 have effectively dwindled and made Japan less important to North Korea than at any time in decades. This created an unfavorable political situation for Abe, who was at the helm in Japan while leading the LDP to decisive general election victories in 2012, 2014, and 2017. But the resolution of the North Korean abduction issue in a manner that is satisfactory to his key supporters remained a pillar of judging his premiership a failure or success. The same was no less true for Suga Yoshihide, who became prime minister after Abe resigned for health-related reasons in September 2020. For Kim Jong-un, meanwhile, the downgrading of Japan's importance has led to a revival of hostile rhetoric and propaganda directed at Japan.

A genuine North Korean opening to Japan was never going to be easy, given that virulent hostility to Japan for its colonial rule over Korea was a driving force in the formation of the communist regime in Pyongyang after 1945. Since 2017, a North Korean opening to Japan has become not just difficult but maybe not even necessary provided the United States and South Korea remain in agreement on the desirability of engaging with North Korea rather than isolating it. Kim Jong-un's own background as the son of the late Ko Yong-hui, an ethnic Korean woman who was born in Japan, provides him with further impetus to demonstrate his anti-Japan views as a way of allaying any doubts that may exist in North Korea about his commitment to the nation.

Therefore, by the end of 2019, the situation had reached the point where the North Korean government publicly called Abe an "idiot" for criticizing yet another missile test carried out by Pyongyang.[18] More tellingly, Abe's sense of anxiety at being seen as shut out of dealing with North Korea was revealed by his expressed desire in the spring of 2019 to meet "unconditionally" with Kim.[19] The invitation was rejected. It is most unlikely that Abe would have extended such an invitation if Donald Trump had not met with Kim first.

Therefore, as of this book chapter's writing, the policy of North Korea toward Japan remains stalemated and even downgraded in importance. Like his predecessor Abe, Suga in 2020 and 2021 publicly expressed his willingness to meet Kim Jong-un without preconditions and received no positive reply.[20] Suga himself resigned as prime minister in October 2021 and was replaced by Kishida Fumio, who stated in a speech at the United Nations in

September 2022 that he was "determined to meet with President Kim Jong-un without any conditions."[21] Japan's overture to Pyongyang again received no reply. But nothing stays in place forever, and so the North Korean pendulum could very well swing back toward at least a grudging desire for engagement with Japan. The next section will discuss possible future scenarios for a shift in North Korean policy toward Japan.

North Korean Policy toward Japan in the Future

The very odd couple of Donald Trump and Moon Jae-in was central to North Korea's diminishing lack of incentives to engage with Japan. This political combination ended when Trump left office in January 2021, but its impact continues to be felt. Moon was constitutionally barred in South Korea from serving more than a single term, so his presidency ended In May 2022. By early 2022, therefore, Moon was a lame duck who did not have the power to launch any major new diplomacy with North Korea. Moon was succeeded as president by Yoon Suk-yeol of the conservative People Power party, but Yoon's first several months as president were marked by so many missteps related to etiquette and gaffes that his professed desire to approach North Korea in a more hawkish manner was undermined.

There are multiple scenarios in U.S. and South Korean politics that could produce different outcomes for North Korean policy toward Japan. In the first scenario, a conservative hardliner who governs effectively and has a clear mandate is the president of South Korea and thus seeks to immediately halt and reverse all steps taken by her or his predecessor toward normalizing relations with North Korea. It is likely that Washington in such a situation would take its cue from the political change in South Korea and also pull back from engaging with North Korea. During his time as U.S. president from 2009 to 2017, Barack Obama did not push his conservative counterparts in Seoul to engage with Pyongyang.

In this kind of scenario, North Korea would have an incentive to restart negotiations with Japan about getting relief from unilateral Japanese sanctions in exchange for further investigation into the abductee issue. But if it is the case that the North Koreans in 2002 did not tell the whole truth about the fate of the remaining abductees that the Japanese government had inquired about, it is difficult to imagine how it would be beneficial for Pyongyang to admit that in the future and come clean. The distrust of North Korea by the Japanese would only grow further. If the North Koreans did indeed lie about the eight abductees whom they claimed had died and the four whom they claimed had never been taken, they have boxed themselves in with that lie and cannot rectify the situation.

On the other hand, if it is conclusively shown that the North Koreans told the whole truth about the abductees then the onus will be on the Japanese government to accept that outcome and move forward. But given the levels of distrust toward North Korea that exist in Japanese political circles, that seems unlikely. And even if Japan somehow does accept the North Korean version of what happened to the abductees, negotiations will still be difficult due to Tokyo's continuing insistence that North Korea fully denuclearize and cease all missile tests. The denuclearization of North Korea will occur only if the United States makes a credible commitment not to attack North Korea for any reason. One source of misunderstanding in Japan is that North Korea's weapons and missile tests are really aimed at sending a message to the United States; Japan just happens to be located in the airspace over which North Korean missiles must travel to frighten the Americans. Prohibited from maintaining offensive military capabilities due to the famous Article 9 of its Constitution, Japan is militarily powerless to stop North Korea from carrying out such tests.

In a second future political scenario, South Korea could elect as president another politician from the left who favors continuing moves toward reconciliation with Pyongyang and has a fresh mandate to do so. With a Democratic president in Washington, this scenario could replicate the environment that prevailed from February 1998 to January 2001 when Kim Dae-jung was South Korean president and Bill Clinton was in the White House. In other words, on paper, it would be a very favorable environment for North Korea to gain further concessions and thus reinforce Pyongyang's inclination to ignore any calls by Japan to discuss the abductees or any other issue.

How a future Republican president, whether that person is Trump or another politician, would react is a bit more of a wild card. That person may very well go along with South Korean initiatives toward North Korea under a left-wing president, just as Trump did with Moon. Certainly, Trump's humiliating treatment of hawkish neoconservative and former national security advisor John Bolton was evidence that he and his most fervent supporters had little use for reviving George W. Bush's policy of opposing leftist South Korean politicians who wish to engage with North Korea.

But much would depend on North Korean policy and provocations, particularly with regard to long-range missile launches that can strike Hawaii or even mainland U.S. territory. A major resumption of such launches could very well lead a future Republican president to become disillusioned with the South Korean progressive camp's approach and demand that they take a harder line against the North. Such a scenario would come to resemble the tensions in U.S.–South Korea relations in 2001 and 2002, which then provided the North Koreans under Kim Jong-il an incentive to pursue an alternative path out of isolation from Japan.

Finally, future scenarios cannot ignore political leadership in North Korea and Japan. Before stepping down, Abe became the longest-serving Japanese prime minister in history.[22] In 2021, his successor and fellow LDP member Suga was criticized among other things for the relatively slow pace of vaccinations in Japan against the coronavirus. This was a factor in his decision to resign. But the LDP is essentially the default ruling party of Japan, having governed the country for all but a handful of years since its founding in 1955. The political opposition in Japan is badly splintered and shows little sign of being able to coalesce around a major second party capable of defeating the LDP in a general election. So in that sense, one should expect continuity in Japanese politics.

There is, however, one potential domestic political change in Japan that could radically alter North Korean policy toward that country. A major objective since the 1950s for hawkish Japanese conservatives has been to see Article 9 of the Constitution either repealed or amended. Abe was a major champion of this objective during his political career, and he was far from alone. As chief cabinet secretary during the entire duration of the second Abe premiership from 2012 to 2020, Suga also supported revising the Constitution. Amending or repealing Article 9 decisively would once and for all lift the prohibition on offensive capabilities that severely constrains Japan's military and makes it impossible for Tokyo to threaten North Korea with the kind of force that can be applied by the United States.

The post–World War II Japanese Constitution has never been amended. One reason for this is because the process of amending the Constitution entails huge risks for any government that supports a drive for change that fails. For an amendment to pass, there must be two-thirds majority support in both houses of the Japanese National Diet followed by a simple majority vote in favor via a national referendum. But a majority vote via a national referendum is not so simple. Britain's Brexit debacle in 2016 demonstrated for the ruling Conservative government there the perils of depending on a national referendum vote. The impact of Britain's voters unexpectedly supporting withdrawal from the European Union by a 52–48 margin was so shocking that not only did David Cameron have to resign as prime minister the day after the vote, but shortly thereafter he resigned from the House of Commons altogether.[23]

Therefore, the bar for amending Article 9 is quite high. But in the event that it somehow did happen, North Korean policy toward Japan would likely change greatly. Pyongyang would find itself confronting a Japan that could respond directly to a provocation such as a missile launch over Japanese airspace. Japan could even threaten a military intervention of some kind into North Korean territory to ascertain the whereabouts of Japanese citizens thought to be living there. Whether it responds with greater belligerence or moves toward another attempt at normalization of relations, North Korea would not be able to simply ignore or ridicule a Japan where Article 9 was repealed or amended. But given the risks involved, the amending of the Japanese Constitution along such lines appears far from the realm of possibility. In his first year as prime minister, Kishida appeared to have little appetite for pursuing such a potentially perilous course.

Finally, there is the question of how a leadership change in North Korea could affect the motivations of North Korean policy toward Japan. Questions surrounding Kim Jong-un's absence from the public eye for a lengthy period in the spring of 2020 led to speculations about his being overweight, in general poor health, and even having contracted the coronavirus. Every individual is different, even members of the Kim family dynasty in North Korea. A sudden leadership change in North Korea cannot be ruled out. Kim Jong-il's death at age sixty-nine in 2011 caught most people by surprise.

A sudden change in supreme power from Kim Jong-un to, for example, his prominent and high-profile sister Kim Yo-jong would not appear by itself to drastically change the motivations of North Korean foreign policy toward Japan. The shift from Kim Jong-il to his son in 2011 did not produce a major break from the past. As siblings a few years apart in age, Kim Jong-un and Kim Yo-jong had similar upbringings with schooling for several years in Switzerland. Therefore, there is no immediate reason to believe they harbor very different attitudes toward Japan. But of course, every power shift in North Korea is a cause for speculation and concern due to the secrecy and unpredictability of the regime.

CONCLUSION

This book chapter has assessed the motivations of North Korean foreign policy toward Japan, mainly since Kim Jong-un became supreme leader in December 2011. At its core, North Korean policy toward Japan is rooted in the determination to extract economic concessions from what is still a very wealthy country. The dissolution of the Soviet Union in 1991 greatly increased North Korea's dependence on China for aid and trade. Despite their close ties, North Korea has never been comfortable with its position of extreme isolation and dependence on China in the post–Cold War era.

But extracting concessions from Japan in the forms of money, food, and access to trade and foreign investment has become inextricably intertwined with one problem that the North Korean government considers resolved (the Japanese abductee issue) and another that the North Korean government considers largely irrelevant to Japan—their nuclear weapons and missile programs aimed at deterring the United States from attempting any kind of regime change. There exists a fundamental disagreement between North Korea and Japan over what matters in their potential bilateral relations. The positions of the two countries have hardened over the years to the point where a shift by either will be viewed by hardliners within each country as an unacceptable capitulation. In other words, on the weapons issue, North Korea cannot agree to fully denuclearize along the lines demanded by Japan and Japan cannot agree to let North Korea maintain any kind of nuclear capabilities.

Because of these two stumbling blocks to full engagement with Japan, North Korean policy toward Japan has largely become a function of whether South Korea and the United States are willing to engage with North Korea. During the reign of Kim Jong-un, this became abundantly clear with the radical political changes in 2017 that occurred first in Washington and then in Seoul. Fixated on resolving to their satisfaction the abductee issue as well as denuclearization as preconditions for any kind of conclusive deal with North Korea, the Japanese were perceived to be sidelined and with regard to North Korea perhaps deeply distressed by the presidencies of Donald Trump and Moon Jae-in.

The Japanese, however, were never entirely sidelined and used their still considerable presence in the region to try and delay if not outright spoil any moves toward an inter-Korean rapprochement that did not address their core interests. A clear instance of this occurred in November 2021, when Tokyo appeared reluctant to endorse President Moon's last-ditch effort at declaring a formal end to the Korean War. Moon's initiative had little chance of succeeding given his own status as a lame-duck executive and thus failed. In line with the Sunshine Policy idea of using carrots and not sticks, Moon believed that the accompanying benefits for North Korea of formally ending the state of war with its neighbor would entice Pyongyang to at least think about denuclearization. But predictably, the Japanese side was "concerned that such a preceding conciliatory move would complicate its position for resolving the issue of past abductions by North Korea of Japanese citizens."[24] Also, Japan would not accept a formal inter-Korean peace that could leave North Korea intact and possessing any nuclear weapons.

Even if, somehow, the government of Japan eventually gives up on further pursuing the abductee issue and accepts the reality of a nuclear-armed North Korea, there is simply no way that North Korean motivations toward Japan will come to resemble those of a more conventional and once-isolated developing country where leaders are either neutral on the legacy of Japanese imperialism or perhaps even inclined to view it in a positive light as an example of an Asian country that managed to achieve parity with the Western powers in the first half of the twentieth century. In other words, North Korea in its interactions with Japan will never be like Myanmar or Vietnam.

The North Koreans, like their counterparts in the South, have strongly negative and hostile feelings about the legacy of Japanese imperial rule over an undivided Korea from 1910 to 1945. The deterioration in recent years in bilateral relations between Japan and South Korea illustrates this point and is due in large part to the view among people in the latter that Japan never sufficiently compensated Koreans for their work during the World War II period as forced laborers in service to the Japanese Empire.[25] There is little reason to doubt that North Korea will pursue such claims against Japan if it gets the opportunity to do so in negotiations.

For North Korea, the motivations to engage with Japan are tempered by an awareness of great pitfalls. It would be a serious mistake to assume that just because Kim Jong-un spent part of his childhood living in Switzerland and has only known a world in which South Korea is wealthy that he is fully convinced of the need for North Korea to completely abandon its way of doing things. In its still fierce competition with South Korea for recognition as the legitimate representative of all Koreans, North Korea's leaders can point with contempt to South Korea's chronic trade deficits with Japan and the presence of a so-called pro-Japan political faction in the country (*chinilpa* in Korean) as a betrayal that North Korea must not follow.

To conclude, Kim Jong-un may have supreme power in North Korea but he cannot act completely independent of the system that was constructed by his grandfather and further consolidated by his father during the first-ever dynastic succession in a communist country after 1994. The system he presides over, but is also a part of, derives its legitimacy in part from hostility to Japan. This rules out falling into the trap of any sort of "core-periphery" relationship of dependence with Korea's former colonial ruler. So long as that is the case, North Korea will be motivated to engage with Japan for the purpose of increasing its economic prosperity through wealth extraction but not for the purpose of establishing truly cordial bilateral relations.

NOTES

1. In 1952, hundreds of thousands of ethnic Koreans who had been residing in Japan since before the end of Japanese rule in Korea were unilaterally stripped of their Japanese citizenship. Many chose to become citizens of North Korea. For more on this topic, see Konrad Kalicki, Go Murakami, and Nicholas A.R. Fraser, "The Difference That Security Makes: The Politics of Citizenship in Postwar Japan in a Comparative Perspective," *Social Science Japan Journal* 16, no. 2 (2013): 211–34.

2. Marcus Noland, "North Korea's External Economic Relations," *Peterson Institute for International Economics*, February 1, 2001, https://www.piie.com/commentary/speeches-papers/north-koreas-external-economic-relations-paper#table1.

3. "Treaty on Basic Relations," *United Nations—Treaty Series*, accessed May 30, 2020, https://treaties.un.org/doc/Publication/UNTS/Volume%20583/volume-583 -I-8471-English.pdf.

4. Sheryl Wudunn, "North Korea Fires Missile over Japanese Territory," *New York Times*, September 1, 1998, https://www.nytimes.com/1998/09/01/world/north-korea -fires-missile-over-japanese-territory.html.

5. David E. Sanger, "Bush Tells Seoul Talks with North Won't Resume Now," *New York Times*, March 8, 2001, https://www.nytimes.com/2001/03/08/world/bush-tells -seoul-talks-with-north-won-t-resume-now.html.

6. Justin McCurry, "Japan's 'Secret' Trip to North Korea Disrupts United Stance against Pyongyang," *Christian Science Monitor*, May 17, 2013, https://www .csmonitor.com/World/Asia-Pacific/2013/0517/Japan-s-secret-trip-to-North-Korea -disrupts-united-stance-against-Pyongyang.

7. James Brooke, "North Korea and Japan Sign a Deal on Abductions," *New York Times*, May 23, 2004, https://www.nytimes.com/2004/05/23/world/north-korea-and -japan-sign-a-deal-on-abductions.html.

8. "Japan-DPRK Pyongyang Declaration," *Ministry of Foreign Affairs of Japan*, September 17, 2002, https://www.mofa.go.jp/region/asia-paci/n_korea/pmv0209/ pyongyang.html.

9. Stephen Evans, "The Saddam Factor in North Korea's Nuclear Strategy," BBC News, September 9, 2016, https://www.bbc.com/news/world-asia-37321686.

10. "GDP Per Capita (Current US$)—China," *The World Bank*, accessed May 30, 2020, https://data.worldbank.org/indicator/NY.GDP.PCAP.CD?locations=CN&name _desc=false.

11. "Measures Taken by Japan against North Korea (Announcement by the Chief Cabinet Secretary)," *Prime Minister of Japan and His Cabinet*, accessed May 30, 2020, https://japan.kantei.go.jp/96_abe/decisions/2013/0405tyoukanhappyou_e.html.

12. Steven Erlanger, "UN Panel to Investigate Human Rights Abuses in North Korea," *New York Times*, March 21, 2013, https://www.nytimes.com/2013/03/22/ world/europe/un-panel-to-investigate-human-rights-abuses-in-north-korea.html.

13. McCurry, "Japan's 'Secret' Trip."

14. "Talks between Japan and North Korea on the Abduction Issue," *Ministry of Foreign Affairs of Japan*, accessed May 30, 2020, https://www.mofa.go.jp/a_o/na/kp /page1we_000069.html.

15. Yoko Wakatsuki and Jethro Mullen, "Japan Eases Sanctions on North Korea after Talks on Abductions," CNN, July 4, 2014, https://www.cnn.com/2014/07/04/ world/asia/japan-north-korea-sanctions/index.html.

16. "North Korea Halts Inquiry into Abductions of Japanese Citizens," *The Guard-ian*, February 12, 2016, https://www.theguardian.com/world/2016/feb/12/north-korea -halts-inquiry-into-abductions-of-japanese-citizens.

17. David E. Sanger and William J. Broad, "North Korea Missile Tests, 'Very Standard' to Trump, Show Signs of Advancing Arsenal," *New York Times*, September 2, 2019, https://www.nytimes.com/2019/09/02/world/asia/north-korea-kim-trump -missiles.html.

18. Doug Stanglin, "North Korea Blasts Japanese PM as 'idiot,' Warns of Ballistic Missile Launch Toward Japan," *USA Today*, November 30, 2019, https://www.usatoday.com/story/news/world/2019/11/30/north-korea-shinzo-abe-warns-future-missile-launch-japan/4339816002.

19. Elizabeth Shim, "Japan's Shinzo Abe Compliments Kim Jong Un While Seeking Summit," United Press International, May 2, 2019, https://www.upi.com/Top_News/World-News/2019/05/02/Japans-Shinzo-Abe-compliments-Kim-Jong-Un-while-seeking-summit/3851556803417/.

20. "Suga Still Game to Meet North Korea's Kim after Biden Rules Out Summit in Near Future," *Japan Times*, March 30, 2021, https://www.japantimes.co.jp/news/2021/03/30/national/politics-diplomacy/suga-biden-kim-meeting/.

21. "Address by Prime Minister Kishida at the Seventy-Seventh Session of the United Nations General Assembly," *Ministry of Foreign Affairs of Japan*, September 20, 2022,
https://www.mofa.go.jp/fp/unp_a/page3e_001242.html.

22. Robin Harding, "Shinzo Abe Becomes Japan's Longest Serving Prime Minister," *Financial Times*, November 19, 2019, https://www.ft.com/content/f4323946-0a9f-11ea-bb52-34c8d9dc6d84#comments-anchor.

23. Stephen Castle, "David Cameron Steps Down from His Seat in British Parliament," *New York Times*, September 12, 2016, https://www.nytimes.com/2016/09/13/world/europe/david-cameron-parliament-britain-witney.html.

24. "Japan Reluctant to Accept Proposal to Declare Korean War Over," *Kyodo News*, November 7, 2021, https://english.kyodonews.net/news/2021/11/8cc01072198e-japan-reluctant-to-accept-proposal-to-declare-korean-war-over.html.

25. Joyce Lee, "South Korean Forced Labor Victims to Seek Japan's Mitsubishi Asset Sale," Reuters, July 16, 2019, https://www.reuters.com/article/us-southkorea-japan-laborers-mhi/south-korean-forced-labor-victims-to-seek-japans-mitsubishi-asset-sale-idUSKCN1UB0HO.

Chapter 5

Seeking Alternative Opportunities

North Korea-Russia Relations

Evgenii Gamerman

The history of this issue, the relations between the Soviet Union (Russian Federation) and the Democratic People's Republic of Korea (DPRK) has a relatively small chronology, which originates from decisions that were made by the anti-Hitler coalition during World War II.

At the Yalta Conference of coalition leaders, U.S. president Franklin Roosevelt formally proposed, after defeating Japan, to establish custody of Korea, which would be carried out with the participation of the USSR, the United States, Great Britain, and China (Chiang Kai-shek regime).

At the Potsdam Conference, in July 1945, a dividing line was established along thirty-eight parallel lines between Soviet and American forces, to the north and south, of which both sides were to defeat the Japanese armed forces. This event was the beginning of the process of folding the two Korean states, oriented, respectively, to the USSR and the United States.[1]

In the directive on September 20, 1945, Stalin's command of the 25th army was instructed not to impede the creation of democratic parties and organizations in Korea, to protect private and public property, not to touch churches, and not to impede the performance of religious rites. Also in the North, the Office of the Soviet Civil Administration was formed (to restore the economy). Immediately after the liberation from the Japanese, local government bodies—people's committees—began to be created. In the initial stage, nationalists dominated them, but soon, with the strong support of the Soviet civil administration, leftists supplanted the nationalists and took leading positions. To coordinate the activities of the people's committees, the administrative bureau of five provinces was established, as well as ten departments that supervised the main sectors of the economy and the social sphere.

In February 1946, the Provisional People's Committee of North Korea was created, headed by Kim Il-sung, the leader of one of the partisan units fighting against the Japanese. In 1946, land reform was carried out in the North, as well as the nationalization of industries, transportation, communications, and banks. By 1947, industrial enterprises were restored and trade was established. In 1946, the Communist Party merged with the New People's Party and became known as the Workers' Party of Korea.

After the landing of U.S. troops on September 9, 1945, an American military administration was created in the south of the Korean Peninsula. However, at the same time, people's committees were formed in the south, and the Communist Party was active. The American command took stringent measures against the leftist parties and organizations operating in the south.[2]

From December 16–26, 1945, foreign ministers of the USSR, the United States, and Great Britain met in Moscow to discuss the question of Korea. The meeting decided to create a joint Soviet-American commission to assist in the formation of a provisional Korean democratic government. In the second stage, the plan was to establish a four-sided government of the country through the organization of guardianship, which was to be carried out by a special administrative body consisting of representatives of the USSR, the United States, Great Britain, and China. Due to grave disagreements, the USSR and the United States could not agree on the conditions for the unification of Korea and began the process of creating antipode states. On August 15, 1948, the creation of the Republic of Korea was proclaimed. In response, elections to the Supreme People's Assembly were held in Pyongyang, and the assembly was formed on August 25. In its first session, from September 2 to 8, the assembly proclaimed the formation of the Democratic People's Republic of Korea and adopted the Constitution. The chairman of the cabinet of ministers was Kim Il-sung. The USSR was the first to recognize the DPRK and established diplomatic relations with it on October 12, 1948, from which the history of the interaction between the two countries began.[3]

In summation, Russia-North Korea relations can be chronologically divided into three periods. (1) The first period, from 1948 to 1953, starts with the formation of North Korea and the establishment of diplomatic relations between the two countries and ends with the Korean War, during which the USSR actively supported Pyongyang. (2) The second period is from 1953 to 1991. This period covers the time from the end of the Korean War and North Korea's involvement in the socialist camp to the collapse of the Soviet Union. This is a time of active cooperation and interaction between the two states in various fields. (3) The third period is from 1991 to 2020, a period of interaction between North Korea and the modern Russian Federation. This period is complex and can be divided (albeit rather conditionally) into two sub-periods: The first is the 1990s when Russia was experiencing the most acute economic,

political, and ideological crisis. In this decade, Moscow minimized its presence in all countries and regions, and in fact, relations with Pyongyang came
to naught. The second, 2000 to present, is the time of Russian revanchism,
a partial recovery of the economy, and attempts to regain lost ground in the
international arena. During this time, Moscow tried to regain its influence on
North Korea, restore military-political and economic ties, and become the
main (or one of the main) partners for the leadership of the DPRK Workers'
Party. It is within the framework of these three periods that we will consider
the relationship and cooperation of the two countries.

It should be noted that throughout the history of Soviet (Russia)–North
Korean relations, the main focus of the bilateral relationship was security and
political support. For Moscow, it seeks to expand its sphere of influence in the
East Asia region. For North Korea, its relationship with Russia is a matter of
national security and diplomatic support. Economic development is a secondary priority for the two countries in the bilateral relationship.

1948–1953: THE FORMATION OF THE
DPRK AND THE KOREAN WAR

This period can be divided into two sub-periods, the prewar sub-period
(1948–1950) and the sub-period of military operations (1950–1953). In the
sub-period from 1948 to 1950, very active military preparations went on both
sides of the 38th parallel, increasing the number of armed forces and deploy-
ing military equipment. In principle, in 1948, all interested parties already
understood the inevitability of a military conflict on the Korean Peninsula.
Therefore, this period is a time of building up forces, building strategies and
tactical lines, and finding the most optimal ways to defeat the enemy. The
influence of the Soviet leadership on the leaders of North Korea was unconditional during this period. In October 1948, the military units of the Soviet
Army were finally withdrawn from the DPRK. However, all Soviet weapons
and military equipment remained on the territory of North Korea. In addition,
Soviet military advisers stayed in North Korea and played a leading role in
the formation of a battle-worthy North Korean army.[4]

At the turn of 1949–1950, the situation sharply worsened. For several
months, the North Korean leadership tried to convince Stalin of the need
to liberate South Korea by military means. Until the beginning of 1950, the
Soviet leader hesitated and did not give his consent. However, after the formation of the People's Republic of China and the creation of atomic weapons
in the USSR, Stalin agreed on a plan for a military solution to the problem of
unification of Korea so that China would support this development of events.

On June 25, 1950, the North Korean armed forces attacked the South Korean army and captured Seoul for three days, and in September approached Busan, where they encountered a well-fortified bridgehead.[5] These events caused a negative reaction from the world. On the day the war began, the United States convened the UN Security Council. There was no representative of the USSR at this meeting (considered by many researchers and diplomats to be one of the most significant diplomatic miscalculations of Moscow of this period). The security council adopted a resolution accusing the DPRK of violating peace and called for an immediate cessation of hostilities. On June 27, 1950, a second UN Security Council resolution was adopted, recommending the UN member states support the South Korean government in repelling the attack. Moreover, the United States decided to send American troops to Korea. On July 7, 1950, the UN Security Council approved a resolution on the deployment of UN forces to Korea, with armed forces from sixteen countries taking part in the war in support of Seoul. By the end of October, UN troops reached the DPRK border with China. Moscow had been negotiating with China so that Beijing would intervene in the Korean conflict and avoid the complete defeat of Pyongyang and the loss of independence. The negotiations were difficult, but they succeeded. On October 25, 1950, detachments of Chinese "people's volunteers" defeated American forces. In addition, by the beginning of 1951, the front stabilized in the region of the 38th parallel. In mid-1951, peace negotiations began, which culminated in the signing of the Korean Armistice Agreement on July 27, 1953. The war brought significant losses for both South and North Korea. In addition to casualties (about 4 million people on both sides), there was considerable material damage. In the DPRK, nine-thousand-plus enterprises, six-hundred-thousand-plus residential buildings, and twenty-eight-thousand-plus cultural and educational institutions were destroyed. The war also led to a deterioration of the situation in the whole region—to the formation of military bloc, and the growth of aggressive aspirations.[6]

Throughout the 1940s and 1950s, in North Korea, with the full support of the USSR, Soviet-style economic and social transformations were adopted and brought about positive results. DPRK underwent radical reforms, in particular, the nationalization of the properties of Japanese colonialists and collaborators, confiscation of land and temple properties without redemption, communization in the agricultural sector industry, and services, and the transition to a planned economy. At the "first leap" stage, gratuitous material assistance and development loans were of great importance for North Korean recovery. In particular, during the 1950s and 1960s, the USSR provided DPRK with credit assistance for 567 million rubles. North Korea went its own way, exploiting the model of import-substituting development, which also yielded certain positive results, and showed, although not indisputably, the effectiveness and viability of such developmental strategy.[7]

1953–1991: RUSSIAN-NORTH KOREAN RELATIONS IN THE BIPOLAR PERIOD

After the Korean War, Pyongyang set about rebuilding the national economy. With the help of the USSR and other socialist countries, 240 industrial facilities were restored, and 80 new ones were built. The socialist bloc also provided gratuitous material assistance of 800 million rubles, of which 292.5 million rubles came from the USSR. Industrial production during the first decade after the Korean War grew by an average of 36.6 percent per year. In 1958, the agricultural cooperatives of peasant farms were completed. In 1960, North Korea was ahead of South Korea in all major economic indicators. However, the North Korean economy emphasized heavy industry. The North Korean population lived very poorly. Nevertheless, little attention was paid to this.

In the economic sphere, the trends of the previous period have been preserved. A significant part of the DPRK's needs were met at the expense of external sources. Industrialization was carried out in the republic. In the postwar period (1954–1956), the socialist countries provided the DPRK with free aid and loans (to purchase industrial equipment and raw materials) to help restore the national economy. The share of goods received because of gratuitous aid and loans amounted to 77.6 percent of DPRK's total imports. Between 1954 and 1960, thanks to the help of socialist countries, about fifty enterprises were restored, and they formed the basis of the national economy.[8]

An important area of foreign economic relations of the DPRK from the very beginning was scientific and technical cooperation. In particular, the Soviet Union acquainted North Korean specialists with scientific, technical, and industrial achievements in more than 2,500 areas. In the 1960s, the DPRK leadership tried to limit external factors in economic development, following the Juche ideology to pursue independence in the economy.

The DPRK leadership, first, allocated funds to create "anti-import" industries, trying to increase the degree of self-sufficiency and isolation of the North Korean economy. Nevertheless, foreign trade continued to play a significant role in the development of the DPRK economy. Because of imports, the republic thoroughly met its needs for coking coal, petroleum products, natural rubber, cotton, wool, sugar, manganese ore, and apatite. North Korea also imported a significant amount of equipment, precision instruments, and other industrial products. The share of socialist countries in 1965 accounted for 84 percent of all DPRK foreign trade, half of which was trade with the USSR.[9]

The result of economic problems (dependence on imports and economic aid from other countries) within North Korea was the adjustment of the DPRK's foreign economic policy at the turn of the 1960s and 1970s. North Korea began to seek to expand and diversify economic ties in several areas: with Western countries, developing countries, and countries of the Council for Mutual Economic Assistance. In the 1970s, Pyongyang managed to get large loans from Western countries to purchase modern technologies and equipment. However, the DPRK was not able to repay the debt on time in the mid-1970s. In the 1960–1970s, the socialist countries provided DPRK with financial loans totaling about 1.1 billion rubles. In addition, economic assistance was provided. In the 1970s, the DPRK received approximately 1 billion rubles. Loans from several Western countries (such as Austria, Finland, Sweden, Germany, and England) were used mainly to purchase equipment in the capitalist market. In the 1980s, North Korea attempted to expand foreign economic relations through the creation of export industries in some sectors such as the clothing industry and attracting foreign investment in joint ventures. In 1984, the Law on Joint Ventures was adopted, which was designed to attract foreign investment and obtain advanced technologies. However, it failed to achieve a substantial expansion of foreign trade.[10]

In general, by the beginning of the 1990s, the DPRK lagged behind most of the former socialist countries in the development of foreign economic relations. According to Russian experts,[11] North Korea's share of exports in its national income did not exceed 10 percent, and commodity turnover per capita was twelve to thirteen times lower than that of Eastern European countries. At this point, the DPRK's specialization in the world market consisted of the supply of raw materials and products with a low degree of processing, such as magnesite clinker, zinc, lead, and cement. As for imports, raw materials and machinery were imported to North Korea. The disproportionately small volume of North Korea's foreign trade indicated the inability of the existing economic complex of the DPRK to actively participate in the international division of labor and the low level of its international specialization. In fact, at the end of the 1980s, North Korea lacked an independent economy and was unable to ensure national economic security. Hence, serious problems arose in the DPRK after the collapse of the socialist camp and the demise of the USSR.[12]

At the turn of the 1950s and 1960s, Kim Il-sung announced that the Workers' Party of Korea was now guided by the Juche ideology, an interpretation of Marxism–Leninism concerning conditions in the DPRK. At the same time, a course of self-reliance was proclaimed. In the mid-1950s, a power struggle escalated in the DPRK leadership. Several leaders of the pro-Soviet

group opposed the imposition of the personality cult of Kim Il-sung and supported strengthening democratic principles in the activities of the party and
the decisions of the Twentieth Congress of the Communist Party of the Soviet
Union. The "pro-Chinese faction" also advocated the removal of Kim Il-sung.
However, Kim's supporters managed to prevail. Domestic political events in
North Korea were accompanied by the closure of economic and military ties
with the USSR.[13]

In 1962, after Khrushchev refused to provide Pyongyang with free military
assistance, Kim Il-sung announced the start of parallel economic and defense
construction to be more independent of Moscow. The 1960s was the period of
the most complex, strained relations between the USSR and the DPRK. This
is also connected with the personality of the Soviet leader Khrushchev who
was not inclined to diplomacy or compromise, and the desire of North Korea
for greater independence.[14]

In 1972, a new Constitution of the DPRK was adopted to consolidate the
changes that took place, such as the official ideology of Juche and the creation of a president position and the Central People's Committee, the highest
authority. In the late 1970s and early 1980s, a slowdown in economic development began followed by an economic crisis. Consequently, the second
Seven-Year Economic Development Plan 1978–1984 was not implemented.
Neither was the third Seven-Year Plan. This was caused by the administra-
tive-command system of management, directive planning, and the reduction
of economic assistance from Moscow as the USSR suffered from its own
crisis, culminating in the collapse of the country. In 1984 and 1986, Kim
Il-sung paid visits to Moscow and concluded many economic agreements.
In addition, military assistance was also provided to Pyongyang. With the
beginning of perestroika and the proclamation of new political thinking in the
USSR, relations with the DPRK began to deteriorate. Against the background
of the desire of the Gorbachev leadership for the normalization of relations
with the West and the Asia-Pacific countries from the capitalist bloc, relations
with the DPRK began to be seen by the USSR as a "headache," while relations with the Republic of Korea (ROK) seemed promising. In North Korea,
the perception of the USSR also became increasingly negative. After his first
meeting with Gorbachev in Moscow in 1985, Kim Il-sung reacted to USSR
with caution. The development of Soviet-South Korean relations on the eve
of and after the 1988 Seoul Olympics convinced the North Korean leadership
of the need to prepare for the worst, despite assurances from the Soviet side.
It was then that the DPRK nuclear program was activated as a backup security guarantee in case the USSR refused allied obligations. In 1990, the KGB
reported "up" on the creation of a prototype nuclear device in the DPRK,
but there was no political reaction. In September 1990, two months after the
meeting between Gorbachev and South Korean President Roh Tae-woo in

San Francisco, E.A. Shevardnadze (Minister of Foreign Affairs of the USSR from 1985 to 1991, and president of Georgia from 1995 to 2003) went to North Korea to announce the USSR's readiness to establish diplomatic relations with South Korea. This decision provoked a strong reaction from the North Korean leadership. For example, Kim Il-sung refused to accept the Soviet delegation, and then DPRK Foreign Minister Kim Yong-nam said plainly, "You are leaving us, and if so, we will create nuclear weapons."[15]

During the Cold War era, the peculiarities of relations between the two countries were approximately at the same level. However, by the end of the 1980s, problems began that turned into a serious economic crisis in North Korea, which resulted in a massive famine and worsening of national security.

1991–2022: RELATIONS BETWEEN RUSSIA AND NORTH KOREA AT THE PRESENT STAGE

In 1991, the DPRK joined the UN. Within a decade, North Korea established diplomatic relations with 150 countries and significantly improved relations with countries in Western Europe. After the collapse of the USSR, North Korea lost its economic and political support. Then, a series of lean years and natural disasters followed. By the end of the 1990s, the economic situation of the DPRK had become very difficult. For instance, there was an acute shortage of electricity and most types of raw materials and fuels. Eighty percent of enterprises were simply paralyzed. The only functional industrial complex was the military, which received about 50 percent of the national budget. There was also a grave food shortage. From 1995 to 1997, the country's population was starving. Approximately 1 million people died from starvation during this period. Amid a tough crisis, the North Korean political elite relied on increased propaganda for Korean nationalism. Strengthening defensive capabilities was declared a vital state affair. The military's position was elevated in all government bodies through the Constitutional amendments in 1998 because of this crisis.[16]

North Korea joined the Treaty on the Non-Proliferation of Nuclear Weapons (NPT) in 1985 but delayed the safeguards agreement with the International Atomic Energy Agency (IAEA). At the same time, in the area of Yongbyon, the construction of nuclear facilities was carried out. On March 12, 1993, the DPRK announced the decision to withdraw from the NPT, explaining this as a response to the U.S. nuclear threat. In addition, since the early 1980s, North Korea has been developing ballistic missile technology. In 1993, its first missile with a range of up to one thousand kilometers—"Nodong-1"—was created. Pyongyang's foreign policy changed dramatically. In the first sub-period, the 1990s, North Korea had a very constructive negotiation process with the United States, which could have had positive results. However, when George W. Bush came to power in the White House, his aggressive rhetoric put an end to all the achievements of the previous period. In the 1990s, relations between Russia and the DPRK were practically curtailed. Russia took the path of establishing relations with Western countries, including South Korea. The Kremlin was outraged by Pyongyang's confrontational stance in inter-Korean relations. Pyongyang could not accept the fact that Russia had embarked on a broad development of ties with South Korea. In addition, Moscow condemned Pyongyang's nuclear program and stopped economic assistance due to the economic crisis in Russia and the political shortsightedness of its leadership. China has become a new pillar and economic donor for the DPRK.[17]

In the second sub-period, since 2000, relations between Russia and the DPRK began to normalize. In February 2000, an agreement on friendship, good neighborliness, and cooperation between the two countries was signed in Pyongyang. It replaced the obsolete 1961 Treaty of Friendship, Cooperation, and Mutual Assistance, which established the military alliance between the Soviet Union and North Korea. Under the new agreement, the parties agreed to maintain normal bilateral relations. For the first time in the history of relations between the two countries, in June 2000, the head of Russia, President Vladimir Putin visited North Korea. For eastern diplomacy, this was a significant step for the further development of the relations. During Putin's visit, the parties demonstrated their determination to leave mutual claims in the past (from 1980 to 1990) and develop cooperation in specific practical areas. In particular, emphasis was placed on the restoration of the railway connection between the two Koreas with the eastern regions of Russia. In the summer of 2001, Kim Jong-il paid a return visit to Moscow. During these two meetings, two crucial documents were signed—the Pyongyang and Moscow Political Declarations. These documents laid out the principles of relations between the two countries and the similarities of their positions on most of the problems of world development. One of the points in the declarations was the peaceful nature of North Korea's nuclear program. These meetings and agreements have become a crucial milestone in bilateral relations. In essence, they symbolized the beginning of a new, modern stage in Russia-North Korea relations, which continues to this day.[18]

A rapprochement and a new era of cooperation began in 2011. Although Russia began to restore economic cooperation with the DPRK, the volume of bilateral trade by 2010 had decreased by 95 percent compared to the late Soviet period and amounted to only $98,670. In the summer of 2011, another meeting was held between Kim Jong-il and Vladimir Putin in the city of Ulan-Ude, Russia, after which the Russian government began working on a list of investment projects aimed at the restoration and modernization of enterprises built on the territory of the DPRK by the Soviet Union.[19]

After Kim Jong-un came to power at the end of 2011, relations between the two countries improved. Russia liquidated $10 billion of credit debt to North Korea (out of a total of $11 billion). The remaining $1 billion of debt was allocated as investments in the development of bilateral cooperation in North Korea. In particular, investments were made in infrastructural development for the Victory project, of which the railway network in the DPRK's territory (with a length of 3,500 kilometers) was modernized. In addition, the Trans-Korean Railway in the eastern part of the Korean Peninsula was connected to the Trans-Siberian Railway. Even though the Korean highway itself between the two Koreas has not yet been restored, the first freight trains began to run along the Trans-Siberian Railway to North Korea in 2013.[20]

In addition, the arrangement of the Rajin-Sonbong free trade zone (Rason FTZ) began. This zone was intended to connect North Korean ports through the Korean railway with the Trans-Siberian Railway for the transportation of North Korean goods. Another area of cooperation is labor migration. In the Far East, the use of North Korean labor has a long history. In particular, in the Amur Region, Koreans were employed in logging and agricultural industries. This allowed Pyongyang to partially alleviate the domestic unemployment problem and the Russian regions get cheap labor. In 2014, Pyongyang increased the number of special economic zones on its territory to nineteen and since then has sought to attract foreign investment in them.

In April 2015, a meeting of the Russian-North Korean intergovernmental commission on economic, scientific, and technical cooperation was held in Pyongyang. The meeting announced that the main areas of Russia-Korea cooperation would focus on energy and rail transportation. Russia would provide North Korea with investments and exports for access to the latter's mineral resources.[21]

One of the main goals and motivations of Pyongyang in developing trade relations with Russia is the need to balance and align the structure of foreign trade operations, which has a very heavy bias toward China. Throughout the 2000s, the DPRK sought to diversify its trade. However, little came of this. As of 2014, trade with China accounted for 90 percent of all of North Korea's foreign trade operations. At the same time, North Korea mainly exports to China minerals, raw materials, and seafood, which negates the prospects for the development of its production capacities. In this regard, the development of trade relations with Russia is key to North Korea, since they have a higher share of manufactured goods.[22]

The year 2014 was another important time in the development of bilateral relations. After Russia annexed Crimea and the outbreak of war in the Donbas, and a serious confrontation with the countries of Europe and North

America, Moscow experienced a very acute shortage of allies in the international arena. Contrary to the expectations of Russia, China took a neutral position. When voting at the UN General Assembly on Crimea, only ten states supported the Russian position (two countries of the former USSR, several countries from Africa and Latin America, and only one country from Asia—the DPRK). All this became a reason for an even closer relationship between the two states. Since then, mutual visits of senior officials of the two countries have become much more active. For example, Chairman of the Presidium of the DPRK Supreme People's Assembly Kim Yong-nam visited Russia in February 2014, Foreign Minister Lee Ryong Nam in June of the same year, Deputy Foreign Minister Lee Soo-young in July, and the special envoy of the head of the DPRK, member of the Presidium of the Political Bureau of the Central Committee of the Workers' Party of North Korea Choe Ryong-hae and Deputy Minister of Agriculture Ko Myung-hee in November. On the one hand, the level of delegations is not so high as to hint at Pyongyang's urge for close relations, on the other hand, it is sufficient to show its solidarity with Moscow.[23]

Return visits were paid by Russian officials to North Korea. For example, in March and April 2014, Minister of Development of the Russian Far East Galushko, and in October of the same year, Deputy Chairman of the Government of the Russian Federation, Plenipotentiary Representative of the President of the Russian Federation in the Far Eastern Federal District Trutnev visited Pyongyang. Moreover, 2015 was declared by the leadership of the two countries the Year of Friendship between Russia and North Korea.

In relations between the two countries, the priority is not economic, but political (and in some places military-political). The similarity of the positions of the two countries lies in the fact that both Moscow and Pyongyang are opposed to American foreign policy, and both countries are subject to sanctions from many countries in Western Europe and North America. North Korea usually supports Russia's position in the international arena. Russia also seeks to support Pyongyang's interests in the international arena. However, it should be recognized that Russia's support for the DPRK is inconsistent, especially in recent years.[24]

Why are the two states striving so hard to build relationships with each other? What is their motivation? Throughout the post–Cold War period and especially after the successful nuclear tests, North Korea has been virtually isolated and faced difficulties in developing the economy and continuing to develop the nuclear missile program. Improving relations with Moscow is an attempt to get out of isolation and add impetus for development. In addition, on the part of Pyongyang, better relations with Russia can reduce political dependency on China.

　　As for the motivation of Moscow, Russia in the 1990s distanced itself from East Asia, which was caused by the serious economic crisis within the country, political destabilization, and conflict in Chechnya. In addition, over the past few years, Russia has been trying to return to the region and restore its position. Building relationships with North Korea is, primarily, the desire to strengthen Moscow's influence in Northeast Asia. In addition, it is a desire for Russia to reduce U.S. influence in the region, an attempt to confront the American bilateral military-political alliances and the missile defense system. After 2014 and the aggravation of Moscow's confrontation with Western countries, relations with Pyongyang also became an attempt for Russia to demonstrate to the international community the presence of allies and partners.

　　The leader of the DPRK, Kim Jong-il, pursued a fairly moderate internal and external policy in the last years of his life. Moreover, his son came to power—the young and ambitious Kim Jong-un. The new ruler seeks to solve the internal and external problems of his country. In 2012, North Korea launched space satellites and joined the club of space powers, thereby violating UN Security Council resolutions 2000 and 2009, and sparking negative reactions from the international community. In February 2013, the DPRK successfully conducted its third nuclear test. In the same year, it canceled the non-aggression pact with the Republic of Korea which was signed in 1953. Consequently, the UN Security Council expanded sanctions against the North Korean regime. The Korean peninsula was again placed in the conditions of impending hostilities. However, opposition by the international community did not affect Kim Jong-un's pursuit of nuclear weapons.[25]

　　Since North Korea's first nuclear test in 2006, the level of confrontation and the sanctions against the DPRK have been rising. The UN Security Council resolution No. 1718 demanded North Korea stop the nuclear test and ban the export of much military equipment to the country. UN Security Council Resolution No. 1874 passed after the second nuclear test in 2009, expanded the arms embargo. In 2013, the UN Security Council resolutions No. 2087 and No. 2094 authorized the search of all ships going to the DPRK for prohibited goods and placed restrictions on money transfers with the country. In addition, after the fourth nuclear test in 2016, resolutions No. 2270 and No. 2321 were adopted to ban exports of gold, silver, vanadium, titanium, rare metals, coal, copper, nickel, and zinc from North Korea. However, this did not stop the North Korean leadership, and nuclear testing continued. In September 2017, the sixth full-fledged nuclear test was conducted and the creation of the DPRK of thermonuclear weapons was announced. In August and September 2017, UN Security Council resolutions No. 2371 and No. 2375 were adopted to ban the export of iron, lead, seafood, textiles, and gas condensate from North Korea and exports of oil and oil products to North Korea, and prohibit

North Korean citizens from working abroad, and ban any government from establishing joint ventures with the participation of North Korean capital. Sanctions were also introduced by individual states, such as the United States, Australia, Japan, the Republic of Korea, and EU countries.[26]

However, the situation with the sanctions does not look so straightforward in its positive consequences. On the one hand, as of 2017, 116 out of 193 UN member countries did not submit their reports on the implementation and enforcement of the sanctions imposed. This suggests the possibility of them not being observed or faithfully executed by all states. On the other hand, over the twelve years of sanctions, it became clear that the measures taken did not prejudice the DPRK nuclear program, especially with loopholes in sanctions. However, the sanctions seriously worsened the situations of ordinary North Korean citizens, carrying threats to food, energy, and migration security, and putting the country on the brink of a humanitarian catastrophe.

The nuclear issue developed in such a negative way that even the few supporters of Pyongyang stopped supporting it. In 2017 and 2018, China and Russia condemned the actions of the DPRK. Russia declared its commitment to sanctions, stopped the work of North Koreans in Russia, and limited the supply of oil products and gas condensates. The absence of North Korean citizens negatively affected the economy of the Russian Far East, reducing competition in many sectors of the economy and leading to higher prices. However, supporting the sanctions, Russia called on the international community to resolve all complex issues at the negotiation table.

In addition, since 2018, China has taken concrete steps to fulfill international obligations. So, North Korea's exports of iron, steel, and precious metals stopped, and the supplies of oil products, minerals, chemical goods, and industrial equipment were significantly reduced.

The situation in the economic, social, energy, and food spheres in the DPRK has become close to critical. However, it can be stated that at the beginning of 2018, North Korea became the de facto owner of nuclear and thermonuclear weapons, with carriers capable of delivering warheads to the United States.

According to Russian President Putin, "Kim Jong-un solved his strategic task: he has a nuclear charge, Kim has a global-range missile (up to 13,000 kilometers) that can reach almost any point on the enemy's territory. He showed himself to be a competent and mature politician." However, after this, he called for the denuclearization of the Korean peninsula through dialogue. It must be noted that Pyongyang retained this stage of the confrontation. No matter how much Washington threatens, talks about preparing for the invasion, and does not lift sanctions, the DPRK nevertheless achieved its goal.[27]

In 2018, the North Korean leader dramatically changed his strategy, both concerning his closest neighbors and on a global scale. The formal reason for this was the Winter Olympic Games in Pyeongchang, Republic of Korea. In January 2018, Kim Jong-un unexpectedly took the initiative to propose to jointly enter the opening ceremony with the South Korean team under one flag (white with a blue silhouette of the Korean Peninsula). And, indeed, the two Koreas marched together under the same flag for the first time in twelve years, in addition to putting up a single team of two states in the women's hockey tournament. Twenty-two athletes from the DPRK received an invitation from the IOC to the Olympics in excess of the quota.

Kim Jong-un also announced his desire to negotiate with South Korea and U.S. president, Donald Trump. The first-ever meeting of the U.S. and DPRK leaders took place on June 12, 2018, in Singapore. On February 27, 2019, the second meeting took place in Hanoi, and on June 30, 2019, the third meeting took place in the demilitarized zone. Trump became the first American president to step into North Korean territory. These summits did not bring any tangible results and were rather a political public relations campaign. Regarding Russian-Korean relations from 2017, the accelerated development of the nuclear missile program by Pyongyang in 2016 and 2017 complicated the relations. Moscow unequivocally declared the impossibility of developing interaction in isolation from the situation on the Korean Peninsula and the nuclear missile experiments of Pyongyang.

Close contact is maintained by the foreign affairs agencies of the two countries. In August 2017, on the sidelines of the ministerial meeting of the ASEAN Regional Security Forum (ARF) in Manila, Russian Foreign Minister Sergei Lavrov held talks with DPRK Foreign Minister Lee Yong-ho.

On June 14, 2018, Russian President Vladimir Putin received in the Kremlin the chair of the Presidium of the Supreme People's Assembly of DPRK, Kim Yong-nam. During the meeting, Kim handed over to Putin a letter from Kim Jong-un.

In April 2018, Lee Yong-ho was on an official visit to Moscow. In May 2018, Sergey Lavrov paid an official visit to Pyongyang, during which he met with the Chairman of the DPRK State Council Kim Jong-un. On September 26, 2018, Russian Foreign Minister Sergey Lavrov held talks with the DPRK Foreign Minister Lee Young-ho in New York on the sidelines of the UN General Assembly.

Inter-parliamentary contacts play a pivotal role in the development of Russian–North Korean relations. In April and November 2017, a delegation of the State Duma of Russia visited North Korea. In October 2017, Deputy Chairman of the Supreme National Assembly, An Don-chun, visited Russia and held talks with the Chairman of the Federation Council, Valentina Matvienko.

In September 2018, the Russian parliamentary delegation led by the Chairman of the Federation Council of the Russian Federation Valentina

Matvienko took part in the celebrations on the seventieth anniversary of the founding of the Democratic People's Republic of Korea and was received by Kim Jong-un. Valentina Matvienko conveyed to the North Korean leader a personal message from Russian President Putin.

As previously noted, Russia is a traditional economic partner of the DPRK. International sanctions, as well as unilateral restrictions imposed by some countries, seriously complicated the further development of bilateral economic ties. In 2017, Russia–North Korea trade amounted to $77.9 million. At the end of 2018, Russia's trade with the DPRK amounted to $34.065 million, a decrease of 56.26 percent from 2017. Russia's exports to and imports from the DPRK amounted to $32.082 million and $1.983 million respectively. Moreover, this is a significant fall that hit the economy of North Korea, the development of the Russian Far East, and bilateral relations.[28] The Russian exports consist of mineral products, food products, and agricultural raw materials; and its imports from North Korea consist of musical instruments, machines, equipment and vehicles, and chemical products.

An important bilateral project is the joint operation of the Khasan (Russia)–Rajin (DPRK) railway section and the third pier of the Rajin port, which was reconstructed by the joint venture Rasonkontrans, a subsidiary of Russian Railways. At present, Russian Railways continues to engage Russian and foreign transport and logistics companies in the project to form a cargo base. In addition, Russia regularly provides North Korea with humanitarian assistance both bilaterally and through international organizations.

Russia and the DPRK are developing cooperation in the field of culture and education. Since 2009, the Russian Center has been successfully operating in the DPRK at the Pyongyang Institute of Foreign Languages, created by the Russkiy Mir Foundation. Since 2015, Republican Russian-language Olympiads have been held annually among North Korean schoolchildren. As part of the Russia Study program (training at the expense of the federal budget of the Russian Federation), forty students from the DPRK have been accepted each year since 2016.

On April 25, 2019, the first in-person meeting between President Putin and Kim Jong-Un took place in Vladivostok. The two main topics for negotiations were the restoration of the previous parameters of economic cooperation between the two countries. In addition, the leaders discussed the construction of new power lines, a gas pipeline, and an oil pipeline from Russia to the DPRK.

In 2019, Russia's trade with North Korea amounted to $47.90 million dollars, an increase of 40.62 percent from 2018. At the same time, Russian exports to the DPRK in 2019 amounted to $44.86 million dollars, an increase of 39.84 percent ($12.78 million dollars) compared to 2018. Moreover, Russia's imports from the DPRK (North Korea) in 2019 amounted to $3.03

million dollars, an increase of 53.12 percent ($1.05 million dollars) compared to 2018.

In the structure of Russia's exports to North Korea in 2019, the main share of supplies fell on the following types of goods: (1) mineral products—61.27 percent of Russia's total exports to the DPRK (68 percent in 2018); (2) food products and agricultural raw materials—27.43 percent of Russia's total exports to North Korea (24.9 percent in 2018); (3) chemical industry products—5.84 percent of Russia's total exports to the DPRK (5.15 percent in 2018); (4) machinery, equipment, and vehicles—4.75 percent of Russia's total exports to the DPRK (1.2 percent in 2018).[29]

In the structure of Russian imports from North Korea in 2019, the main share of supplies fell to the following types of goods: (1) machines, equipment, and vehicles—23.83 percent of Russian imports from the DPRK (14.54 percent in 2018); (2) chemical products—16.33 percent of Russia's total imports from North Korea (11.25 percent in 2018); (3) metals and products—1.61 percent of Russia's total imports from the DPRK (1.09 percent in 2018); (4) food products and agricultural raw materials—1.08 percent of Russia's total imports from the DPRK (0.07 percent in 2018).

The most significant gains in Russia's imports from North Korea in 2019 compared to 2018 were recorded for the following product groups: (1) nuclear reactors, boilers, equipment, and mechanical devices; parts thereof—an increase of $478,250; (2) pharmaceutical products—an increase of $422,019; (3) musical instruments; parts and accessories thereof—an increase of $157,999; (4) furniture; bedding, mattresses, mattress basics, sofa cushions, and similar printed furniture; lamps and lighting equipment not elsewhere specified or included; light signs, light plates with a name or title, or address and similar products; prefabricated buildings—an increase of $93,372.[30]

After the meeting of the leaders of Russia and North Korea, as well as after the beginning of the international detente and the closure of the nuclear test site in the DPRK, there was a noticeable improvement in mutual economic cooperation between the two countries. However, at the same time, the share of North Korea in Russian foreign trade in 2019 amounted to only 0.0072 percent (0.0050 percent in 2018). In Russian trade in 2019, the DPRK ranked 137th place (in 2018, 144th place). The volumes of mutual trade are insignificant and occupy a very modest place in Russian foreign trade. For North Korea, the share of Russia in its trade is about 1.5 percent, which is insignificant compared to that of China.

The COVID-19 pandemic seriously disrupted North Korea's foreign trade. With the breakout of the pandemic in North Korea in May 2020, Pyongyang will need the humanitarian assistance that Beijing and Moscow are likely to provide. Russian–North Korean economic cooperation and trade volume will steadily recover when the pandemic eases.

More important for both sides are political relations. For the Russian Federation at this stage, it is important to achieve the lifting of sanctions against the DPRK and return this country to normality. There has been a question of food security and a humanitarian catastrophe. According to rough estimates, about 10 million people are deficient in food in the country. Moscow provided humanitarian assistance to Pyongyang in 2019 and 2020. In 2019, Russia transferred eight thousand tons of wheat worth $ 8 million to the DPRK through the UN. And in May 2020, Russia transferred twenty-five thousand tons of selected grain to North Korea through the UN World Food Program.

On January 5–12, 2021, the 8th Congress of the Workers' Party of Korea was held in Pyongyang. There were no radical changes in the party congress. Kim Jong-un was elected as general secretary, and the political and economic course remained unchanged, while criticism of economic development was voiced, as well as the fact that the five-year plan was not fulfilled (for the first time since 1993). The need to strengthen the military potential, especially its nuclear missile component, was also emphasized.

The North Korean leader's report highlighted the need to develop priority relations with Russia and China. For North Korea at this stage, relations with Russia are a matter of national security. Without the Russian Federation, it will be very difficult to resist the United States and China's unilateral influence.

In 2022, Russian–North Korean relations received a new impetus. The aggressive foreign policy of the Kremlin and the beginning of the military operation in Ukraine, which did not find understanding almost anywhere in the world, found support in Pyongyang. North Korea is one of the few countries that has fully supported Russia's position in its conflict with Ukraine. In March, at the UN General Assembly, this country, along with Syria, Belarus, Eritrea, and, in fact, the Russian Federation, voted against a resolution condemning the Russian operation. In July 2022, Kim Jong-un took a demonstrative step to support the Kremlin. The DPRK recognized the independence of the DNR and LNR. In response, Ukraine severed diplomatic relations with Pyongyang. The North Korean leader had the opportunity to take relations between the two countries to a new level by supporting the Kremlin's policy. This is an opportunity to at least partially get out of the situation of international isolation and full-scale sanctions, to receive economic assistance from Moscow, to establish previous cooperation, and in the longer term, to receive recognition from Russia of its nuclear status.

On August 15, 2022, the parties exchanged telegrams on the anniversary of Japan's surrender. In addition, if the telegram of the Russian leader was sustained in a purely official tone, then the response telegram was replete with powerful allied messages. Kim Jong-un not only sent "warm greetings to the President of the Russian Federation, the Russian government and people," wishing Putin "good health, as well as a great success in responsible work to protect the sovereignty and interests of the country and people," but also noted that Pyongyang and Moscow are now "on a common front to disrupt the military threat and provocation, arbitrariness and self-will of hostile forces."

On August 1, 2022, in an interview with RBC, Russian Deputy Prime Minister Khusnullin called the North Korean labor market "very interesting." A few days earlier, DPR leader Pushilin announced plans to recruit North Korean workers to rebuild Donbass. It is quite possible that Moscow, already under severe international sanctions, will take this step (in violation of UN resolutions), given that Russia is experiencing a labor shortage (both because of the pandemic and because of the events in Ukraine).[31]

In October 2022, the DPRK Foreign Ministry welcomed the entry of new regions into Russia and declared respect for the will of their inhabitants. Reuters reported this concerning the words of the director general of international organizations in the Pyongyang Foreign Ministry, Jo Chol-soo. "The referendums were legally held under the UN charter, but the United States maintains gangster double standards to maintain its own supremacy," the diplomat said.

As a consequence of Pyongyang's strong support for Moscow's position, North Korea decided to take the next step. On September 9, 2022, the DPRK authorities adopted a new law that gives the republic the right to launch a preventive strike against the enemy if there is a threat to the republic from outside. The law secured the nuclear status of North Korea. In addition, the law specifies that the DPRK undertakes the obligation to non-proliferation with its nuclear weapons. Moreover, in October, Pyongyang carried out another test of cruise missiles.[32]

CONCLUSION

The relations between North Korea and the USSR/Russia are historically developed in the bipolar period. The two states today are economic and political partners for each other. During the Cold War, the Soviet Union was the locomotive that drove the North Korean economy. Politically, the DPRK was an outpost of the socialist camp in East Asia. However, after the collapse of the Soviet Union, relations between the two countries almost completely ceased. The DPRK economic situation has become critical. During this period, Beijing becomes a key partner of Pyongyang, which remains to this day. In the last decade, Russia has made every effort to "return" to North Korea. Russia established economic cooperation (though insignificant), provided humanitarian assistance, tried to come up with international initiatives, and supported Pyongyang in the international arena, with the exception of Pyongyang's nuclear program. For Russia, North Korea is almost the only opportunity to influence the situation in East Asia, to try to play a more significant role there, and to integrate into the processes that are taking place in the region today. Efforts to denuclearize the Korean peninsula and integrate the DPRK into the global economic and political space can significantly increase Moscow's prestige in the international arena. For Pyongyang, relations with Moscow are an opportunity to diversify foreign economic relations, get rid of the one-sided full dependence on Beijing, an opportunity to solve their humanitarian, economic, and foreign policy tasks, namely, to achieve the lifting of the sanction, to obtain security guarantees, and to break international isolation. There are prospects for expanding bilateral ties. In the post-coronavirus world, the economic and political ties between Moscow and Pyongyang will develop in an upward direction.

Despite the common borders of Russia and North Korea economic interaction has not become a top priority. Pyongyang primarily seeks international support and military-political interaction from Russia. Moscow is trying to expand its influence in the region. In the context of the Sino-American competition, the interaction between Russia and North Korea has a chance for a positive agenda and obtaining their desired results.

In the context of the pandemic, the economic interaction between Russia and North Korea has almost come to naught, however how much political interaction has intensified in 2020 and, especially, in 2022. Apparently, in the near future, in the context of the existing transformations, this interaction will increase, and Pyongyang will receive even more support from Moscow, both political and economic.

NOTES

1. A. V. Torkunov, *Mysterious War: Korean Conflict 1950–1953* (Moscow: Russian Political Encyclopedia, 2000).

2 *History of the East in 6 volumes. Volume 6: The East in the Newest Period (1945–2000)*, edited by V. Belokrenitsky (Moscow: Institute of Oriental Studies RAS, 2008).

3 Ibid.

4 Torkunov, *Mysterious War.*

5. Belokrenitsky, *History of the East*

6. Ibid.

7. M. T. Haggard, "North Korea's International Position," *Asian Survey* 5, no. 8 (1965): 375–88.

8. Foreign Trade of Russia, *Russian Foreign Trade Reviews*. Available at https: //russian-trade.com/reports-and-reviews/2020-02/torgovlya-mezhdu-rossiey-i-kndr -severnoy-koreey-v-2019-g/. Accessed April 20, 2020.

9. D. S. Zagoria, "The USSR and Asia in 1984," *Asian Survey* 25, no. 1 (1985): 21–32.

10. Ibid.

11. Zakharova, L., "Russia-North Korea Economic Relations," *Joint U.S.-Korea Academic Studies* (2015), 212–22.

12. L. Zakharova, "North Korea's International Economic Ties in the 21st Century and Prospects for Their Development under Kim Jong Un," *Far Eastern Affairs* 3 (2013): 142–43.

13. Belokrenitsky, *History of the East.*

14. Ibid.

15. P. Cherkashin, "Current Russian-North Korean Relations and Prospects of Their Development" (2016). Available at http://russiancouncil.ru/en/blogs/dvfu/?id_4 =2022. Accessed February15, 2019.

16. Zakharova, *Economic Ties.*

17. Cherkashin, "Current Russian-North Korean Relations."

18. Doug J.Kim, "Russian Influence on North Korea: Views of Former South Korean Ambassadors to Russia," *The Korean Journal of Defense Analysis* 24, no. 3 (September 2012): 391–404.

19. Foreign Trade of Russia, *Russian Foreign Trade Reviews.*

20. Cherkashin, "Current Russian-North Korean Relations."

21. "Russia Largest N. Korea WFP Donor in 2015—Corrected," NK News, https://www.nknews.org/pro/russia-largest-n-korea-wfp-donor-in-2015-corrected/. Accessed February 12, 2020.

22. Kim, "Russian Influence on North Korea."

23. Cherkashin, "Current Russian-North Korean Relations."

24. Zakharova, "Russia-North Korea Economic Relations."

25. Cherkashin, "Current Russian-North Korean Relations."

26. *North Korea and the Republic of Korea—70 years.* Moscow: Institute of the Far East of the Russian Academy of Sciences, 2018.

27. Ibid.

28. Ibid.

29. Foreign Trade of Russia, *Russian Foreign Trade Reviews.*

30. Ibid.

31. "Is Russia Ready to Violate UN Anti-North Korean Sanctions," https://www.ng .ru/world/2022-08-15/1_8513_cooperation.html. Accessed October 3, 2022.

32. "North Korea Announced Its Nuclear Status," https://deita.ru/article/523091. Accessed October 3, 2022.

Chapter 6

North Korea and Iran

Kim Jong-Un's Dilemma

Alon Levkowitz

Since the 1980s, the relationship between North Korea and Iran included cooperation over conventional and nonconventional weapons as well as economic and diplomatic relations. The missile industry was one of the best examples of their mutual collaboration. Over the years, there have even been indications of chemical and nuclear cooperation between the two countries, also including Syria.[1] The nomination of Kim Jong-un as the leader of North Korea after the death of his father, Kim Jong-il, in 2011 begged the question of whether he would change Pyongyang's Iranian policy or continue with the existing policy. During the 2015 Joint Comprehensive Plan of Action (JCPOA) deal between Iran and the P5+1, scholars asked whether the JCPOA would influence security relations between Pyongyang and Tehran. The question was raised once again when Kim Jong-un decided to pursue a new policy toward Washington and to sign the Singapore declaration in June 2018. This chapter analyzes relations between North Korea and Iran during the Kim Jong-un era and how they have been influenced by JCPOA and the new U.S.–North Korea relationship.

The diplomatic, economic, and military relations between North Korea and Iran, especially the North Korean military export to Iran and other parts of the Middle East, serve Pyongyang's vital interests: It allows North Korea to increase its foreign income by exporting military equipment and technologies to the region. The foreign currency allows Kim Jong-un's regime to strengthen the North Korean economy and the survival of the regime, especially with the decline of economic assistance from other countries and the increasing sanctions on Pyongyang. The relations with Iran, allow the regime to legitimize and finance the army and the military industry, which play an important role in maintaining the stability of the regime. The relations with Iran allow North Korea to look for new alliances in the Middle East and to demonstrate its foreign independent policy.

NORTH KOREAN–IRANIAN RELATIONS

Despite the geographic distance between North Korea and Iran and the lack of common religious or ideological backgrounds, the two countries share other interests that have allowed them to be allies since the 1980s. While diplomatic relations began in 1973 during the Iranian Shah and Kim Il-sung eras, the two countries did not share any ideological, strategic, or economic interests in those days. The relationship improved, however, after the 1979 Islamic Revolution due to internal, regional, and global changes that influenced the interests of both parties.[2]

Internal changes in Iran—the fall of Shah Mohammad Reza Pahlavi and the rise of Ayatollah Khomeini—led to a change in Iran's foreign policy. The regional environment changes due to the war between Iran and Iraq (1980–1988) forced Iran to look for allies and new weapon suppliers, particularly as, in the global arena, the collapse of the Soviet Union led to a decline in Soviet military exports to Iran. While the West had been willing to sell weapons to Iran during the Shah era, they proved less enthusiastic during Ayatollah Khomeini's regime, leaving Tehran desperately seeking other sources.

At the same time, North Korea was searching foreign markets for its military equipment in an attempt to increase its foreign currency income.[3] It was willing to sell weapons with no restrictions and, unlike Washington, Moscow, and Paris, with no hidden agenda of trying to influence its buyers. Another advantage was that North Korean military exports were less expensive than their competitors. The Iran–Iraq War was indeed very profitable for North Korea, which became Iran's biggest weapons exporter.[4] Due to their growing need for missiles to respond and deter Iraqi missile attacks,[5] North Korea first sold Scud Bs and Scud Cs to Iran,[6] later moving on to short-range ballistic missiles (SRBM) and medium-range ballistic missiles (MRBM).[7] Military and technological cooperation between the two countries also helped to upgrade the Iranian missile industry.[8] Mutual interest thus brought Iran and North Korea much closer in the 1980s despite the two countries' stark ideological differences.[9] Iran was not the only country in the Middle East to which North Korea sold missiles: Syria, Yemen, and other Middle East countries were also their customers.[10]

The relationship between North Korea and Iran was maintained after the death of Kim Il-sung. Their missile and nuclear cooperation continued, even though North Korea signed agreements with the United States and was expected to limit military cooperation.[11] This cooperation included military exports and technological cooperation on conventional and nonconventional weapons,[12] allowing a partial win-win for both states: North Korea was looking for foreign income and oil, while Iran needed missiles and other military equipment and was willing to pay in cash and oil.[13] As various reports have hinted, relations between North Korea and Iran extended also to other countries such as Syria. The Syrian nuclear project that was bombarded by Israel in 2007 was, in fact, funded partially by Iran.[14]

The Kim Jong-un era began with partial optimism—or wishful thinking as some experts would say—that his European education might lead him to pursue more liberal changes in North Korea, which in turn might prompt a change in his policy toward South Korea, the United States, and Iran.[15] This optimistic view was shattered once Kim Jong-un began to upgrade the missile and nuclear projects at a fairly high speed in comparison to his predecessors and even continued the conventional and nonconventional military cooperation despite U.S. suspicions that Iran was developing a nuclear program.[16]

Kim Jong-un and Iran—Why?

Why should Kim Jong-un maintain relations with Iran despite regional and global changes? There are a few economic, diplomatic, and military motivations for continuing with this relationship that began in Kim Il-sung's era.

From an economic perspective, North Korea's main export and import partner is China. The end of the Cold War reduced the number of states that North Korea could trade with, primarily because North Korea had not prepared its economy for the changing economic environment and the fall of the communist bloc.[17] Its economic dependency on China, especially since the 1990s, limits its policy options. North Korea has searched over the years for foreign markets with which it could trade its products and technological know-how for cash and oil. Some of the sanctions that were imposed by the United Nations Security Council (UNSC), the United States, and other states on North Korea restricted its international bank services (SWIFT),[18] forcing Pyongyang to find illegal ways to transfer money. The Middle East, Africa, and even South America became important markets for North Korean military exports. Iran was able to sell oil to North Korea, which allowed Pyongyang to not just rely on Beijing for its oil imports.

Iran's economic importance was not just as an "end user" of North Korea's military equipment and technology; it also served as a hub for North Korea's military exports to other parts of the Middle East (Syria). Iran, as discussed below, also served as a hub for other state and non-state terrorist organizations (Hezbollah) in the Middle East supported by Iran.[19] It also funded some of the arms deals and the military cooperation between North Korea and

Syria, for example. Iran thus boosted the incentive of Kim Jong-un's regime to continue their economic and diplomatic relations. The technological cooperation between North Korea and Iran, mainly in the area of missiles, benefits both states and allows them to increase their deterrence capabilities against foreign threats and upgrade their missiles in order to export them.

Although George W. Bush tagged North Korea and Iran as the "axis of evil," this unofficial alliance has continued for decades, allowing North Korea to get diplomatic, economic, and technological support from Iran.[20] High official visits between the two countries help both states to legitimize their regional importance, while their cooperation enables them to bypass the U.S. and UN sanctions imposed on them without breaching agreements that both have signed with foreign countries (the JCPOA, Agreed Framework, etc.). Iran gives North Korea a backdoor through which to continue exporting weapons and to maintain nonconventional (nuclear) and conventional (missiles) weapon cooperation without being seen to violate the sanctions.[21] Likewise, Iran uses its relations with North Korea to bypass the constraints that it faces.[22]

The Joint Comprehensive Plan of Action (JCPOA), which was signed on July 14, 2015, during the Obama administration, demonstrated that nuclear issues that threaten regional and global security can be solved through diplomatic dialogue without the need for military action. Some would say that without the harsh sanctions, Iran would have never considered signing the JCPOA. The JCPOA opened a window of economic opportunities for Iran; delegations from all around the world landed in Iran seeking oil contracts, infrastructure projects, and other business deals facilitated by the signing of the JCPOA. Once the U.S. veto on doing business with Iran was lifted, everyone was looking for economic opportunities—even South Korea. In fact, in May 2016, President Park Geun-hye flew to Iran with a huge economic delegation in search of the "Second Middle East Boom."[23] The billion-dollar contracts that Iran signed with foreign states and companies and the potential of more after the lifting of the sanctions due to the signing of the JCPOA raises the question of whether the economic logic of the trading state will convince Iran to change its foreign and security policy.[24] Will Iran try to breach the JCPOA and continue its conventional and nonconventional military cooperation with North Korea, and, in doing so, endanger the billion-dollar contracts that it signed? Or will it find ways to bypass the JCPOA restrictions in order to continue its trade with North Korea? While the JCPOA dealt with the Iranian nuclear program, it did not include the issue of missiles and thus enabled Iran to continue its missile cooperation with North Korea without being seen to violate the agreement.[25] Despite negotiating the deal with Iran, the U.S. Department of the Treasury imposed few times sanctions on Iran due to its missile cooperation with North Korea during the Kim Jong-un regime.[26]

The JCPOA prompted calls for a new deal requiring North Korea to freeze or dismantle its nuclear program.[27] However, the difference between Iran and North Korea and their nuclear programs make it harder to reach the same deal with North Korea. Indeed, President Trump later discovered that dismantling the North Korean nuclear program was more difficult than he had anticipated.

Over the years, the "axis of evil" link between North Korea and Iran, originally coined to refer to the nuclear issue, has extended to also include the missile issue. Almost every time Washington tries to reach a deal with Pyongyang or Tehran, it must also consider the implications for the other country. The JCPOA was seen by the European Union and the Obama administration as a diplomatic success, as it convinced Iran to freeze its nuclear program for ten years without using force. It was seen as a potential model for pressurizing North Korea to similarly freeze or dismantle its nuclear program. The Singapore declaration was seen at the beginning as a deal that would lead to the disarming of North Korea and might even bring peace to the Korean Peninsula and, later on, prevent Iran from developing a nuclear program without the need to use military force. While North Korea has developed and tested its nuclear power, Iran is at an earlier stage. In the last decade the debates between experts have been about whether Iran is two or three years away from becoming a nuclear state. The current debate is on how many weeks will it take Iran to become a threshold state.[28] However, there is no doubt that military cooperation between North Korea and Iran on conventional and nonconventional weapons will hasten Iran's process of becoming a nuclear state.[29]

Missiles Cooperation

Despite the positive economic indications that the North Korean economy is growing,[30] the North Korean economy is still dependent on the Chinese market, even when the economic sanctions imposed by the United Nations and the United States were not lifted. Having been shown to be one of the weakest economies in the world in spite of its huge natural resources, North Korea's military industry might be expected to be very small and not very productive. However, its technological achievements and global cooperation with Pakistan, Iran, Russia, China, and others have enabled the establishment of an industry that can manufacture a variety of missiles from short-range to middle- and long-range missiles.[31] These missiles have become an important pillar of North Korean exports and one of the foundations for the cooperation between Iran and North Korea. If one were to analyze the number and variety of missile tests under Kim Jong-un relative to Kim Jong-il or Kim Il-sung,[32] or even to other middle-power states, one could say that North Korea's missile industry, has become a vibrant and successful market for developing a wide variety of missiles.

North Korea and Iran have cooperated on various issues; the two most relevant to this chapter are missiles and nuclear weapons which, despite its exports of light weapons as well, have provided North Korea's main income. With Iranian assistance this cooperation has extended to include other countries, for example, Libya and Syria, regarding, in particular, the export of Nodong and Scud missiles.[33]

As mentioned above, North Korea produces a variety of missiles. These missiles can be launched from static launching pads, which are easier to intercept, or from mobile launching vehicles, which are harder to intercept because of their mobility. North Korea also manufactured the Pukkŭksŏng-1 (KN-11), the submarine-launched ballistic missile (SLBM), which extends North Korea's capability to attack the United States.[34] North Korea's ability to build the SLBM and to compete with the small number of countries that can export these missiles could boost its exports and perhaps be sold to Iran, which sees it as a means to expand its deterrence.

The achievements of the North Korean missile industry are a result of its technological successes, some of which were acquired from reverse engineering and some from global cooperation with its allies including Iran.[35] But for Kim Jong-un, the game changer will be North Korea's development of intercontinental ballistic missiles (ICBM) that can reach not just U.S. bases in Japan, South Korea, or Guam but the American mainland. As he stated in his January 2018 New Year address,

> On this platform one year ago, I officially made public on behalf of the Party and government that we had entered the final stage of preparation for the test launch of an intercontinental ballistic missile. In the past one year we conducted several rounds of its test launch, aimed at implementing the program, safely and transparently, thus proving before the eyes of the world its definite success.[36]

Once Pyongyang launched successfully the Hwasong-15 (ICBM) in November 2017,[37] the ICBM strengthened its deterrence capabilities against the United States and became one of the reasons why Washington was willing to negotiate as an equal partner, according to Pyongyang. The development and manufacturing of the ICBM demonstrate North Korea's technological capabilities and as suggested by analysts, Iran's assistance.[38]

Once North Korea developed and produced long-range missiles, the next phase was to develop the nuclear warhead. In the next part of the chapter, I talk about the nuclear cooperation between Iran and North Korea. There is a debate between analysts over whether North Korea has developed a nuclear warhead that will be able to reenter the atmosphere. In an interview with the media, John Bolton stated a few times that one of his biggest concerns about relations between North Korea and Iran is that any of North Korea's technological achievements in the missile and nuclear fields will be shared with Iran.[39]

Military experts have found many similarities between North Korean and Iranian missiles or examples of technological cooperation between North Korea and Iran. Some of the missiles, launch pads, or launch vehicles are in some cases Soviet brands, but the missile themselves demonstrate the cooperation between the two states. One example is Musudan (KN-10), the North Korean ballistic missile, which was tested in 2016; another is Khorramshahr, the Iranian ballistic missile, which was tested in January 2017 and could be said to have some "fingerprints" of the Musudan.[40] The North Korean Nodong-2 and the Iranian Shehab-3 have also been regarded as demonstrating the cooperation between the two countries.[41] The two countries not only codeveloped missiles but also satellite launchers,[42] a cooperation which enabled them to both share data and knowledge and reduce the cost of development. The satellite launchers allow both states to develop long-range capabilities without the need to be dependent on foreign states.

Another example of cooperation between North Korea and Iran during Kim Jong-un's regime is submarines. Submarines allow the state to project its military power without detection. During a failed Iranian missile test conducted from a submarine in May 2017, analysts were able to identify the Iranian Ghadir-class submarine, finding huge similarities to the North Korean Yono-class submarine and thus indicating another long-term cooperation between North Korea and Iran.[43] If both states had cooperated on the submarine, no one would be able to prevent North Korea from sharing its technology of the submarine-launched ballistic missile (SLBM) that it tested in 2015. Purchasing SLBM from North Korea or developing it in Iran with North Korean assistance will allow Iran to expand its deterrence capabilities.[44]

The cooperation on the development of the North Korean and Iranian missile industry has included over the years visits by officials such as Kim Yong-Nam,[45] diplomats, and experts from both countries.[46] U.S. intelligence reports presented many indications that the missile cooperation between North Korea and Iran continued during the administrations of Kim Jong-un and Barack Obama.[47]

The Honeymoon with Trump

While, on the one hand, one could say that the relationship between Donald Trump and Kim Jong-un began with the possibility of catastrophic regional conflict,[48] the second part of Trump's presidency demonstrated a change in attitudes, and a peaceful Korean Peninsula was seen as almost in reach.[49] The

declaration signed in Singapore was supposed to be discussed and its implementation detailed at the Hanoi summit, however, the Singapore, Hanoi, and
even the meeting at the demilitarized zone (DMZ) failed to achieve any of the
changes in the North Korean–United States relations that Kim Jong-un was
trying to achieve,[50] such as lifting sanctions and improving relations with the
United States without losing North Korea's main strategic assets. Despite the
conciliatory words that President Trump used when speaking about Kim after
the Singapore summit, he did not lift the sanctions, which carry a very high
cost for the North Korean economy.

The continuation of the sanctions limits North Korea's trade options and
explains the growing number of reports on North Korean attempts to smug-
gle, trade North Korean merchandise, and import oil.[51] Being dependent on
smugglers increases the price of products that North Korea purchases while
decreasing the price of products sold to the smugglers. The rising cost of the
smuggling networks thus raises the cost of the sanctions. Kim Jong-un therefore needed to find new creative ways to increase state income that would
allow him to bypass the sanctions without being identified as breaching them
or being seen as the source of the smuggled merchandise. Trade with China
thus became North Korea's main economic pipeline, as the sanctions pre-
vented even South Korea from initiating cooperative economic projects with
North Korea despite President Moon Jae-in's attempts. Any such attempts are
blocked by Washington.[52] South Korean President Yoon Suk-yeol, stated that
he was willing to cooperate with Pyongyang, but his preconditions for North
Korean disarmament, indicate that Kim Jong-un will receive any economic
assistance during Yoon's presidency.

Kim's need for other trading partners explains the role of Iran as an important economic partner for, in particular, military exports and oil imports.
While the dialogue between Kim Jong-un and Donald Trump might have
been expected to limit the military trade between North Korea and Iran, as
part of North Korea's charm diplomacy,[53] a report by Hugh Griffiths and Matt
Schroeder that was published in September 2020 as well as the *Report of
the Panel of Experts Established Pursuant to Resolution 1874 (2009)* which
was addressed to the UNSC provide a long list of sanctions violations and
smuggling between the two countries.[54] The reports reveal the existence of an
institutionalized smuggling network via air, sea, and land and even via the
diplomatic core. The increasing number of violations sends a clear indication
that the continuation of the sanctions forces North Korea to look for illegal
ways to boost its income and that Iran is one of North Korea's most important
trade partner. Kim Jong-un is aware that the UN and Washington are monitoring illegal transactions with Iran; nonetheless, he continues to trade with Iran
and bypass the sanctions due to his limited trade options.

Despite the "love letters" between Kim Jong-un and Donald Trump,[55] Washington has signaled that violating the agreements and sanctions will have a price tag. The decision (September 2020) by Washington to impose sanctions on two dozen people and entities in Iran that are linked to the missile and nuclear industries, some of which are linked to North Korea, makes it very clear that Pyongyang and Tehran are continuing with their conventional and nonconventional military cooperation. As an anonymous official from the U.S. government stated on September 20, 2020, "Iran and North Korea have resumed cooperation on a long-range missile project, including the transfer of critical parts."[56]

While relations between the United States and North Korea have partly improved during President Trump's mid-term, U.S. relations with Iran have deteriorated and Washington's decision to impose sanctions on Iranian companies that trade with North Korea and withdraw from the JCPOA and sends a clear message that the United States opposes the military cooperation between Tehran and Pyongyang.[57] Teheran and Pyongyang now face the same dilemma: both are paying a huge economic price due to the sanctions and both want to continue their cooperation, in light of their limited alternatives, but need to find ways to bypass the sanctions despite the costly penalties of their violation.

Kim Jong-un and Donald Trump's "honeymoon" did not sever relations between Tehran and Pyongyang. The statement by Iranian president Hassan Rouhani on June 24, 2020, which included criticism of the U.S. sanction policy against Iran, also condemned U.S. sanctions on North Korea.[58] Another indication of the Iranian support of North Korea can be seen in the Iranian press comments on the Kim–Trump summits. The Iranian press praised Kim Jong-un's tactics during the negotiation with President Trump.[59] Further evidence of the bond between North Korea and Iran can be seen in the statement of North Korea's new ambassador to Iran, Han Song-u, a few days later that the two countries share a "common enemy" and that Kim and Rouhani "must stand stronger than ever against their [U.S.] extravagance and bullying."[60] These harsh words by Iranian and North Korean officials against the United States and, especially, the Trump administration demonstrate the importance that Kim Jong-un places on relations with Iran despite his attempts to improve relations with President Trump.

Nuclear

North Korea's nuclear project, which began during the Kim Il-sung era, is another layer of cooperation between North Korea and Iran. The two countries are in different phases of the nuclear program: while North Korea held six nuclear tests between October 9, 2006, and September 3, 2017, Iran has not yet held any official nuclear nor does it have a similarly advanced nuclear program.

Kim Jong-il held two nuclear tests on October 9, 2006, and May 25, 2009. Kim Jong-un hastened the nuclear program despite the increasing sanctions and held his first nuclear test on February 12, 2013, and then, three years later, held two nuclear tests in one year, on January 6 and September 9, 2016.[61] Kim Jong-un's decision to speed up the program demonstrates his determination to build a credible nuclear deterrence capability. The more recent nuclear test, held on September 3, 2017, demonstrates yet another attempt by Kim Jong-un to springboard the nuclear program by building a hydrogen bomb;[62] most experts, however, have expressed doubts about this claim.[63] North Korea's six nuclear tests have shown the world that, despite U.S. reluctance to accept it, North Korea is indeed a nuclear power state.[64]

Despite the differences between the Iranian and North Korean nuclear programs, both cooperated not only in missile technology and industry but also in the nuclear field North Korea's willingness to cooperate with Iran in the nuclear field does not come from an ideological or altruistic position;[65] rather, as mentioned above, North Korea sees its nuclear program as not just a deterrence or bargaining chip but also a military capability that can be exported and gain money.

The latter point is, in fact, the link between North Korea's nuclear and missile programs. Developing nuclear capabilities is the first phase, which North Korea has already achieved. The second or parallel phase is to develop long-range missiles that can carry nuclear warheads. There have been ongoing debates about whether Pyongyang has already developed nuclear warheads. Indications from intelligence agencies suggest that North Korea is currently overcoming the technical issues and progressing with its nuclear warheads,[66] despite negotiations with the United States. As John Bolton and other experts have stated, the cooperation between North Korea and Iran will give Iran access to North Korean developments and vice versa, thus allowing both to leap forward with their nuclear and missile technology and capabilities.

Both countries are facing harsh sanctions, and both are looking for ways to lift, cancel, or ease some or all of these. In the Iranian case, the JCPOA led to the freezing of their nuclear program and an increase of investments and trade with Iran, until President Trump decided to withdraw from the JCPOA and reimpose the sanctions. In the North Korean case, negotiations between Kim and Trump were intended, from the former's point of view, to ease and prevent additional sanctions in the short run with a view to lifting the sanctions after the Singapore summit.[67]

Despite the fact that Iran has not yet become a nuclear state, it can become a threshold state without breaching the JCPOA or facing new U.S. sanctions. Over the years, Iran and North Korea have cooperated in the nuclear field, as was seen by Iran's participation in the North Korean nuclear test in 2013.[68] This cooperation gives Iran a "backdoor" plan to continue developing its nuclear program without being detected and provides North Korea with financial support and oil from Iran until the sanctions are lifted.[69]

The Biden Administration—A New Opportunity for Kim?

The election of President Joe Biden, and the negotiation between the United States, Iran, and the other members of P5+1 on the return to the JCPOA agreement, will raise the question about what might be the implications for the relations between Iran and North Korea. Will the new JCPOA include a reference to the Iranian missile capabilities? By doing so, Washington will constrain the missile cooperation between Iran and North Korea. Iran will prefer to sign the JCPOA without adding any additional limitations on its military industry. From Pyongyang's interests, any constraints on the military cooperation between North Korea and Iran pose a potential threat to its foreign income, which is important to the stability of the regime. President Biden's decision to nominate Ambassador Sung as the special envoy to North Korea, sends a clear message to Pyongyang, that Washington wants to restart the negotiation with Pyongyang. But President Biden is currently occupied with the Russia-Ukraine war, the tension between China and Taiwan, the U.S. economy and elections, and the Middle East crisis. North Korea is not the first issue on his agenda. Kim Jong-un will face difficulties to convince Washington to reopen the negotiation when his precondition will include not giving up its nuclear capabilities. The failure to restart the negotiation with Washington will prevent the easing of the sanctions. If Pyongyang will continue to launch middle-long-range missiles and conduct a nuclear test, the Biden administration will impose additional sanctions. The failure to ease the sanctions will force Kim Jong-un to increase the military export to Iran and other parts of the world, in order to overcome the potential economic crisis that might threaten the stability of his regime.

CONCLUSION

The October 10, 2020, military parade in Pyongyang demonstrated North Korea's military might, including the new multiple independently targetable reentry vehicle (MIRV). It served as an internal and external legitimization tool, showing the world what North Korea's military industry can develop and produce for potential customers despite, as Kim Jong-un stated, the economic sanctions and COVID-19.

This does not, however, solve the huge economic challenges facing North Korea. The sanctions, which Kim Jong-un had hoped would be lifted after his meeting with Donald Trump, remain in place at a rising cost to the North Korean economy, which suffers from the constraints on North Korean exports and the lack of countries willing to trade with it. That is one of the main reasons why Iran was and still is an important ally of North Korea. The "axis of evil" alliance has become an important economic lifeline for Pyongyang, therefore critical for the survival of the regime. The new reports on smuggling attempts between North Korea and Iran and the new sanctions imposed by Washington on Iranian people and companies that trade with North Korea demonstrate that Kim Jong-un sees relations with Iran as important enough to risk new sanctions. As stated in the chapter, the economic relations with Iran, especially the military export, are very important for the North Korean economy and the stability of the regime. It is another layer in the survival of the Kim Jong-un regime. It is not the only economic source, but it is an important one.

The Biden administration will not lift the sanctions on North Korea until Pyongyang will be willing to change its precondition for the negotiation. The threat to the stability of Kim Jong-un's regime will continue to increase. In order to survive, Kim Jong-un needs to continue the economic, diplomatic, and military relations with Iran, even if it might breach some of the sanctions that both states face.

The influence of the new JCPOA agreement, if signed, on the relations between Iran and North Korea, will depend on what will be included in the new agreement and if the United States will lift some of the economic sanctions on Iran. If the new JCPOA will not include any additional restrictions on the missile and civilian trade between Iran and North Korea, then one could estimate that both states will continue to trade without any limitations. This will allow Kim Jong-un to continue to stabilize his regime. But, if the Biden administration will include harsh sanctions as part of the new JCPOA and continue the sanctions on North Korea, then Pyongyang and Teheran will have to find new ways to bypass the sanctions in order to gain economic and technological benefits that both states need.

NOTES

1. Bruce E. Bechtol, *North Korea and Regional Security in the Kim Jong-un Era* (London: Palgrave Macmillan, 2014), 23–24; Samuel Ramani, "The North Korean-Iran Relationship: An Anti-American Alliance or Transactional Partnership?"38 North, November 24, 2021, https://www.38north.org/2021/11/the-north -korea-iran-relationship-an-anti-american-alliance-or-transactional-partnership/.

2. Virginie Grzelczyk, *North Korea's New Diplomacy: Challenging Political Isolation in the 21st Century* (London: Palgrave Macmillan, 2018), 84–85, 107.

3. Richard Halloran, "Iran Is Said to Get North Korea Arms," *The New York Times*, December 19, 1982, https://www.nytimes.com/1982/12/19/world/iran-is-said-to-get -north-korea-arms.html.

4. Halloran, "Iran Is Said to Get North Korea Arms," 1.

5. Kamran Taremi, "Ballistic Missiles in Iran's Military Thinking," Wilson Center, October 14, 2003, https://www.wilsoncenter.org/event/ballistic-missiles-irans -military-thinking.

6. Nelson Hansen, "North Korean-Iranian Cooperation," in *Assessment of the Nuclear Programs of Iran and North Korea*, edited by Kang Jungmin, (New York: Springer, 2013), 115–28, 116.

7. Associated Press, "North Korea Cancels Scud-D Sales," January 4, 1994.

8. Michael Elman, "North Korea–Iran Missile Cooperation," 38 North, September 22, 2016, https://www.38north.org/2016/09/melleman092216/; Paul K. Kerr, Steven A. Hildreth, and Mary Beth D. Nikitin, "Iran-North Korea-Syria Ballistic Missile and Nuclear Cooperation," CRS Reports, February 26, 2016, https://fas.org/sgp/crs/nuke /R43480.pdf.

9. Shirzad Azad, *Korean in the Persian Gulf* (London: Routledge, 2015), 72–74.

10. Joshua Pollack, "Ballistic Trajectory," *The Nonproliferation Review* 18, no. 2 (2011): 411–29.

11. Associated Press, "Kim Jong Il Says," August 14, 2000, http://web.lexis-nexis .com.

12. Louis Charbonneau, "North Korea Provides Nuclear Aid to Iran," Reuters, July 7, 2005, https://www.iranfocus.com/en/wpen/nuclear/2760-nkorea-provides-nuclear -aid-to-iran-intel-reports/.

13. *Jerusalem Post*, "North Korea and Iran," July 6, 2006, https://www.jpost.com/ opinion/editorials/north-korea-and-iran-27246.

14. Erich Follath and Holger Stark, "The Story of 'Operation Orchard,'" Spiegel Online, November 2, 2009.

15. The same optimistic view was expressed about Bashar al-Assad and his British education.

16. Alon Levkowitz, "North Korea's Missile Program," BESA Center Perspectives Paper, No. 680, December 10, 2017, https://besacenter.org/perspectives-papers/north -korea-missile-program/.

17. E. Kwan Choi, E. Han Kim, and Yesook Merrill, *North Korea in the World Economy* (London: RoutledgeCruzon, 2003).

18. Tom Bergin, "SWIFT Messaging System Cuts Off Remaining North Korean Banks," Reuters, March 16, 2017, https://www.reuters.com/article/us-northkorea -banks-idUSKBN16N2SZ.

19. Yoram Evron, "A Threefold Cord Is Not Readily Broken: North Korea's Military Bond with Iran and Syria," *Strategic Assessment* 11, no. 1 (June 2008): 76–83.

20. Ankit Panda, *Kim Jong Un and the Bomb* (New York: Oxford University Press, 2020), chapter 5.

21. Refael Ofek and Dany Shoham, "Iran's Korean Nuclear Backdoor," AIJAC, March 31, 2017, https://aijac.org.au/australia-israel-review/iran-s-korean-nuclear-backdoor/.

22. Dan De Luce, "U.N. Investigating Suspected North Korean Arms Dealers in Iran," NBC News, March 12, 2019, https://www.nbcnews.com/news/north-korea/u-n-investigating-suspected-north-korean-arms-dealers-iran-n982016.

23. Alon Levkowitz, "Can South Korea Capitalize on a Second Middle East Boom?" The Diplomat, No. 332, August 25, 2016, http://thediplomat.com/2016/08/can-south-korea-capitalize-on-a-second-middle-east-boom/.

24. In the same way that President Obama justified the JCPOA's economic logic as bringing change to Iran, so can the Sunshine Policy be seen as the basis for change in North Korea. Valérie Gelézeau, Koen De Ceuster, and Alain Delissen, eds. De-Bordering Korea Tangible and Intangible Legacies of the Sunshine Policy (London: Routledge, 2013).

25. Ephraim Asculai, Emily B. Landau, Daniel Shapiro, and Moshe Ya'alon, "Strengthening the JCPOA," INSS Insight, No. 1048 (April 26, 2018): https://www.inss.org.il/publication/strengthening-the-jcpoa/.

26. 기자 백성원 미 전문가 "북-이란 군사협력 전방위 확대 . . . ICBM·핵 커넥션 고도화" [Reporter Baek Baek-won, a U.S. expert, "Expanding North Korea-Iran military cooperation in all directions . . . Advancement of ICBM and nuclear connections"] https://www.voakorea.com/korea/korea-politics/iran-military.

27. Manit Shah and Jose Trevino, "The Iran Deal: A Pathway for North Korea?" Federation of American Scientists, October 14, 2015, https://fas.org/pir-pubs/the-iran-deal-a-pathway-for-north-korea/; U.S. Department of the Treasury, "Treasury Sanctions Those Involved in Ballistic Missile Procurement for Iran." January 17, 2016, https://home.treasury.gov/news/press-releases/jl0322#:%7E:text=Musavi%20is%20the%20SHIG%20commercial,coordinates%20KOMID%20shipments%20to%20Iran.

28. Emily B. Landau, Ephraim Asculai, and Shimon Stein, Confronting Nuclear Proliferation Challenges: Iran and North Korea (Tel Aviv: Institute for National Security Studies, 2018). Andrea Stricker, "Iranian Official Claims Tehran Has Nuclear Threshold Status," July 21, 2022, http://www.fdd.org/analysis/2022/07/21/iranian-official-claims-tehran-has-nuclear-threshold-status.

29. Chung Min Lee, The Hermit King: The Dangerous Game of Kim Jong Un (New York: All Points Books, 2019), chapter 3.

30. "North Korea's Economy Grew in 2019—First Time in 3 Years," Aljazeera, July 31, 2020, https://www.aljazeera.com/economy/2020/07/31/north-koreas-economy-grew-in-2019-first-time-in-3-years/?gb=true.

31. Alon Levkowitz, "North Korea's Missile Program." BESA Center Perspectives Paper, No. 680, December 10, 2017. https://besacenter.org/perspectives-papers/north-korea-missile-program/; Michael Elman, "North Korea–Iran Missile Cooperation," 38 North, September 22, 2016, https://www.38north.org/2016/09/melleman092216/; Michael Elman, "Iran's Missile Test: Getting the Facts Straight on North Korea's Cooperation," 38 North, February 3, 2017, https://www.38north.org/2017/02/melleman020317/, 122.

32. NTI, "The CNC North Korea Missile Test Database," March 31, 2020, https://www.nti.org/analysis/articles/cns-north-korea-missile-test-database/.

33. Virginie Grzelczyk, *North Korea's New Diplomacy: Challenging Political Isolation in the 21st Century* (London: Palgrave Macmillan, 2018), 128.

34. Matthew McGrath and Daniel Wertz, "North Korea's Ballistic Missile Program," *NCNK*, August 2015, https://www.ncnk.org/sites/default/files/NCNK_Missile_Issue_Brief_Aug2015.pdf.

35. Elizabeth Shim, "North Korea Procuring Iranian Missile Technology, Israeli Analyst Says," UPI, April 20, 2016, https://www.upi.com/Top_News/World-News/2016/04/20/North-Korea-procuring-Iranian-missile-technology-Israeli-analyst-says/5281461158692/.

36. Kim Jong Un, "Kim Jong Un's 2018 New Year's Address," NCNK, January 1, 1998, https://www.ncnk.org/node/1427.

37. Mary Beth D.Nikitin and Samuel D. Ryder, "North Korea's Nuclear Weapons and Missile Programs," CRS Reports, July 14, 2020, https://fas.org/sgp/crs/nuke/IF10472.pdf.

38. Nelson E. Hansen, "North Korean–Iranian Cooperation in Ballistic Missile Development," in *Assessment of the Nuclear Programs of Iran and North Korea*, edited by Kang Jungmin (New York: Springer, 2013), 115–28, 126.

39. John Hayward, "John Bolton: If North Korea Gets Nuclear Missiles, 'Iran Could Have That Capability the Next Day by Writing a Check.'" Breitbart, April 28, 2017, https://www.breitbart.com/radio/2017/04/28/john-bolton-if-north-korea-gets-nuclear-missiles-iran-could-have-that-capability-the-next-day-by-writing-a-check/.

40. Elman, "North Korea–Iran Missile Cooperation"; Uzi Rubin, "What Parades in Pyongyang Ends Up in Tehran," BESA Center Perspectives Paper No. 598, September 28, 2017, https://besacenter.org/perspectives-papers/parades-pyongyang-ends-up-tehran/.

41. Nathan Beauchamp-Mustafaga and Scott W. Harold, "Through the Looking Glass: Chinese Open Source Assessments Of North Korea's Ballistic Missile Capabilities," KEI special report, September 10, 2020, http://www.keia.org/sites/default/files/publications/kei_sma_mustafagaharold_200827.pdf, p. 12.

42. Elman, "North Korea-Iran Missile Cooperation."

43. Samuel Ramani, "A Closer Look at Iran and North Korea's Missile Cooperation," The Diplomat, May 13, 2017, https://thediplomat.com/2017/05/a-closer-look-at-iran-and-north-koreas-missile-cooperation/.

44. McGrath and Wertz, "North Korea's Ballistic Missile Program," 5; Ben Cohen, "Failed Submarine-Launched Cruise Missile Test Boosts U.S. Concern over Iran–North Korea Military Alliance," Algemeiner, May 5, 2017, https://www.algemeiner.com/2017/05/05/failed-missile-test-boosts-us-concern-over-iran-north-korea-military-alliance/.

45. NCRIStaff, November 29, 2017, "Iran Regime and North Korea's Collaboration Exposed," NCRI, https://www.ncr-iran.org/en/news/iran-regime-and-north-korea-s-collaboration-exposed/.

46. Staff Writer, March 28, 2016, "North Korean Arms Exporters Visit Iran after U.N. Slaps Sanctions," Yonhap, https://www.ncr-iran.org/en/news/north-korean-arms-exporters-visit-iran-after-u-n-slaps-sanctions-yonhap/.

47. Paul K. Kerr, Steven A. Hildreth, and Mary Beth D. Nikitin, "Iran–North Korea–Syria Ballistic Missile and Nuclear Cooperation," CRS Reports, February 26, 2016, https://fas.org/sgp/crs/nuke/R43480.pdf.

48. Alon Levkowitz, "Giving Pyongyang a 'Bloody Nose,'" BESA Center Perspectives Paper, No. 756, March 1, 2018, https://besacenter.org/perspectives-papers/pyongyang-bloody-nose/.

49. Alon Levkowitz, "The Korean Peninsula: Peaceful Change or Back to Square One?" BESA Center Perspectives Paper, No. 840, May 21, 2018, https://besacenter.org/perspectives-papers/korean-peninsula-optimism/.

50. John Bolton, *The Room Where It Happened* (New York: Simon & Schuster, 2020); Louis Charbonneau, "North Korea Provides Nuclear Aid to Iran—Intel Reports," Reuters, July 7, 2005, chapter 4, https://www.iranfocus.com/en/wpen/nuclear/2760-nkorea-provides-nuclear-aid-to-iran-intel-reports/

51. Project Sandstone, "Anatomy of a North Korean Coal Smuggling Operation," The Diplomat, April 16, 2020, https://thediplomat.com/2020/04/anatomy-of-a-north-korean-coal-smuggling-operation/.

52. Bolton, *The Room Where It Happened*, chapter 3.

53. Christopher Green, "The Modest Diplomatic Promise of North Korea's Charm Offensive," International Crisis Group, March 11, 2018, https://www.crisisgroup.org/asia/north-east-asia/korean-peninsula/modest-diplomatic-promise-north-koreas-charm-offensive.

54. Hugh Griffiths and Matt Schroeder, "Covert Carriers: Evolving Methods and Techniques of North Korean Sanctions Evasion," Small Arms Survey, September 2020, http://www.smallarmssurvey.org/fileadmin/docs/T-Briefing-Papers/SAS-BP-DPRK-Covert-Carriers.pdf; United Nations Security Council, Report of the Panel of Experts Established Pursuant to Resolution 1874 (2009), https://www.undocs.org/S/2010/571.

55. John Haltiwanger, "Kim Jong Un Told Trump Their Friendship Would 'Work as a Magical Force' in Personal 'Love Letters,' New Woodward Book Says," Business Insider, September 9, 2020, https://www.businessinsider.com/kim-jong-un-told-trump-friendship-would-be-magical-force-2020-9.

56. Jeremy Binnie, "U.S. Official Says Iran, North Korea Have Restarted Long-Range Missile Co-Operation," Janes Defense Weekly, September, 22 2020, https://wwwjanes.com/defence-news/news-detail/us-official-says-iran-has-restarted-missile-co-operation-with-north-korea.

57. Steve Holland and Arshad Mohammed, "Exclusive: U.S. to Slap Sanctions on over Two Dozen Targets Tied to Iran Arms," Reuters, September 20, 2020, https://www.reuters.com/article/us-usa-iran-exclusive/exclusive-u-s-to-slap-sanctions-on-over-two-dozen-targets-tied-to-iran-arms-idUSKCN26B0QE.

58. Guy Taylor, "Iran's President Expresses Solidarity with North Korea against 'Common Enemy' U.S." *The Washington Times*, June 25, 2020, https://www

.washingtontimes.com/news/2020/jun/25/hassan-rouhani-iran-president-expresses
-solidarity/.

59. Balazs Szalontai, "'This is Iran, Not North Korea': Conflicting Images of North Korea in Iranian Public Discourse," *North Korean Review* 17, no. 1 (2021): 79–95, page 89.

60. Colin Zwirko, "New North Korean Ambassador to Iran Meets Rouhani, Talks 'common enemy' U.S." NK News, June 29, 2020, https://www.nknews.org/2020/06/new-north-korean-ambassador-to-iran-meets-rouhani-talks-common-enemy-u-s/.

61. Nikitin, *North Korea's Nuclear Test*, CRS Reports, https://crsreports.congress.gov/product/pdf/IF/IF10472.

62. BBC News, "North Korea Nuclear Test: Hydrogen Bomb 'Missile-Ready,'" September 3, 2017, https://www.bbc.com/news/world-asia-41139445.

63. Lee, *The Hermit King*, 144.

64. Lee, *The Hermit King*, 146.

65. Ronen Bergman and Ronen Solomon, "Assad's Atom Program," Yediot Aharonot, April 4, p. 17; C. Pyon, "Syria, Iran Main Buyers of North Korean Chemical Weapons," Radio Free Asia, October 3, 2013, http://www.refworld.org/docid/5261031f8.html.

66. Yonhap News Agency, "N. Korea's SLBM to Complicate Denuclearization Efforts: Ex-Defense Official," October 7, 2020, https://en.yna.co.kr/view/AEN20201007000200325.

67. Lee, *The Hermit King*, 104–5.

68. Times of Israel, "Iranian Nuke Chief was in N. Korea for Atomic Test," February 17, 2013, https://www.timesofisrael.com/iranian-nuke-chief-was-in-n-korea-for-atomic-test/.

69. Alon Levkowitz, "North Korea Did It Again," BESA Center Perspectives Paper, No. 328, February 2, 2016, https://besacenter.org/9785/.

Chapter 7

External Legitimacy in North Korean Survival Diplomacy

Global South and International Organizations

Roberto Dominguez

The North Korean political system remains unique among the authoritarian countries due to the long-lasting personalistic practices around the Kim Dynasty: Kim Il-sung (1948–1994), Kim Jong-il (1994–2011), and Kim Jong-un (since 2011).[1] The extensive literature about the Korean peninsula has covered a wide variety of topics, including the political and economic isolation of North Korea and nuclear security in North-East Asia. The analysis of the external relations of North Korea has also received significant attention, particularly about the countries that play a central role in the strategic calculations of the supreme leader Kim Jong-un: China, South Korea, the United States, Russia, Japan, Germany, and Iran, among others. Less attention has been paid to the relationship between North Korea and countries in the Global South, which is the focus of this chapter.

Numerous Global South countries shared with North Korea some views about the world under the Cold War as the label of Third World represented a comprehensive movement reactive to the bipolar order. However, the world experienced tectonic shifts in the early 1990s marked by advancements and contestations to globalization. The conceptual transit from Third World to the Global South meant to describe the various transformations of political choices of the countries that once were fully committed to the principles of the Conference of Bandung and the Non-Alignment movement. Global South countries have experienced significant changes in a variety of directions.

Some have moved from authoritarian to democratic governments; others have implemented economic policies that produced development, while others have reversed democratic achievements or contested full-fledged market economies. While the academic and political concept of Global South remains operational in analytical terms, it is essential to explain that the diversity of national political, economic, and security calculations greatly varies the relationships between North Korea and Global South countries. Overall, the liberal order remains the general trend of global politics despite the current contestations from some Global South countries. At the same time, North Korea remains centered on implementing policies primarily anchored in the mindset of the Cold War and guided by the third successor of the Kim Dynasty. The result is that North Korea has been self-isolated from the world community and countries in the Global South opted for lowering the profile of relations with North Korea.

This chapter addresses three main questions: (1) What are the changes and continuities between the Kim Jong-il and Kim Jong-un regimes in foreign policy? (2) What are the causes of them? (3) What are the implications for future development in North Korean foreign policy and bilateral relationships? In answering these questions, the chapter argues that the primary rationale of North Korean foreign policy to the Global South is finding external legitimacy, which can be focused on security, economic, or ideological agendas. To develop the argument, the first part reviews some of the premises of the analysis to study the relationship between North Korea and the Global South. The second examines the relationship between North Korea and a selection of Global South countries that, at some point, have played a significant role in North Korean foreign policy. The third part deals with the work that intergovernmental organizations have conducted in North Korea over several years, even though most of them left the country due to conditions of the COVID-19 pandemic in 2020–2021.

EXTERNAL LEGITIMIZATION THROUGH SURVIVAL DIPLOMACY

The role of Global South countries in North Korean foreign policy is marginal compared to the dominant position of South Korea, China, the United States, and Russia, to name a few countries. The literature on North Korean foreign policy is extensive, particularly concerning South Korea, the United States, and China.[2] On the other hand, the research or collection of systematic reflections about North Korean and Global South ties is limited to short academic analyses or case studies and journalism pieces. In the context of the diplomacy of survival and the overwhelming role of the concentration of

North Korean foreign policy in a few key players or usual suspects, Global South countries have increasingly found it difficult to enhance relations with North Korea due to the North Korean pariah's diplomatic status. From the North Korean perspective, countries in the Global South represent limited valves of escape that provide external legitimization and, eventually, some economic and, in some cases, modest security gains.

Based on the thin North Korean–Global South relationship, the realist and liberal theories provided little explanation. From the perspective of this chapter, the literature about North Korean foreign policy provides some elements to understand North Korean diplomacy of survival. Woo has developed the concept of the balance of dependence.[3] In his view, particularly after the end of the Cold War, Pyongyang's foreign policy under Kim Jong-il had been attuned to the rise and fall of assistance from other nations. It sought to disperse its dependence on a host of potential sponsors to not be exclusively reliant on a single donor state, fearing restrictions on its political autonomy. The rationale behind such a strategy included avoiding exclusive dependence, obtaining insurance, and eliciting competition among donors. The balance of dependence argument is constructive to explore the shifting strategies of North Korea toward its main and significant allies, adversaries, and by extension, the limited role of Global South countries.

On the other hand, like the analyses of the foreign policy of authoritarian regimes, North Korean foreign policy behavior is an enigma to many observers. Bae presents a theory of how politics within personalist regimes influence foreign policy and tests whether the logic of enhancing domestic stability drives North Korean conflict behavior under the personalist rule of the Kims.[4] The diversionary war theory posits that leaders have an incentive to initiate conflict when facing domestic turmoil to divert attention from the source of discontent and boost support for the leader.[5] Against this background, some contextual elements characterize the Global South and North Korea relations. The first is that the geopolitical and ideological position of North Korea limits the options for diversification with underdeveloped countries. Compared to the Eastern European countries at the end of the Cold War, North Korea tried to keep itself from being too dependent on the Soviet Union and China.[6] In the past two decades, North Korea has become very reliant on China and, to a lesser extent Russia. Second, this dependency has been reinforced. The North Korean siege mentality has been self-initiated by a national leader who voluntarily isolates his or her society from the international.[7] Third, relations with underdeveloped countries are motivated by very narrow niches of opportunities in the political, economic, and humanitarian areas to legitimize the North Korean regime. With notable exceptions (Pakistan), most of the actions of North Korea in the Global South are driven by limited economic exchanges in the areas of trade or military exchanges, ideological reinforcement (Cuba), or humanitarian cooperation (WHO or India). The chapter explores the relations between North Korea and the Global South and embraces the notion of external legitimization, following the research of Del Sordi and Dalmasso,[8] as part of the diplomacy of survival. In the last few years, the scholarly literature on authoritarian legitimation has made significant headway in understanding how regimes try to achieve a certain level of widespread belief in the justness of their rule within the *selectorate* and the *ejectorate*.[9] The authoritarian quest for legitimacy has an international dimension, too, in which authoritarian elites observe the global context and produce discourses and policies that aim to create a positive country brand. Following Del Sordi and Dalmasso's argument,[10] authoritarian leaders use the international recognition they obtain to legitimize their rule at home. However, due to the personalistic nature of the North Korean regime, the internal dimension is difficult to operationalize. Nonetheless, the argument explores the international legitimization of North Korean gains concerning Global South countries to reinforce North Korean positions against the policies of great powers and the UN sanction regime.

Countries

The overwhelming role of China, Russia, and the United States in North Korean external relations leaves a small room to maneuver global South countries for political, security, and economic ties. Subject to some nuances in specific cases, Global South countries have increasingly observed the North Korean nuclear policy as a political and security liability, and ideological alignments or disagreements have often guided diplomatic relations.

Economic relations are indicative of the priorities in foreign policy. In the case of North Korea, due to its centralized and authoritarian characteristics, the major caveat is the reliability of economic data. For identifying the main economic partners of North Korea in the Global South, table 7.1 compiles information from 2000, 2005, 2010, 2015, and 2020 based on the Observatory of Economic Complexity. In the case of imports, one can draw general trends from the table. First, China has an increasing and consistent role in North Korean imports, representing 27.2 percent in 2000 and 95.7 percent in 2018. Second, some Global South countries have ranked consistently in the list of the top-ten partners of North Korean imports, but in a minimal percentage: Russia, India, and Thailand. Third, other countries have inconsistently been in and out of the list of the leading North Korean import partners: Brazil, Qatar, Ukraine, Gabon, and South Africa. Regarding North Korean exports, trade relations are more diversified but still highly concentrated in China, representing 62.5 percent of all North Korean exports in 2018. The Global

Table 7.1: Main Export Destinations of North Korea (2000–2020). Main Countries Exporting to North Korea (North Korea Imports) (2000–2020).

	2000			2005	
	Exports to (in US million)	% of total exports		Exports to (in US million)	% of total exports
Japan	251	22.5	China	469	35.1
Mexico	155	13.9	Thailand	130	9.73
Brazil	118	10.6	Japan	128	9.58
Ghana	65.4	5.86	Brazil	70.1	5.24
Spain	64.2	5.76	Mexico	67.1	5.02
Saudi Arabia	56.2	5.04	Dom. Rep.	56.9	4.25
Bangladesh	50.3	4.51	Saudi Arabia	35.7	2.67
Hong Kong	45.6	4.09	France	29.8	2.23
China	34.8	3.12	Poland	29.4	2.2
France	25.6	2.3	Germany	27.8	2.08

	2010			2015	
	Exports to (in US million)	% of total exports		Exports to (in US million)	% of total exports
China	1.11B	59.4	China	2.36B	82.4
Brazil	117	6.22	India	97.9	3.42
Netherlands	79.9	4.26	Pakistan	43.4	1.52
Egypt	65.4	3.49	Burkina Faso	33.1	1.16
Mexico	44.8	2.39	Chinese Taipei	27	0.94
India	44.7	2.38	Saudi Arabia	25.4	0.89
Venezuela	42.1	2.25	Chile	24.3	0.85
Sri Lanka	35	1.87	Paraguay	16.6	0.58
Germany	33.7	1.8	Brazil	15.5	0.54
Saudi Arabia	24.4	1.3	Zambia	13.8	0.48

	2020	
	Exports to (in US million)	% of total exports
China	44.1	31
Burma	24	16.9
Poland	20.6	14.5
Nigeria	6.57	4.61
Luxembourg	5.09	3.58
Uganda	4.21	2.96
Mozambique	4.15	2.91
Togo	3.29	2.31
Costa Rica	2.29	1.61
Burkina Faso	1.73	1.21

Source: Own elaboration with the collaboration of Rafal Stanislaw Fryc based on data provided by the Observatory of Economic Complexity: https://oec.world/en/profile/country/prk.

South top destinations of North Korean exports have been inconsistent, but some countries have experienced some stability as destinations: Pakistan, India, Saudi Arabia, and Zambia, among others.

The review of the relations between North Korea and some Global South countries can indicate some general trends in the diplomacy of survival. Asia, India and Pakistan have been consistent North Korean partners defined by two elements. First, Pyongyang's closeness with China produces two opposite effects in Pakistan (positive) and India (negative), primarily explained by the competitive or cooperative relationship between the two South Asian countries with China. Second, while the North Korean nuclear policy is a concern for both Pakistan and India, the former has been inclined to cooperate with North Korea. In contrast, the latter has taken a cautious distance.[11] In the realm of trade, Pakistan and India are two of the most important partners of North Korea in Asia. In 2018, Pakistan (27.8 million USD) and India (25 million USD) were the top export destinations of North Korea after China (1.58 billion USD), which received more than 90 percent of North Korean exports.[12]

In the context of the Cold War, Pakistan and North Korea started diplomatic relations in the 1970s. Prime Minister Zulfikar Ali Bhutto Zulfikar (1973–1977) visited North Korea as part of his foreign policy campaign to strengthen relations with socialist states. During the Iran–Iraq War (1980–1988), still under the Cold War, North Korea and Pakistan found common interests in supporting Iran and have informally cooperated in nuclear policy. In 2002, information leaked that Pakistan had been the source of North Korea's development of nuclear warheads. Pyongyang gave missile technology to Islamabad, and Pakistan transferred nuclear technology to North Korea through the network of Pakistani nuclear engineer Abdul Qadeer Khan.[13] Beyond the scandal related to AQ. Khan, Tierney indicates that from the North Korean perspective, the Pakistani model must look compelling, mainly because Pakistan's nuclear weapons have successfully deterred India.[14] After refusing to sign the Non-Proliferation Treaty, Pakistan faces restrictions on importing civilian nuclear technology, but nuclear weapons have deterred India.

The other relevant South Asian country is India. North Korea and India maintain their open diplomatic representations, and the meetings are cordial regarding Indian humanitarian assistance. Yet, there is no bilateral agreement regarding good North Korean relations with Pakistan.[15] While North Korean civilians were allowed to take courses related to nuclear weapons development, advanced physics, computer science, and aviation engineering at Indian schools, India began to move away from those policies in 2017. Also, India indicated that it would implement North Korean sanctions and ban North Korean military officers from training in the country in response to South Korean pressure to implement UNSC sanctions resolutions.[16] While India has repeatedly condemned North Korean nuclear tests and views its nuclear program as a threat to regional security, in humanitarian assistance, India is sensitive to the shortage of medical supply situation in North Korea. The Indian mission in Pyongyang continues providing medical aid delivered under the WHO's anti-tuberculosis program,[17] even in the context of the COVID-19 pandemic.[18]

Relations between North Korea and some African countries operated under the ideological alignment characteristic of the Cold War. For the past three decades, the relationship has been relatively marginal in general, and the scattered information allows us to identify two main areas linking up North Korea and some African countries. The first is the conflict between technical and military cooperation on the one hand, and the implementation of UNSC Resolutions, on the other. The second is the role of some African countries as recipients of North Korean exports. In November 2018, U.S. Secretary of State Rex Tillerson called for African nations to take additional measures to pressure the DPRK by downgrading their diplomatic relations with Pyongyang, urging them to sever economic ties and expel all North Korean laborers.[19]

The reports of the Panel of Experts (PoE) that monitor UN resolutions have presented evidence of the problems African countries are experiencing in implementing UNSC resolutions regarding North Korea. Overall, unresponsiveness from the African continent has stymied the UN's efforts, particularly regarding the late submissions of national implementation reports (NIRs).[20] One example is UNSC Resolution 2270 (2016).[21] In the area of military cooperation, according to the UN, Pyongyang has conducted military training in Angola, Uganda, and the Democratic Republic of the Congo (DRC); attempted to ship military communications equipment to Eritrea; imported arms to Mozambique; repaired military equipment in Tanzania; and built military-related facilities in Namibia.[22] In response, some countries accused of violating the sanctions have denied wrongdoing or dismissed the UN's legitimacy, while others have provided some evidence of cutting military cooperation with North Korea.

Sudan, Angola, and Tanzania are three examples of the tensions between military cooperation and UNCS resolutions. Sudan committed to cutting ties with North Korea in 2016 to improve its relationship with Washington. In a positive gesture, in July 2017, Washington said that it had extended the review period of its sanctions against Sudan to ensure it was fulfilling its international obligations to the DPRK. Some of Sudan's previous military cooperation with North Korea came to light in 2011 when a WikiLeaks cable revealed U.S. concerns over a weapons deal between the two countries.[23] Along the same lines, Angola stopped importing any small arms or light weapons from North Korea, a move that marked a significant shift in the relations between Luanda and Pyongyang, with the two having maintained close ties since the 1970s.[24] In the case of Tanzania, the UN Panel of Experts reports indicated investigations of a contract worth 10.4 million Euros to repair and upgrade the surface-to-air missile Pechora (S-125) and the P-12 systems. While Tanzania has said since then that the contract terminated in 2014, it appears, according to the PoE, that in July 2016, military cooperation resumed.[25]

Regarding the area of trade, most of the contracts with African countries represent small amounts considering the dominant position of China in North Korean imports and exports (see table 7.1). From Senegal and Guinea, North Korea imports frozen and fresh fish; from Benin, North Korea imports raw cotton and scrap iron; South Africa imports refined petroleum and various other goods. And, from Burkina Faso, North Korea imports vegetable products. Exported goods from North Korea are similarly diverse. North Korea exports refined petroleum to Burkina Faso and Benin. To Zambia, Mozambique, and Egypt, North Korea exports cars, plastics, rubbers, and dozens of other goods.[26] However, UN sanctions, particularly after Resolution 2371 in August 2017, have imposed some limits on North Korean trade relations. Angola terminated all contracts with North Korea's Mansudae Overseas Projects (MOP),[27] as indicated in the 2017 Angolan report on the implementation of the UN Security Council (UNSC) resolutions 2321, 2356, 2371, and 2375. Despite such limitations, a delegation led by Ho Yong Bok, a foreign ministry official, visited the country intending to increase cooperation in public health, construction, and IT fields.[28] On the other hand, Namibia, a significant hub for MOP operations, also provided the PoE with a 350-page response to the group's inquiries on November 17, 2017. It announced that "all DPRK workers have left the country" and—like Angola—supplied supporting documentation.[29]

One of the most documented cases of the inner workings of North Korean relations with Africa is Mozambique. In 2020, the Permanent Mission of the Republic of Mozambique to the United Nations submitted a report on the implementation of sanctions imposed by the Security Council on North Korea under resolution 1718 (2006).[30] The issue of North Koreans earning income abroad, which officially became a prohibited activity under UN sanctions, was addressed in the report, with Mozambique claiming extensive, deliberate actions to prevent any violation. It also indicated that except for medical doctors working under a specific protocol in the health sector, no citizen of that country had been hired since 2015. Mozambique defended ongoing medical cooperation and North Korea's contributions as vital toward fulfilling UN Sustainable Development Goals but did say it would necessarily end in 2021.[31]

When the analysis of North Korean–Global South relations turns to Latin America, the evaluation is that North Korea faces increasing isolation. Ideological reasons influence North Korean foreign policy drivers to the region in the cases of Cuba and Venezuela. At the same time, many Latin American countries have opted to lower the profile of diplomatic relations and condemn the North Korean nuclear policy. From the economic perspective, Brazil is the Latin American country with a more consistent presence in the external trade of North Korea, followed by Mexico. Other Latin American countries have ranked among the top-ten North Korean trade partners in an episodic way, largely explain for short-term increases and decreases in the trade of one or a few specific goods. These are the cases of Chile, Paraguay, the Dominican Republic, and Colombia (see table 7.1). In addition to the structural weakness of the economic and diplomatic relations of Latin America with North Korea, the United States has called on Latin American countries, particularly Brazil, Mexico, and Peru, to sever ties with North Korea, as U.S. Vice President Mike Pence, did during a visit to Chile in 2017.[32]

Regarding the two main North Korean ideological allies, Cuba has been one of the most consistent partners since 1960, when both countries established diplomatic relations. Both countries have forged a bond of solidarity based on their militant positions opposing American power from the Cold War to the Trump administration. After Fidel Castro died in 2016, the North Korean government declared a three-day mourning period and sent an official delegation to his funeral. Cuban President Miguel Díaz-Canel visited Pyongyang in 2018 for the first state visit by a Cuban leader to North Korea in over thirty years, joining the country's leader Kim Jong-un in condemning the foreign policy of the United States.[33] North Korea and Cuba signed a trade agreement in 2016 to exchange goods via a barter system, helping North Korea with the problems of scarcity of foreign currency. The international community questioned Cuban-North Korean solidarity when a North Korean vessel was infamously caught smuggling weaponry and military systems, hidden under ten thousand tons of sugar, through the Panama Canal in 2013.[34]

In contrast to Cuba, Venezuela has developed an ideological affinity since Hugo Chavez was elected. In 2015, North Korea reopened its embassy in Caracas, as solidarity between Caracas and Pyongyang has strengthened. The two countries also signed a bilateral agreement to build a giant statute in Venezuela and for cooperation in agriculture and the food industry.[35] In 2018, the president of the Supreme People's Assembly, Kim Yong-nam, visited Venezuela to meet with President Nicolás Maduro as part of Yong-nam's tour to Cuba, Mexico, and Venezuela. In the 2019 Venezuelan presidential crisis, North Korea was among the twenty-two countries recognizing Nicolás Maduro as the president of Venezuela.[36]

North Korea has kept a low profile in Mexican, Brazilian, and Peruvian policies. Mexico has repeatedly condemned all missile launches from North Korea. In June 2009, as a nonpermanent member of the UNSC, Mexico voted in favor of United Nations Security Council Resolution 1874,[37] which imposed further economic and commercial sanctions on North Korea and encouraged UN member states to search North Korean cargo ships. While Mexico and North Korea established diplomatic relations in September 1980, it wasn't until 1993 that North Korea opened an embassy in Mexico City. However, the bilateral relationship has faced several diplomatic disagreements. In July 2014, a 6,700-ton cargo called the Mu Du Bong ship was stranded on the reef nine miles from Tuxpan, Veracruz. Mexico detained the vessel after discovering it belonged to a blacklisted shipping firm. The merchant ship was never released back to North Korea, and in 2016, Mexico began scrapping the boat and releasing the crew members back to their home country.[38] In September 2017, the Mexican government declared persona non grata the ambassador of North Korea in Mexico, Kim Hyong-gil, and expelled him, a decision that followed the sixth nuclear test carried out by Pyongyang. In December 2018, bilateral relations improved when Kim Yong-nam, president of the Presidium of the Supreme People's Assembly of North Korea, arrived in Mexico City to attend the inauguration of President Andrés Manuel López Obrador.

Brazil has consistently condemned the North Korean nuclear program. In July 2009, Brazil announced the inauguration of the embassy in Pyongyang, making Brazil one of the only twenty-five countries with an embassy in North Korea. Few knew at the time that it had been President Fernando Henrique Cardoso (1995–2003) who decided to open an embassy in North Korea in the context of South Korea's Sunshine Policy[39] toward the North, in a move welcomed by leaders in Seoul. While Brasilia decided to open an embassy at the height of the Sunshine Policy, it was only opened in 2009, by the time the rapprochement in the Korean peninsula had vanished.[40] In the case of Peru, bilateral relations have deteriorated over time. Both established diplomatic ties in 1988. North Korea supplied the Peruvian government with rifles to combat the Shining Path insurgency. Regarding North Korean nuclear tests, the government of Peru has repeatedly called on the government of North Korea to stop these types of actions immediately. In September 2017, Peru expelled the North Korean diplomats due to the violations of because of UNSC resolutions, including Resolution 2397.[41]

International Organizations

This section reviews the role of international organizations in North Korea. While most of the literature refers to UN resolutions, the role of the UN and its agencies in North Korea is quite significant. On several occasions, UN

Secretary-General Guterres has expressed his deep concern at the evolution of nuclear policies in the DPRK as well as the dialogue between the two Koreas.[42] The UN Security Council has enacted numerous resolutions regarding North Korean nuclear policies and sanctions as well.[43] But some other agencies have also played a significant policy in implementing engaging diplomacy.

UN resolutions constrain the relationship of Global South countries with North Korea in several forms. For instance, UNSC resolutions target North Korea's trade in coal, iron, lead, and seafood. Also, resolutions target the DPRK's use of foreign labor, another of the North Korean government's sources of foreign currency. It is estimated that more than fifty thousand North Korean workers are employed throughout Asia, the Middle East, Europe, and Africa.[44] In 2020, the UN Security Council (UNSC) committee overseeing North Korean sanctions published an annual report on the DPRK's alleged efforts to evade the UN's rules and keep cash flowing into the country through illicit means.[45] Regardless of the loopholes, UN resolutions have established coercive restrictions. Still, in parallel, the overall goal of UN agencies is to support and reinforce national efforts to ensure people's health and well-being, especially the most vulnerable, and to build their resilience. The work of the six UN agencies operating in North Korea is too complicated because of three restrictions. First, the North Korean government monitors and eventually restricts staff and mobility outside Pyongyang.[46]

Secondly, UN resolutions impose restrictions on the work of the international organization inside North Korea, particularly regarding imports of goods prohibited by UNSC resolutions. The third layer of complexity is how the global context and internal discussions of North Korean influence the decisions to increase or decrease the freedom of action of international organizations operating in North Korea. For instance, because of the COVID-19 pandemic in 2020, workers from the six UN agencies in Pyongyang have been unable to implement or monitor projects in rural areas, creating significant obstacles to humanitarian operations in North Korea in 2020 and potentially beyond.[47]

Although the obstacles to the work of international organizations in North Korea, the diplomacy of engagement provides several benefits for paving the way for a peaceful transition or openness of the North Korean regime, the first is that UN agencies develop communication and coordination with North Korean agencies, leading a better understanding of how policies work inside North Korea. Second, the UN network has created an interagency model of collaboration with numerous partners within and outside the United Nations, including the United Nations Development Program (UNDP), the United Nations Population Fund (UNFPA), the World Food Program (WFP), the Food and Agriculture Organization (FAO), the World Health Organization

(WHO), the Swiss Development Cooperation (SDC) as well as the embassies of Germany, the United Kingdom, and Sweden, to mention a few.[48] In sum, the role of the UN and UN agencies goes far beyond the nuclear policy and the UNSC sanctions. The demand for improving the living conditions of North Koreans opens a gateway between the North Korean government and the international community.

Over the past three decades, FAO has cooperated with North Korea providing agricultural technical assistance ranging from agroforestry, fruit and crop production, and marine aquaculture to transboundary pest and disease control. Emergency support has been a significant feature of cooperation in the past. More comprehensive program approaches to development have been adopted since the second half of the 1990s, including an increasing focus on issues such as food safety. FAO work covers eight out of eleven provinces, spread across sixty-six counties. Policymakers, government staff, and researchers in North Korea have benefited from various international study tours and regional FAO programs that have enabled the exchange of experiences and expertise. During the early years of 1985 to 2000, the United Nations Development Program (UNDP) funded seventeen long-term technical cooperation projects with a total value of close to 12 million USD, while more than fifty FAO were financed and implemented in agriculture, livestock, forestry, and fisheries. More than twenty large-scale FAO programs for double cropping were implemented during the 2000s with a value of well over 17 million USD, with Sweden, Norway, Denmark, and Italy as the leading donors. During the decade, the double-cropping program evolved into the National Special Program for Food Security, and the Italian government provided funding to support it.[49]

North Korea has been a member of the WHO since 1973. In 1997, a WHO Emergency and Humanitarian Action (EHA) office was established to deal with the deteriorating health and humanitarian situation in DPR Korea. The collaboration between the government of North Korea and the WHO has developed positively over the years and expanded after establishing the WHO Country Office in Pyongyang in November 2001. WHO supports the public health program in the country based on the WHO Country Cooperation Strategy (2014–2019), which is an organizational requirement, and as guided by WHO's Global Program of Work (GPW) 2014–2019 and the biennial program budget approved by all member states of WHO.[50]

The partnership between UNICEF and WHO brings many benefits to implementing Gavi HSS support in the Democratic People's Republic of Korea. This is a win-win arrangement for all parties involved, including MoPH, Gavi, UNICEF, and WHO (WHO 2020). With organizations such as Global funds for AIDS, tuberculosis (TB), and malaria (GFATM) and Global Alliance for Vaccine and Immunization (GAVI), and the adoption of innovative communication for development strategies.[51] Sustained high and equitable vaccination coverage of more than 96 percent across the country for the last three years helped North Korea achieve measles-free status, attested by the World Health Organization (WHO) Regional Verification Committee in 2018. However, WHO has defined DPRK as one of the countries most affected by TB. Tuberculosis has been recognized as one of the biggest public health problems in North Korea. In 2017, WHO reported some 131,000 cases of TB in North Korea, with some 16,000 individuals succumbing to the disease in the same year.[52]

The UNICEF country program seeks to enhance the development of a national policy environment conducive to children through advocacy, increased technical support to key ministries, and building strategic alliances. Despite the limitations of the isolated North Korean economy, recurrent food crises, and the gap between rural and urban, some development has been made. UNICEF data show significant improvements in key indicators of child survival compared to previous data, with a high degree of equity in most basic service indicators.[53] According to the United Nations Inter-Agency Group for Child Mortality Estimation, between 2000 and 2017, the DPRK under-five mortality rate decreased steadily from sixty to nineteen deaths per one thousand live births, while the official national estimate puts it at eighteen per one thousand live births.[54]

The World Food Program (WFP) has been in DPR Korea since 1995. From the distribution of cereals and biscuits for the nutrition program in the sixty most vulnerable counties across nine provinces to the assistance of children in nurseries, kindergartens, hospitals, and boarding schools, as well as pregnant and lactating women and girls, the WFP provides a wide range of humanitarian actions. More importantly, from the perspective of diplomacy of engagement, it involves the participation of multiple stakeholders. On the one hand, to a great extent, the North Korean government provides the input that determines the UN Country Team requirements. On the other, the work of the WFP sets in motion a network of donors to implement humanitarian commitments. In 2020, for instance, out of the 107 million USD needed for humanitarian assistance, WFP's funding requirements represent 50 percent, which will depend on continued resource partnerships with its long-term partners, including Switzerland, Russia, Sweden, Canada, France, as well as new partners who reengaged as donors in 2019, such as Republic of Korea, India, Norway.[55]

Within the United Nations family, the International Atomic Energy Agency (IAEA) is a crucial organization related to North Korean nuclear developments. Even though the North Korean government does not allow IAEA inspections, the agency continues to monitor the nuclear program of North Korea, using open-source information and satellite imagery. While no significant recent changes have been observed, the IAEA remains ready to resume verification of North Korea's nuclear program if a political agreement is reached among the countries concerned.[56]

In the area of human rights, the United Nations Human Rights Council established the Commission of Inquiry on Human Rights in the Democratic People's Republic of Korea (DPRK) in 2013. The mandate was to investigate the DPRK's systematic, widespread, and grave human rights violations to ensure full accountability, particularly for violations that may amount to crimes against humanity. The establishment of the Commission of Inquiry must also be seen considering the DPRK's limited cooperation with the existing human rights mechanisms. The DPRK is a state party to the International Covenant on Civil and Political Rights (ICCPR), the International Covenant on Economic and Social Rights (ICESCR), the Convention on the Rights of the Child (CRC), and the Convention on the Elimination of All Forms of Discrimination against Women (CEDAW). However, since 2009, the DPRK has failed to submit reports to the different UN human rights mechanisms. Since the publication of the report in 2014, which presented evidence of systematic, widespread, and grave human rights violations, the cooperation between the DPRK and the UN Human Rights Council has been limited and sporadic.[57]

Regarding regional organizations, ASEAN Regional Forum (ARF) has approached North Korea with a two-fold strategy. On the one hand, ASEAN keeps North Korea as a member and opens the dialogue about regional security concerns. On the other, it helps to build a bridge between North Korea and other ARF partners such as the United States or the European Union. For several years, Pyongyang regularly sent its foreign minister to the ARF until 2018, when it started dispatching less-senior officials, which can be interpreted as a sign of distancing from the ARF. In 2022, South Korean Foreign Minister Park Jin called for an unconditional dialogue between the two Koreas during his brief exchange with a North Korean envoy participating in the ASEAN Regional Forum in Phnom Penh. Following the pattern of sending less-seniors officials, North Korea sent An Kwang-il, the North's ambassador to Indonesia, rather than the minister of foreign affairs.[58]

International organizations in North Korea have been one of the most effective aid instruments to alleviate the problem of isolationism. However, the global pandemic deeply affected North Korea, which faced its worst economic and food crises in over two decades. In contrast to the return of other countries to the post-pandemic "new normal," North Korea has fewer instruments at its disposal. Typically, North Korea would aim to meet the shortfall through a combination of food aid and commercial imports. But trade with China remains very slow as of mid-2021, and the last two international staff members for the United Nations WFP left Pyongyang in March 2021, as part of an exodus of foreigners caused by the strict lockdowns there.[59]

CONCLUSIONS

This chapter addressed three interrelated questions about North Korean external relations toward Global South countries: (1) changes and continuities in foreign policy, (2) causes, and (3) prospects. The research conducted in this chapter finds that the general trend in the North Korean–Global South / international organizations' relationship is that North Korea has become more isolated. The causes of the general direction of isolation resulted from domestic and international factors. The unrelenting nuclear policy and the lack of adaptation to the changing global circumstances are domestic options primarily determined by the roles of a deep-seated exclusive ideology, personalistic political practices, and the vicious circle of zero-sum game mindset in security and stability. The international factors that exacerbate and reinforce North Korean isolation are the UNSC resolution regime and the marginalization of North Korea in the foreign policy of countries in the Global South. On the other hand, international organizations around the UN agencies delivering humanitarian aid face the double restrictions from the UNSC resolution regime and the North Korean regime.

The legitimation of survival diplomacy faces a bleak future. This chapter argues that the primary rationale of North Korean survival diplomacy to the Global South and the UN system of agencies is finding external legitimacy, which can be focused on security, economic, humanitarian, or ideological agendas. From the cost-benefit analysis, the gains of exchanges with Global South countries are limited but essential for the North Korean regime. However, in a three-decade period, underdeveloped countries have taken some distance from the North Korean government for two reasons, at least. First, there is increasing condemnation of nuclear tests and policies from countries with a traditionally adverse approach to atomic arms (Latin America). Second, some countries are more inclined to implement UNSC Resolutions (Africa/Asia) due to international or domestic pressure. As table 7.1 indicates, there is a general concentration trend of North Korean exports to and imports from China. On the other hand, Global South countries tend to have a marginal and irregular trade volume of exchanges with North Korea.

Despite the seemingly conciliatory diplomacy of the United States with North Korea, there is no clear evidence of a significant change in North Korea. It remains in self-isolation mode, anchored in a metastasized authoritarian and personalistic regime, and frozen in the nuclear strategy is crucial for survival. For Pyongyang, as Tierney[60] argues, the Pakistani atomic design is a model to follow, as opposed to the Libyan or Iraqi models that faced the perils of disarmament. In this regard, Islamabad and Pyongyang share essential similarities. They both face an enduring rivalry with a far more powerful democratic state that used to be part of the same country (India and South Korea). Both are formal sideliners of international law in nuclear weapons: in 2003, North Korea withdrew from the Non-Proliferation Treaty, while Pakistan never signed the treaty. For decades, North Korea and Pakistan have been informal allies, trading conventional weapons and supporting Iran in the Iran–Iraq War.[61]

Overall, the potential future transformations in the Korean peninsula remain marginal, primarily for Global South countries. The debate about the future and the stability of North Korea has envisioned two opposing scenarios. On the one hand, there is the soft-landing perspective. This option suggests that the ideology and system of a unified Korea should be constructed through compromise and negotiation between the two Koreas. On the other hand, we have the hard-landing theory, which emphasizes the broader economic benefits of rapid unification.[62] Both potential strategies are mainly contingent on the decision of the main stakeholders, and the Global South plays a marginal role in it. From the perspective of the UN system of agencies, the limits of their work inside North Korea recurrently lack funding for human rights and humanitarian operations. In 2019, the UN calculated that international aid operations remained critical for over 10 million people, around 40 percent of the population and about 120 million USD dollars were required for life-saving humanitarian operations in the country, having a funding gap of 87 million USD.[63] In 2018, the WFP indicated a massive 73 percent shortfall in funding, hurting critical programs such as nutritional support for children.[64]

Further survival diplomacy and isolation in a context of limited information are detrimental to engagement diplomacy. One of the challenges with the increasing isolation of North Korea is the loss of international understanding of domestic events in North Korea. Diplomats and officials of international organizations can at least ask for official briefings on policy and events, question officials directly, and also maintain contact with people who can at least give some sense of the preoccupations of the upper levels of the North Korean government.[65] In 2020–2021, the COVID-19 pandemic reinforced the isolation and mobility of diplomats and UN officials, which is detrimental to learning about significant development in North Korea.

One of the challenges is to shift from survival diplomacy to engagement diplomacy. The North Korean acceptance of the 113 recommendations from the 2019 Universal Periodic Review and the advent of the 2030 Development Agenda are two examples that provide strategic opportunities to drill a loophole in isolated North Korea.[66] The silent role of engagement is discreet and potentially can pave the way for opportunities if a tectonic event alters the current approaches of the North Korean regime. The insistence of the world community, generically understood, in continuing humanitarian assistance has been quite beneficial for learning from, engaging with, and persuading the North Korean regime.

NOTES

1. Rafal Stanislaw Fryc conducted research for this chapter. My appreciation for his feedback and work as a research assistant.
2. Weiqi Zhang, "Pursuing Interdependence and Independence: North Korea's Foreign Policy on China," 2021, chapter 2 in this volume.
3. Seongji Woo, "Balance of Dependence: The Making of North Korean Foreign Policy under Kim Jong Il," *The Korean Journal of Defense Analysis* 30, no. 4 (2018): 475–92.
4. Joonbum Bae, "The North Korean Regime, Domestic Instability and Foreign Policy," *North Korean Review* 14, no. 1 (2018): 85–101.
5. Ibid.
6. Samuel Yee, "Surviving through the Post–Cold War Era: The Evolution of Foreign Policy in North Korea," *Berkeley Undergraduate Journal* 21, no. 2 (2008).
7. Bomi Kim, "North Korea's Siege Mentality: A Sociopolitical Analysis of the Kim Jong-un Regime's Foreign Policies," *Asian Perspective* 40 (2016): 223–44.
8. Adele Del Sordi and Emanuela Dalmasso, "The Relation between External and Internal Authoritarian Legitimation: The Religious Foreign Policy of Morocco and Kazakhstan," *Taiwan Journal of Democracy* 14, no. 1 (2018): 95–116.
9. Zhang, "Pursuing Interdependence and Independence."
10. Del Sordi and Dalmasso, "The Relation between External and Internal Authoritarian Legitimation."
11. Megha Bahree, "Look Who's Helping North Korea," *Forbes*, June 22, 2010.
12. Katharina Buchholz, "Who Is North Korea Trading With?" *Statista*, September 6, 2019, https://www.statista.com/chart/10683/north-korea-trading-partners/.
13. Sharon A. Squassoni, "Weapons of Mass Destruction: Trade between North Korea and Pakistan," *CRS Report to Congress*, 2006.
14. Dominic Tierney, "North Korea Wants to End up Like Pakistan, Not Libya," *The Atlantic*, May 26, 2018.
15. World Politics Review, "India's Ties with North Korea Cordial but Limited," *World Politics Review*, April 23, 2015, https://www.worldpoliticsreview.com/trend -lines/15604/india-s-ties-with-north-korea-cordial-but-limited.
16. Elizabeth Shim, "India Delivers $1M in Medical Assistance to North Korea," United Press International, July 22, 2020, https://www.upi.com/Top_News /World-News/2020/07/22/India-delivers-1M-in-medical-assistance-to-North-Korea /1691595430966/.
17. According to 2018 WHO data, there are an estimated 131,000 tuberculosis patients in North Korea (Shim, "India Delivers $1M.").

Chapter 7

18. Prashasti Awasthi, "India Extends Medical Support of $1 Mn to North Korea to fight TB," *The Hindu Business Line*, July 25, 2020, https://www.thehindubusinessline.com/news/india-extends-medical-support-of-1-mn-to-north-korea-to-fight-tb/article32190273.ece#.

19. Dagyum Ji, "Angola Terminates 'All Contracts' with North Korea's Mansudae Company: Report," NK News, January 29, 2018, https://www.nknews.org/2018/01/angola-terminates-all-contracts-with-north-koreas-mansudae-art-studio-report/.

20. NIRs detail how member states are carrying out approved sanctions.

21. The United Nations Security Council unanimously adopted Resolution 2270 on March 2, 2016, with approval of all the five permanent members and the ten non-permanent members in response to North Korea's fourth nuclear test on January 6, 2016, and its launch of a long-range missile carrying what it said was a satellite on February 7, 2016.

22. Salem Solomon, "Africa's Ties to North Korea Extend beyond Isolated Military Deals," Thai News Service, September 17, 2017.

23. Leo Byrne, "Sudan Ready to Cut Ties with North Korea: Local Media," NK News, November 16, 2017, https://www.nknews.org/2017/11/sudan-ready-to-ties-with-north-korea-local-media/.

24. Ji, "Angola Terminates 'All Contracts.'"

25. Hamish Macdonald, "North Korea's Illicit Activities in Africa Remain Pervasive, UN Report Shows," NK Pro, February 7, 2018, https://www.nknews.org/pro/north-koreas-illicit-activities-in-africa-remain-pervasive-un-report-shows/.

26. Solomon, "Africa's Ties to North Korea."

27. MOP was blacklisted in Resolution 2371 in August 2017.

28. Ji, "Angola Terminates 'All Contracts.'"

29. Macdonald, "North Korea's Illicit Activities in Africa."

30. Permanent Mission of Mozambique to the United Nations, "Note verbale dated 30 April 2020 from the Permanent Mission of Mozambique to the United Nations addressed to the Chair of the Committee," in *S/AC.49/2020/33*, edited by United Nations Security Council (New York: UNSC, 2020).

31. Colin Zwirko, "Mozambique Denies North Korea Sanctions Violations, Defends Medical Cooperation," NK News, May 26, 2020, https://www.nknews.org/2020/05/mozambique-denies-north-korean-sanctions-violations-defends-medical-cooperation/.

32. Seungmock Oh, "Peru to Expel Two North Korean Diplomats," NK News, December 25, 2017, https://www.nknews.org/2017/12/peru-to-expel-two-north-korean-diplomats/?t=1598370479497.

33. Colin Zwirko, "Cuba, North Korea Reaffirm Historic Ties at First Summit in Thirty Years," NK News, November 4, 2018, https://www.nknews.org/2018/11/cuba-north-korea-reaffirm-historic-ties-at-first-summit-in-thirty-years/?t=1598358336390.

34. Leo Byrne, "Cuba, North Korea Sign Barter-Based Trade Deal," NK News, January 29, 2016, https://www.nknews.org/2016/01/cuba-north-korea-sign-barter-based-trade-deal/.

35. Paul Antonopoulos, "Venezuela and North Korea Consolidate Alliance with New Agreements," *Fort Russ News*, October 1, 2019, accessed on June 20, 2021: https://fort-russ.com/2019/10/major-venezuela-and-north-korea-consolidate-alliance-with-new-agreements/.

36. Colin Zwirko, "Venezuelan President Could Visit North Korea Soon, Official in Pyongyang Says," NK News, September 27, 2019, https://www.nknews.org/2019/09/venezuelan-president-could-visit-north-korea-soon-official-in-pyongyang-says/?t=1598365849415.

37. United Nations Security Council Resolution 1874 was adopted unanimously by the United Nations Security Council on June 12, 2009. The resolution, passed under Chapter VII, Article 41, of the UN Charter, imposes further economic and commercial sanctions on the Democratic People's Republic of Korea (the DPRK, or North Korea) and encourages UN member states to search North Korean cargo, in the aftermath of an underground nuclear test conducted on May 25, 2009.

38. Elizabeth Shim, "Mexico Repatriates All 33 North Koreans on Board Ship Mu Du Bong," United Press International, July 17, 2015, https://www.upi.com/Top_News/World-News/2015/07/17/Mexico-repatriates-all-33-North-Koreans-on-board-ship-Mu-Du-Bong/3291437184768/.

39. Sunshine Policy was the name of South Korea's policy toward North Korea from 1998 until 2008. Articulated by South Korean President Kim Dae Jung, the policy temporarily resulted in greater political and cultural contact between the two Koreas.

40. Oliver Stuenkel, "Why Brazil Is Right to Have an Embassy in North Korea," OliverStuenkel.com, June 27, 2013. Accessed July 10, 2020, https://www.oliverstuenkel.com/2013/06/27/should-brazil-have-an-embassy-in-north-korea/.

41. The UNSC unanimously adopted Resolution 2397, which limits North Korea's importation of refined petroleum to five hundred thousand barrels for twelve months starting on January 1, 2018. The resolution also caps crude oil imports at current levels for the same period and compels member states to return all North Korean laborers working within their borders and their handlers within two years.

42. António Guterres, "Secretary-General's Full Transcript of His Press Conference on the Launch of the UN Comprehensive Response to COVID-19 [as delivered]," United Nations Secretary-General, June 25, 2020, https://www.un.org/sg/en/content/sg/press-encounter/2020-06-25/secretary-generals-full-transcript-of-his-press-conference-the-launch-of-the-un-comprehensive-response-covid-19-delivered.

43. Some of the most important resolutions include the following: 825 (1993), 1540 (2004), 1695 (2006), 1718 (2006), 1874 (2009), 1887 (2009), 1928 (2010), 1985 (2011), 2050 (2012), 2087 (2013), 2094 (2013), 2141 (2014), 2207 (2015), 2270 (2016), 2276 (2016), 2321 (2016), 2345 (2017), 2356 (2017), 2371 (2017), 2375 (2017), 2397 (2017), 2407 (2018), and 2464 (2019), and 2515 (2020).

44. Andrea Berger, "Resolution 2375: Strongest Ever Sanctions, or a Very Small Step?" NK Pro, September 13,2017, https://www.nknews.org/pro/resolution-2375-strongest-ever-sanctions-or-a-very-small-step/.

45. Jacob Fromer, "After UN Worker Ban Took Effect, Russia Granted 753 Work Visas to North Koreans," NK Pro, April 21, 2020, https://www.nknews.org/pro

/after-un-worker-ban-took-effect-russia-granted-753-work-visas-to-north-koreans/?t =1598303679492.

46. John Everard, "Embassies in North Korea Are Quickly Closing Down—and That's a Big Problem," KN News, August 24, 2020, https://www.nknews.org/2020 /08/embassies-in-north-korea-are-quickly-closing-down-and-thats-a-big-problem/?t =1598282244386.

47. Chad O'Carroll, "UN Agencies Unable to Leave Pyongyang, Creating Unprecedented Obstacles," NK News, July 19, 2020, https://www.nknews.org/2020/07/un -agencies-unable-to-leave-pyongyang-creating-unprecedented-obstacles/.

48. UNICEF, *Analysis of the Situation of Children and Women in the Democratic People's Republic of Korea* (Pyongyang: UNICEF, 2019).

49. FAO, "FAO in the Democratic People's Republic of Korea," *FAO Representation in DPR Korea*, 2020, https://www.fao.org/democratic-peoples-republic-of-korea /fr/.

50. WHO, "World Health Organization in Democratic People's Republic of Korea," *WHO, South-East Asia Democratic People's Republic of Korea*, 2020, https: //www.who.int/dprkorea/about-us.

51. WHO, *Evaluation of the Gavi Health Systems Strengthening Support to the Democratic People's Republic of Korea* (DOR Korea: WHO, 2018).

52. Awasthi, "India Extends Medical Support of $1 Mn to North Korea."

53. UNICEF, *Analysis of the Situation of Children and Women in the Democratic People's Republic of Korea*.

54. UNICEF, *Annual Report for 2018. UNICEF DPR Korea Country Office* (Pyongyang: UNICEF, 2018).

55. World Food Programme, "Where We Work: Democratic People's Republic of Korea," *UN World Food Programme*, 2020, https://www.wfp.org/countries/ democratic-peoples-republic-korea.

56. Elodie Broussard, "Despite Lockdown, IAEA Continues Nuclear Verification and Supports Countries Fighting COVID-19 in Largest Ever Operation, Director General Tells Agency's Board," IAEA Office of Public Information and Communication, July 22, 2020.

57. UN Human Rights Council, *Report of the Detailed Findings of the Commission of Inquiry on Human Rights in the Democratic People's Republic of Korea* (New York: UN/HRC/25/63, 2014).

58. Yonhap, "FM Calls for Inter-Korean Dialogue during Brief Encounter with North's Envoy at ASEAN Meetings," *The Korea Herald*, August 6, 2022, https:// www.koreaherald.com/view.php?ud=20220806000065.

59. Simon Denyer, "North Korea's Kim Calls Food Situation 'Tense' as Reports of Shortages Mount," *The Washington Post*, June 16, 2021, https://www.washingtonpost .com/world/asia_pacific/northkorea-food-shortage-kim/2021/06/16/fb745272-ce5a -11eb-a224-bd59bd22197c_story.html.

60. Tierney, "North Korea Wants to End Up Like Pakistan, Not Libya."

61. Tierney, "North Korea Wants to End Up Like Pakistan, Not Libya."

62. Kiyoung Changa and Choongkoo Leeb, "North Korea and the East Asian Security order: competing views on what South Korea ought to do," *The Pacific Review* 31, no. 2 (2018): 245–55.

63. UN News, "North Korea Missile Tests 'Deeply Troubling': Senior UN Official," UN News, December 11, 2019, https://news.un.org/en/story/2019/12/1053281.

64. UN News, "Critical Food Programmes in North Korea Can't Wait for 'Diplomatic Progress,' UN Food Agency Warns," UN News, October 9, 2018, https://news.un.org/en/story/2018/10/1022612.

65. Everard, "Embassies in North Korea Are Quickly Closing Down."

66. UNICEF, *Analysis of the Situation of Children and Women in the Democratic People's Republic of Korea.*

Index

abductions, 80–82, 84, 86, 89
Abe, Shinzo, 44–45, 82–86, 88–89, 91
Africa, 141–42, 149. *See also*
    specific countries
Albright, Madeline, 80
allies, 10–14, 16–17, 35–36,
    60–61, 140, 143
American exceptionalism, 13–14
An Don-chun, 110
Angola, 141–42
Arduous March, 40
Asia: Africa and, 149; allies in, 10,
    140; ASEAN Regional Security
    Forum, 110, 148; Banco Delta Asia,
    38; to China, 77–78, 99–101, 115;
    communism in, 83; economics in,
    67; Hanoi summit and, 72; Japan
    to, 94; Korean War and, 93; Non-
    Alignment movement in, 135–36;
    North Korea to, 14; Russia and, 108;
    transportation in, 106; treaties in,
    22, 81–82; U.S., in, 135. *See also*
    specific countries

Bae, Joonbum, 137
balance-of-power theory, 11, 16
Banco Delta Asia, 38
banking, 119
beliefs, 19–20, 58

Biden, Joe, 46, 69, 127–28
bilateral trade, 40, 46, 83, 105–6
Bolton, John, 123
Brazil, 144
Bretton Woods, 15
Brexit, 91
Brezhnev, Leonid, 35–36
brinkmanship diplomacy, 6, 54,
    56–62, 74n8
Britain. *See* United Kingdom
Bush, George W., 80, 83, 87,
    90, 105, 120
byungjin policy, 41–42, 54

Cambodia, *67*
capitalism, 15–16, 25–26
Cardoso, Fernando Henrique, 144
Castro, Fidel, 143
CCP. *See* Chinese Communist Party
Central Committee of the
    Workers' Party, 23
chaju (independence), 1, 8
charip (self-sustenance), 1, 8
charm diplomacy, 124
Chavez, Hugo, 143
chawi (self-defense), 1, 8
China: Asia to, 77–78, 99–101, 115;
    bilateral trade with, 40; Chinese
    Civil War, 34; Chinese Cultural

Soviet Union (USSR): China and, 32, 35–36, 60–61, 99–100; in Cold War, 5, 8, 99–101; demise of, 8–9; diplomacy with, 114–15; Eastern Europe to, 59; Iran and, 118; in Korean War, 35; military of, 16, 34; North Korea and, 3–4, 97–99, 101–4; South Korea and, 80; trade with, 101–2. *See also* Russia
SRBM. *See* short-range ballistic missiles
Stalin, Joseph, 97–100
state-sponsored media. *See* Korean Central News Agency
strong and prosperous great power (*Kansong Daekuk*), 5, 57–58
submarines, 122–23
Sudan, 141–42
Suga, Yoshihide, 88, 91
Sunshine Policy, 3, 87, 144, 153n39
survival. *See specific topics*
suryong leadership, 71–72
Sweden, 146
Swiss Development Cooperation, 146
Syria, 119–20

Taiwan, 10
Tanzania, 142
tension diplomacy, 42–43
terrorism, 11, 16, 119–20
Thermal High Altitude Area Defense (THAAD) anti-ballistic missile system, 44–45
Third World countries. *See* Global South
Tillerson, Rex, 141
trade: bilateral, 40, 46, 83, 105–6; with China, 59, 78–79; free, 16; imports and, 111–12; politics of, 148–49; Rajin-Sonbong free trade zone, 106; with USSR, 101–2
Trans-Siberian Railway, 106
treaties: in Asia, 22, 81–82; at Conference of Bandung, 135–36; JCPOA deal, 117, 120–21, 125–28, 130n25; Korean Armistice Agreement, 35; peace, 32, 73–74

Treaty on the Non-Proliferation of Nuclear Weapons (NPT), 9–11, 22, 27n1, 37–39, 104–5
Trump, Donald: Abe and, 44–45; diplomacy with, 110; grand bargaining by, 25; Kim Jong-un and, 22, 77–78, 87–88, 123–25, 128; leadership of, 45; Moon and, 89–90, 93; nuclear weapons to, 121
tuberculosis, 146–47

Ukraine, 73, 114, 127
Ulchi Freedom Shield, 69
UN. *See* United Nations
UNICEF, 146–47
United Kingdom, 10–13, 15, 91, 97–98
United Nations (UN): China and, 17–18; Crimea to, 107; economic sanctions to, 23–24, 42, 44, 145–46, 153n37; Geneva Agreed Framework to, 22, 37, 56; globalization and, 88–89, 144–45; humanitarian assistance and, 113, 145–46, 148–50; human rights to, 85–86; Korean War to, 99–101; North Korea to, 152n21; nuclear weapons to, 108–9; Panel of Experts on, 141–42; Security Council, 39–40, 44, 62, 65, 100, 119, 141–44, 149; Sustainable Development Goals, 142
United States (U.S.): Africa to, 141–42; allies of, 14, 36; in Asia, 135; authority of, 21–22; Biden for, 46, 69; Bush for, 83; capitalism to, 15–16, 25–26; China and, 22, 37–39, 45–46, 66, 70, 100; in Cold War, 3, 12, 16; denuclearization policy to, 72; diplomacy, 25, 54, 67–68, 77–78, 80; economic sanctions to, 108–9; European Union and, 148; Forces Korea, 27n2; foreign policy of, 6, 107; Geneva Agreed Framework to, 60; hegemony of, 8, 12, 20–21, 44, 47; Iran and, 124–25; Iraq and, 81; Japan and, 2–3, 15, 56; to Kim Jong-il, 24; Kim Jong-un and,

About the Contributors

Dr. Jun Kwon is an associate professor at the Department of Political Science at Utica University, New York. He earned a PhD in political science from the University of Georgia and a master's in Asian studies from Cornell University. His research interests lie in the fields of comparative politics and international relations with an emphasis on East Asia (including China, Taiwan, North Korea, South Korea, and Japan). He can be reached at jtkwon@utica.edu.

Dr. Weiqi Zhang is an associate professor at the Department of Political Science and Legal Studies of Suffolk University (Boston, MA), and an associate in research at the Fairbank Center of China Studies at Harvard University. He earned his PhD in political science from the University of Georgia. His research focuses on political and economic liberalization in closed societies (with a focus on North Korea and China) and international relations in East Asia. He is also passionate about applying data science in social science research.

Dr. Sukhoon Hong is an associate professor in the Department of International Relations at Changwon National University (ROK). He worked as the director of planning and coordination division and was a research fellow at the Institute for National Unification (KINU). In terms of his research interests, he is keenly interested in U.S.–North Korea relations and North Korean foreign policy as well as the Asian "peace regime." He received his PhD in political science from the University of Georgia (United States). Hong's existing work in this area has been published in KINU's policy reports, *International Area Studies Review*, the *Korean Journal of International Studies*, *National Security and Strategy*, the *Journal of Peace Studies*, and in various book chapters.

Dr. Anand Rao is an assistant professor of political science and international relations at the State University of New York at Geneseo. He lived in Japan for nearly ten years and has published articles in *Asian Politics & Policy* and the *Japan Studies Association Journal*. Dr. Rao is a member of Cohort 5 of the U.S.-Japan Network for the Future, a program run by the Maureen and Mike Mansfield Foundation and the Japan Foundation.

Dr. Evgenii Gamerman is an international scientist. He graduated from the Faculty of History of the Blagoveshchensk State Pedagogical University. He defended his PhD thesis on the history of the Far East at the Institute of History of the Russian Academy of Sciences. He taught at the Universities of Blagoveshchensk, Vladivostok, and Moscow. He lectured at Sofia University (Bulgaria). In 2014–2015, he did an internship at the Institute for the Humanities in Vienna (Austria), at the University of Uppsala (Sweden), and at the London School of Economics (UK).

His research focuses on modern political processes in Northeast Asia, international and regional security, and nontraditional security threats.

Dr. Alon Levkowitz is a senior lecturer and the head of the social science and civics studies department at Beit-Berl College, a senior lecturer in Asian studies at Bar-Ilan University, and a research associate at the Begin-Sadat Center for Strategic Studies. His research focuses on politics and foreign relations in East Asia, the Korean foreign and security policy, and Northeast Asian security. His current projects focus on North Korean military cooperation with Middle Eastern states, the economic and diplomatic relations between South Korea and the Middle East relations, South Korea's African policy, and the North Korean missile industry. He has published articles in a number of academic journals.

Dr. Roberto Dominguez is a professor of international relations at Suffolk University in Boston, Massachusetts. He was a Jean Monnet fellow at the European University Institute in Florence and was a researcher at the European Union Center of Excellence of the University of Miami. He holds a doctoral degree from the University of Miami. His current research interest is comparative regional security governance, security governance in Latin America, and European Union–Latin American relations. He is one of the associated editors of the *Encyclopedia of European Union Politics* (2021). Professor Dominguez has also contributed as a consultant for projects for the European Parliament, the European Commission, Transparency International, the U.S. Library of Congress, and the U.S. Fulbright Commission.